WILD HERITAGE

Books by Sally Carrighar

One Day on Beetle Rock
One Day at Teton Marsh
Icebound Summer
Moonlight at Midday
Wild Voice of the North
The Glass Dove
Wild Heritage

by Sally Carrighar

WILD
HERITAGE

with illustrations by
Rachel S. Horne

HOUGHTON MIFFLIN COMPANY BOSTON
The Riverside Press Cambridge

1965

Never, no never, did nature say one thing
and wisdom another.

Johann Christoph Friedrich von Schiller

Foreword

THE NEW SCIENCE of ethology — the science of animals' normal behavior — has brought up the whole question of what ways, and to what extent, human beings behave like the simpler creatures from which we evolved. What do we do that they do? What similar impulses (if any) move both animals and men? Emotions can sometimes be surmised from performance, but ignore for the present the question of "feelings." Which of our *actions* are carried over from subhuman ancestors?

With the knowledge recently gained by ethologists, problems like these have become inescapable. They are embarrassing, however, because they falsely revive the deep distaste for anthropomorphism. Anthropomorphism — the attributing of human emotions to animals — is the ultimate horror to many biologists. It is a horror to *all* biologists when it includes the assumption that animals rule themselves with values exactly like ours. There are many kinds of activity, nevertheless, which can be studied without drawing conclusions about the state of any animal's consciousness.

The value of understanding our behavioral roots is slowly becoming recognized, and yet ethologists are still, sometimes, accused of anthropomorphism. The charge is not really logical. For many decades it has been known that those high forms of animal life, the vertebrates, are related in such anatomical structures as skeletons. The wings of birds and the forelimbs of bats, horses, whales, and men are all, of course, built on the same general plan, as no one now denies. More recently glands have been seen as related in many species. The hormones secreted by ductless glands are so similar that those of one species are often injected therapeutically into a quite different species; when our own hormones are deficient, many human diseases are relieved or cured by hormones extracted from animals. Those hormones control much of the seemingly voluntary behavior of the animals — and of us — and yet the ban on anthropomorphism has prevented the recognition of likenesses between human activities and those of our subhuman forebears. The fiction has still been maintained that the way human beings behave is no more related to the way animals do than our functioning is related to the functioning of an egg beater or an electric saw. It would be outrageous, for example, to suggest in some scientific quarters that there is any analogy between a human mother feeding cereal to her infant and a mother sparrow putting seeds into the beak of her fledgling. To see a faint similarity in the postures of the two mothers and their two young would be ridiculed, and to intimate that the human mother might learn something from the sparrow about the emotional weaning of her child would — to many biologists — seem so sentimental as not even to merit comment.

Most ethologists think more boldly. Of necessity they are men of very wide and meticulous biological background. And one of the most eminent of them, William H. Thorpe of Cambridge University, states unequivocally that "there is hardly any aspect of the behaviour of animals which may not have some reference to problems in human behaviour."

Indeed, speaking literally, it is not anthropomorphic at all to say that our behavior is related to that of the animals. The point is not that the animals are like *us* but that we are like *them*. That is a thought which arouses profound antagonism in a number of minds; and is the reason a feeling of insecurity which seeks relief in asserting our human superiority? Some rather renowned thinkers have strained to define unique qualities possessed only by human beings. As the animal behaviorists have suggested, however, the process of evolution is denied if we say that human beings suddenly acquired traits that were not even foreshadowed in pre-human species.

Since similarities have, in fact, been proved beyond doubt to exist in the behavior of all the more complex forms of life, we can gain invaluable understanding of ourselves by observing animals as the ethologists do. When we watch these creatures living naturally in the wild, and then confirm by experimentation what we have seen, we can discover tendencies in ourselves that otherwise we might never suspect. It is a purpose long since made respectable by the psychologists.

This too must be said. In some ethological studies, carried out very precisely and carefully during the last fifteen years, it has happened that we have had to give some of the animals credit for higher mental faculties than we once believed they were capable of. Curiosity is an example. Formerly denied as an attribute of any but human minds, curiosity now is recognized as the motivation for various subhuman activities. Some biologists call it by terms such as visual exploring and manipulation, but others don't shrink from the frank use of the word curiosity. Its existence in some animal minds has been demonstrated both in the field and in biological laboratories. Some of the experiments, and others like them, will be described in the pages that follow.

To reassure any reader who might feel that he is being asked to grope back into Victorian sentimentality, a bibliography of scientific sources has been provided. It is a guide to recent and reliable information about the study of human and animal behavior — to the records in which the ethologists are showing for the first time, ever, what animal life is truly like.

Only a very small part of what they have learned is described in this book, but even that little can be enlightening.

1964   SALLY CARRIGHAR

Contents

I

ANIMALS AND MEN

The Blurred Borderline

The Blurred Borderline

O N A SPRING DAY of a recent year a neighbor of mine cut his own telephone line. He could not endure one more night of bombardment by suitors of his wife's niece, who lived with them. The niece is a small, dark, intense girl. Sharp and fine as a new moon, she aroused such a yearning in young male breasts that her side of the street was lined with cars day and night, and the boys who were not there kept trying to shoulder in via the telephone.

Magnetism so great is a dubious gift. The girl was reluctant to settle down, but her uncle's cutting the wire convinced her she had to choose one from among all those candidates; and in the same week she announced that she would be married in June, in two months.

The very air seemed to vibrate with love, then in April. Another conspicuous evidence of it was the continuous flight of three

swallows, a female and two males pursuing her. All day they were skimming, soaring, and plunging above the brook. When swallows are out to forage, they try to funnel into their gaping mouths whatever insects are in the air, and since we can't see those minute bites, the birds' flight seems erratic. But during that courtship the grace of the swallows, darting and turning, with sunlight glinting on white throats and metallic blue wings, was an aerial dance of distracting beauty. It soon ended. By the first of June there were only the food-gathering flights, by a mated pair who were at home in their hole in a dead tree farther along the brook.

The man was saying, "The time's come when we're talking about a house again. We seem to get into this every spring."

And his wife said, "I've been driving around in the last few weeks looking at rooflines. They're very expressive. The terribly steep ones are whimsical—they make me think of a mother inside baking gingerbread cookies all day. Under a flat roof I seem to see cocktails and sandals and men in Hawaiian shirts. What Fred and I want, I guess, is the kind I call the New England roof. A sedate slope. Everything about houses is fascinating!"

"In the spring," he said. "It's a springtime obsession."

Would this be the year these people did build? Twice before —in the spring—they had asked me to be on the watch for a good lot in the area where I live. Both years I had found one they liked and negotiations were started. But the weeks passed and somehow the urgency faded. When the lots went to other buyers, my friends were not disappointed. They were not sure they wanted to build a house after all. Summer had come by then.

As we talked, that warm Sunday in May, however, we were sitting out on my porch. In the nearest pin oak a pair of mourning doves worked on a nest. The male would gather their stalks of dried bits of vines and grass, and the female would weave them into the nest while her mate perched on the bough near her, giving encouragement. Of all the trees here, a maple, a beech, elms, spruces, pin oaks, and dogwood, their oak had the most level branches and the most open and limber shade. Its loosely hung leaves would yield to the breezes and let them through, keeping the nest cool all summer. The doves were connoisseurs, like the woman, of rooflines.

The whole countryside was a vast housing project that day: thousands of nests and burrows, old ones being cleaned out and repaired, new ones made, for the young then arriving. My guests, who do not have children, were not concerned about sheltering offspring, but the primeval instinct is very persistent, as proved by the records of real estate sales by months. The peak comes in May.

Summer is for the young, all the young everywhere, those who are seeing the world for the first time, such as fawns, cubs, and fledgling birds, and for boys and girls who are enjoying it for the second or third year, or even the tenth. It is a new world for them, and no wonder they fall in love with it, so that they never will want to leave it and therefore will try to live for as long as they can.

With its seasons and weather all evened out, the world is not quite that lovely. Breezes are not always tossing the sunlit leaves, little minnows don't always pause beside glossy wet rocks, looking up at a child's eyes with boldness in their own. Summer, however — with sheep moving over the hillside meadow, accompanied at the same slow pace by shadows of fleecy clouds; summer when butterflies dance in the air seeming delirious, like ecstatic small girls at parties, flinging their arms about as they run on the grass — summer will work a spell. In the winter the fawns will huddle with their tense mothers under cold trees, and the young sheep will stand through many long boring days in dimly lit barns. The children too will be under roofs and behind doors. But their hearts will have been won for the long pull of a lifetime by the world they have known in June.

Summer play, for those of all ages, is likely to mean exploring.

Small youngsters may feel that exploring the next field is excitement enough, but their parents will probably want to see other parts of the continent, or indeed the world. Fifty years ago only the affluent could explore — "travel" was part of their yearly routine — but automobiles have given to almost everybody the chance to move out on strange landscapes, and millions do.

It's an extremely old impulse. As far down the evolutionary scale as some fishes, there is a summer urge to venture into new waters, and many species of birds and mammals wander about for no known reason except to satisfy curiosity. Some birds, for example the little blue heron and the southern bald eagle, travel north *after* their nesting season. Others, like flocks of male eider ducks, make an early southward migration and do it by devious routes, roaming here and there, whereas their spring migrations are much more direct.

In the last half of the summer, in August, the impulse is strongest. The most strenuous work of bearing and raising an animal brood has ended, and often the young go along on the exploring trips, which might be considered a part of their education. Human families, then crowding the turnpikes, may know that the flocks of birds streaming above their cars probably have the same motive for making their flights; and in woodlands along the highway, in underbrush and in streams, there is a smaller and unseen movement.

In Alaska it is impossible not to compare the influx of summer tourists, who arrive in plane-loads at some of the Eskimo villages, with the summer visits of countless fishes, whales, many kinds of birds. Even the creatures that live in the arctic all year are inclined to wander, to the very edge of the frozen sea, where their stay always is brief. The human travelers don't remain very long either. Most are gone by the first of September. Many Alaska residents think that the spring, fall, and winter are the best parts of the year, but almost no visitors come at those times. They are not the seasons when one is impelled to explore.

The immense modern organizations that freeze and can summer foodstuffs relieve most of us of the necessity to stock larders for winter. But several women I know — and I am another — put up a few jars of fruit every year. It is a token activity, a slight deferring to an old urge, though we say that we do it because we like the smell of the sweet, hot juices that fills the house while the kettles are bubbling.

One can wonder too about the popularity of deepfreezes: is it possible that the chief need they fill is instinctual? There is a kind of vague feeling of insecurity in buying the food for a family from day to day, even week to week, and on the other hand a reassurance in having a freezer stored full to the lid.

People in country places who don't have easy access to super-markets still "put up" fruits and vegetables and "put down" the root crops, and sometimes the pleasant activity goes beyond what is required. Out in the valley at Jackson Hole, where a few families, not many, remain through the winter, some of the wives bake as many as fifty loaves of bread and two dozen cakes at a time, as soon as the temperature is dependably below freezing. These foods, which can be baked in all seasons of course, are stored with some effort in wire cages slung with pulleys from boughs of trees, the only sure way to keep them out of the reach of bears. When they are thawed, incidentally, the bread and cakes seem to taste better than when they are fresh, but I never heard that reason given for the fall baking-in-quantity.

In Jackson Hole and Alaska and other remote northern places, husbands hope to secure, and often do, the whole winter's supply of meat with their rifles during the hunting season. It seems likely that hunting as carried on in the warmer states by city men, some of whom can hardly tell one end of a gun from the other and have been known to shoot horses and cows for deer, is due to the same urge which prompts arctic foxes and wolves to cache mice in the fall — although with the men, now, apparently there is also a prestige factor.

One September day I circled the north shore of Leigh Lake in
Jackson Hole towards a rocky point. The morning was dazzling.
Fresh new snow mantled the mountain peaks, the gold of aspen
leaves glittered around the shore, and the lake was a blue so intense
one would say it had given its hue to the paler sky. The trail I
was on had been made by moose, as proved by the way it
meandered, keeping clear of the branches lower than antler-height.
The shade was dense back among the dark spruces, but up ahead
flashes of sunlight on waves showed that the path was approaching
the beach. It came out on a tumble of boulders, and I sat down on
one to enjoy the warmth of the stone.

A surprising thing: laid out with some order on most of the
flatter rocks were little hay-piles, stalks of fireweed, lupine, golden-
rod, and some twigs of chokecherry. A pile near me was fan-shaped,
with the seedheads all at the outer edge, facing the sun. Who
would be drying those plants?

The question was answered by a small, aggrieved, nasal voice:
why do you have to sit HERE? Sometimes a friendly tone in a
human voice reassures the wild creatures, and so I said, "I wish I
could see you." I meant it, for this hay could have been gathered
by only one kind of animal — pikas, often called conies (but not
the Biblical conies, which are hoofed animals of the desert).
Pikas are tiny rabbits that dry quantities of plants which they store
under rock piles for winter. They do not hibernate and therefore
must have enough food to last until spring.

Usually pikas are seen only by mountain-climbers, for they live
on the upper slopes, to at least an altitude of 17,000 feet. They
are found very seldom as low as Leigh Lake, 6900 feet. Since I
had known them only by reputation, I stayed, an intruder inter-
fering with urgent harvesting, until three of the pikas came out
of their crannies to make their protests at closer range.

They were so small that one could have crouched comfortably
in my hands; with soft rock-colored fur, whitish below, gray-buff
above, and with large round ears and wide eyes, they looked like

adorable toys. Although they would be quite helpless unless close to an opening in the boulders, they came rather near, like young children who sense that innocence in itself can be a defense.

Their complaints were not harsh, only sounding unhappy, and after several minutes one of the pikas dared to go on with his haying. He left and before long came back with sheaves of stalks carried in his mouth crosswise. These he dropped in a careless pile, which apparently he would spread out later for curing. The other two pikas had drawn back into their crevices, and, feeling guilty about delaying an activity so important, I left.

In the early fall many animals are engaged in laying up winter stores. One is apt to think only of squirrels, digging holes to hide acorns in carefully tended lawns, but some of the other creatures preparing for the cold months are lemmings, field mice of various species, hamsters, muskrats, beavers, pocket gophers (they store only Jerusalem artichokes!), and various birds like the familiar jays. The question often is asked: do these creatures remember where they have left the food? Watching a red squirrel retrieve his acorns, I have an impression that he has known in general where he buried them but that he finds them individually by scent. The northern species of birds called nutcrackers are more exact. P. O. Swanberg watched nutcrackers digging 351 times in snow eighteen inches deep, and found that they came up with the nut they sought more than 80 per cent of the time. (Konrad Lorenz says that ravens do not like to have people observe them when they are hiding food. If they know that they have been seen, they recover the food and hide it somewhere else, out of sight.)

The animals that spend the winter aboveground do not usually bury their food very deep, but those that make burrows often have elaborately constructed storerooms. That is the case with the lesser mole-rat, a European species, whose burrows include, besides the main galleries, special chambers for storing food (onions, potatoes, carrots, and other roots), sanitary rooms which are walled up when they have been filled with droppings, and a nest-room furnished with soft, dry grass.

Finally and most remarkably, there is a nuptial chamber, on which work is started several months before pairing takes place. The little room, about eight inches across, has walls covered with clay. After the mating takes place there, Bodnar Bela reports, this room and the gallery to it are walled off from the rest of the complex burrow.

Our view of winter as barren, with nature asleep, is due to a curious emphasis on plant life rather than animal life. It is true that while sap is withdrawn into roots and seeds are dormant, some animals likewise hibernate. Far more are active and, most important, in winter many animals of the future are being conceived and are starting their secret growth in the dark of animal wombs.

With great efficiency nature has so arranged it that most animals will be born in the spring. During their first vulnerable weeks and months, then, they will not have to cope with storms and cold. The sun's warmth will allow them to move around, learning the techniques of flying, running, swimming, crawling, the activities their particular kind need to know. And food is abundant beginning in spring: food for the parents that may be feeding the young and later the food that the offspring secure for themselves. With all the facts faced, it would seem nearly impossible for most animals to be born and thrive in any season *except* the spring; and that is the season when most of them make their appearance.

Since mother animals vary extremely in the length of their pregnancies, the times when their young are conceived must vary accordingly — and they do. Moose, with a gestation period of seven months, mate in September; elk, which carry their young about thirty days less, come into their breeding season a month later. In wolves and foxes pregnancy lasts for sixty days or so, and usually they mate in February. Even those species that bear several litters a year, like mice, tend to have an infertile period which prevents the birth of young in the most severe weather.

Nature would seem to have complications enough in tallying the love-making seasons with the desired season of births. But that's not the only problem. For many animal parents are hibernating, in deathlike sleep, at the time when conception should take place for the young to come forth in the spring. The solution: most of these animals copulate during the previous summer, relying on several mechanisms for slowing the growth of the fetus.

In badgers, martens, perhaps bears and several other mammals, the fertilized egg does not become attached to the uterus wall and start its development until some time in the winter. And there are still different arrangements. In certain species of bats that hibernate, copulation takes place in the fall, and the sperm is stored, alive, all winter in the female's uterus, with the fertilization of the egg not taking place until spring. In other bats the embryo is fertilized and even implanted during the fall, but by a very special adaptation its development is greatly slowed down while the mother is hibernating. In one way and another, therefore, young animals are prevented from first seeing the light of day under cold winter skies.

Does all this have anything to do with human births, which occur during every month in the year? As we shall see in a moment, it does.

In those parts of the sea that are open all winter, and in the tropics, newborn animals do not have to encounter freezing temperatures, and there the patterns of reproduction are somewhat different. In sea otters and most land mammals near the equator, it is practical for births to take place in all seasons; they are determined by the time of conception and pregnancies proceed at the normal pace. Monkeys and apes, most of which are found in tropical climates, are among those that are free from the strict schedules of reproduction in colder habitats. The females come into breeding condition — the period called the oestrus — at each lunar cycle of about twenty-eight days, and human beings have inherited from these primate ancestors their reproductive pattern, even though most of us now live farther north or south and experience winter weather.

In even the tropical species, however, the number of births reaches a peak in the spring — or during the rainy season, when insects are abundant, for birds. The young animal and the young year seem to belong together (although the real explanation is probably the prosaic one that during the glacial periods even the tropics were cold). Moreover there is a situation which suggests that nature prefers to have human, as well as animal young born in the spring. About twenty-five years ago Ellsworth Huntington published some figures, now largely forgotten, which proved that a significant proportion of talented and successful men have been born in February and March. Seeking the reason, he found that the vitality of human beings reaches a climax nine months before the February-March period, and he concluded that a child conceived during the annual peak of its parents' health would be given the best qualities that its parents could ever transmit. That opinion was no doubt justified — in any planned-parenthood program perhaps the advantages of May-June conceptions ought to be emphasized. What Huntington did not investigate were the factors that make May and June so beneficial to the physical well-being of human fathers and mothers. Why is that the time when their vitality is the highest? He believed that the chief reason is weather, the pleasant days of May and June "which are especially favorable to the smooth functioning of the glands, nerves and other organs."

But those are not the months when most animals are in a state of maximum fitness. In May and June male deer, moose, and elk are so low in energy that they often stay by themselves, as if they were sick. The explanation has sometimes been made that all their strength is going into the growth of their antlers, and to some extent that may be true. Three and four months later, at the time when these hoofed species are mating, they are like different creatures — proud and strong and with glistening coats. Trappers know that such animals as foxes are in their prime during their breeding season. If, therefore, human adults do reach their peak of health during late spring, the reason may be that this is the natural season for the conception of human young. Though in practice human reproduction seems emancipated from animal origins in its timing, perhaps nature's ancient arrangement is best for the children. (The suggestion is offered tentatively. More studies are needed and some are now being made. They show that the brightest children tend to be born in the few months following March.)

With the growing or resting embryos provided for, adult animals come to the time of year when the black storms begin rising behind the horizon. Winter: some will not survive it. Others, in order to live, will make their incredibly long and difficult journeys to warmer climates. The climate where I am living is snowy but moderate and must seem mild to some birds, for their southward migration stops here. One of the smallest birds is a tree sparrow, which nests in the Far North. I know that country. Once I drove down from it, 5200 miles, in a car that performed well and required no more effort of me than steering around the rocks on the road. At the time I felt that the trip was a modest achievement, but I have discarded that notion ever since I have had the chance to look out at this six-inch bird that makes the same trip twice each year with its own muscle power.

It would be interesting to know whether birds and animals have any sense of dread at the approach of winter and its adjustments. One adjustment is the widening of their sociability from the family or small clan typical of the summer to that of the larger flocks and herds. The hazards of frigid weather seem to make the company of one's own kind, or even the company of other species, almost a necessity. The extreme cold of very high altitudes is like the strain of deep winter; and it is said that some species of birds that elsewhere are found in only the wildest places become almost tame in villages of the high Himalayas. There they live around the very doorsteps of human houses.

For us, too, custom has made the dark months the time when our interests and sympathies expand beyond our immediate families. We reach out for friendship — all we mean when we say that the social season has arrived. Parties, club activities, church socials, committee meetings, concerts, plays: all are enjoyed not alone for their entertainment or whatever action has been accomplished, but also because of the warmth of association with other people. It is a precedent that apparently goes far back beyond human beginnings.

Several ways have been suggested in which human beings follow the seasonal patterns that govern the lives of animals. We do not adhere to them closely; some of us start to build houses in August; some courtships come to a climax in January; a few vacations are taken in off-months like October; and the storing of food is not always done in late summer. When I thought on a spring day that I'd like to freeze some of the new rhubarb and strawberries then coming into the market, I could not buy any plastic containers, however. "People don't fill up their freezers at this time of year — not till later on," explained the clerk. We make some of our plans regardless of season, but we do have a clear tendency to adapt old, inherited habits to our so-different civilized living.

"I pricked up my ears at that!"
"He's not for me — too much of an eager beaver."
"He bristled each time she spoke."

Such enduring clichés, derived from our human association with animals, still are coming into the language. Boys use the scornful epithet "Chicken!" who never saw a real chicken until it was cut up and wrapped in cellophane. It would be interesting to know whether the boys have, from ancestral memories, any fleeting

image of hens in timorous, flapping flight. How many of the
following familiar terms click on in the reader's mind any picture
of the animal activities that they represent?

Feather one's nest	To go bats
Bark out orders	A snake in the grass
Monkey around	Turtle doves
Get my hackles up	Wolf whistle
To weasel out	Wildcat strike
To louse up	A cute chick
To crab	Catty
To skunk	Bullish, bearish

And many others. Few of these phrases may now bring up any
images of their actual origin; yet we cannot doubt that men started
to use them because of their recognition that our affairs and those
of the animals are related.

The above expressions are slang. But similar links between
man and his subhuman ancestors were described nearly a hundred
years ago by Charles Darwin in his book *The Expression of the
Emotions in Man and Animals*. We can guess that it offended
more people than even his *Origin of Species*, because it is so
specific. A preacher thundering from his pulpit about the uniqueness of human beings with their God-given souls would not like
to realize that his very gestures, the hairs that rose on his neck, the
deepened tones of his outraged voice, and the perspiration that
probably ran down his skin under clerical vestments are all
manifestations of anger in mammals. If he was sneering at Darwin
a bit (one does not need a mirror to know that one sneers), did
he remember uncomfortably that a sneer is derived from an
animal's lifting its lip to remind an enemy of its fangs? Even
while he was denying the principle of evolution, how could a
vehement man doubt such intimate evidence?

Owing to more recent investigations we are all now aware
of the internal fight or flight mechanisms. We know them in

theory and know that all mammals share them. Darwin's details are more immediately impressive than the information about release of adrenalin, interruption of digestive processes, and changes in circulation when we are terrified, for no one actually feels the adrenalin pouring into his bloodstream; yet we can recognize in ourselves the effects that Darwin described for animals badly frightened. They tremble, grow pale (the skin around their mouths loses color), perspire, take quick, light breaths; and their hearts beat more quickly, even wildly and violently "but probably not efficiently." "It was a hair-raising experience": the animals' hair comes up and so does ours, literally.

An aggressive animal tries to frighten opponents. He growls or snarls and his eyes flash a warning. Above all, he tries to give an impression of larger size. In mammals the fur is raised and shoulders are raised to suggest maximum height. Birds puff out their feathers; frogs pump themselves full of air. One thinks also of sergeants.

In extreme pain all of us groan and writhe about with movements which, Darwin says, express an involuntary attempt to escape from the suffering.

Changes in voices, too, are a form of expressiveness that we share. They deepen in rage; and in both human beings and animals voices become high, with a whining tone, when one feels aggrieved. Animal mothers use voices when they address their young which are quite unlike their voices on other occasions. And human mothers — all human females — have special voices for speaking to babies. I once tried an experiment: to talk to a month-old infant in the same matter-of-fact tone I would use in ordering groceries. It was simply not possible. The voice in which one would say, "And send me a head of lettuce" is so abnormal in one's relationship with a tiny child that it even sounds threatening. The one that I held in my arms puckered up and cried.

The *mmmmm* with which many babies murmur when they are nursing is almost exactly the same hum that some newborn mammals use. The very word mammal has been derived from it.

Expressions of the emotions and even the emotions themselves may not seem very significant links with the animals from which we have evolved. But the likenesses go much deeper. In this book, which is a survey of some of the habits, "ways," tendencies of animals in the four fields, especially, that we share with them — parenthood, sex, aggressiveness, and play — the similarity between our human and their subhuman natures will not often be emphasized or even mentioned. I believe that in many cases it will nevertheless be evident. To any naturalist it is plain that in understanding animals we can see some of our own dangers and opportunities much more clearly. For animals' problems often parallel ours, and they solve them with such success, their lives in general follow such smooth courses, and their societies are so permanent, they work so well, that it seems not only interesting but helpful to realize that human beings have the same possibilities of living effectively.

We have some enormous advantages over the animals; I hope those too will become more apparent, as well as the fact that those advantages are the very things which make it possible for us to wreck our own lives and even to wreck the world. There would also be hazards in trying to adopt uncritically all of nature's programs. It is not realistic to portray the animals' world as invariably wholesome and "right." It can even be said that nature makes a mistake in not providing for failures of instinct; and here at the start one or two of those might be considered. But first, a look at a situation that nearly always is satisfactory in a wilderness and can cause much confusion in a sophisticated human society.

One does not have to go out and live in the woods; it is only necessary to have a bird-feeding station to know that female creatures, when attracting a mate, often revert to the mannerisms of infancy. In that situation many female birds crouch and seem small, their voices sound almost like those of a fledgling, they quiver their wings in that dazzling, attention-getting motion which is so irresistible to a parent, and they may even open their mouths and beg for food. Some male birds do feed the appealing adult babe: the gift has been likened to the box of chocolates which is a standard offering of human suitors. Among mammals too, such as wolves, there frequently is a gift of food from the male to the female when she suggests with her new sweet, high voice and her enchanting, playful manner that she is a puppy. There are exceptions; the reactions of domesticated female cats seem to be one, but in general the mating female animal sloughs off her maturity for a little while.

These actions are highly ritualized. Among all the inborn habits of animals there may be no others in which the rules are laid down as strictly as those of courtship. The actions of male and female must dovetail with an exquisite precision: for everything that he does she has an answering gesture, which in turn triggers his next step, with alternating responses of the pair continuing all the way. This behavior pattern differs in its details with every species and is one of the means by which species remain distinct, since a misstep at any point, by either partner, is enough to throw the whole affair off.

The important point here is that during the mating stage babylike mannerisms are the custom with a great number of female animals. This behavior is quickly discarded when the young arrive and need care that is altogether adult. The appealing bird or animal bride is not expected to keep up her nuptial allurements after the family life is established. She will return to them on succeeding years, briefly, but her mate does not require — he probably would not want — a companion that he would have to woo continuously for an indefinite future. He may even find her emotional versatility one of her greatest attractions.

When that has been said it should be added that the female animal is at most times recognizably feminine: more quiet than males, much less inclined to aggression, more gentle, more soft in her ways. To some degree these are also the characteristics of infant animals, although the mature female in her non-sexual cycle does not have the motions or postures or voice of the young. During the time that these are not suitable she, being in harmony with nature's purposes, drops them. While the season of romance lasts, she probably does sincerely feel vulnerable and helpless and drawn to a masterful male (who may remind her of the masterful male that perhaps helped to take care of her when she was an actual infant). The short return to the courtship ways is really, however, no more than playing — a game, and a game cannot last forever. Can it?

The switch between sexual phases, so easy for birds and animals, may have been accountable for that infinite variety which, in Shakespeare's time, was considered one of woman's great charms. That kind of variety is not often seen now, for showmen and advertisers, exploiting sex, have saturated our social scene with the thought that femininity has no attraction except in the wing-quivering (eyelid-fluttering) phase. The pressure on women to maintain themselves in a nubile stage permanently is one of the strains of being a modern female and is probably one of the reasons why older American women are sometimes described as lost. They have been made to feel that the chances of still being desired are hopeless.

This complication is of our own devising. Nature does not often allow sexuality to run off the track, although it has done so to some extent in some of the subhuman primates.

There are a few other warnings: One of the strangest of animal traits, so impractical as to make one suspect a sense of humor in nature, is a taste for the supernormal, as biologists call it. So far it has not been investigated for many species, but several creatures, it has been found, are fascinated by what is too big, too bright, too flashy, or just too extreme to serve any useful purpose for them. In some cases what is naturally beneficial is ignored in favor of what is more titillating, and the preference then becomes "dysgenic" — meaning unfavorable for the continuing of the species.

That nature could be so frivolous could hardly be believed when the first discovery was made by O. Koehler and A. Zagarus in 1937. Trying to learn whether birds always recognize their own eggs, they tested ringed plovers both with their normal eggs, which are light brownish with darker brown spots, and with eggs about the same size that had a clear white background and larger, *black* dots. The birds showed a definite preference for the showier eggs even though they belonged to a different species.

Five years later Professor Nikolaas Tinbergen and three associates decided to investigate the question of whether a supernormal quality has any appeal for other creatures. First they undertook tests with the birds called oystercatchers. When an oystercatcher (*Haematopus ostralegus*) has laid three eggs, no more, her egg-laying normally ceases and she begins to incubate them. The limit of three is no doubt determined by some internal influence, probably hormonal, and is not a conscious choice. Tinbergen and his colleagues, however, presented certain females with clutches of five eggs and found that they would desert their own clutches of three for the more numerous ones. Far more surprising, a female oystercatcher would abandon any normal oystercatcher's eggs for a herring gull's egg, which is comparatively enormous for an oyster-

catcher, and would even leave the herring gull's egg for an egg
that was twice the size of that one — indeed, an egg that was as
large if not larger than the body of the brooding bird herself and
which she could only straddle in a most awkward way. A predilec-
tion for pure bigness? What would have happened if the scientists
had presented her with an ostrich egg? Or a sixteen-cylinder
Cadillac?

Would this strange tendency apply to any other species, to a
butterfly, for example? A familiar butterfly in Europe is the
grayling (*Eumenis semele*). Even a dummy female made of
paper will stimulate the male grayling to pursue it if the grayling
motion is imitated skillfully. Dummies of different shades of gray
were used. The male responded more readily to the darker ones,
in shades progressively darker, well beyond the color of the normal
females — with the attractiveness proving to be in direct ratio to
the darkening until a black model produced the most response
of all.

Meanwhile the males were tested also for their susceptibility
to size, and the larger the models, the more inclined the males were
to follow them. They felt that about four times the true size would

be about right. Since there are no huge black female grayling butterflies, the male still mates with his own kind — but suppose this butterfly had the ability now envisioned by scientists, that of controlling genetic factors, then what would become of the original grayling species? To the scientists the prospect may be exciting; to the rest of us it is more liable to be terrifying. And there remains this peculiar urge in an oystercatcher to sit on an egg so large she could not possibly hatch it. Perhaps only the jealous guarding of the very large eggs by the rightful mothers prevents the oystercatcher species from dying out.

Rather strange too, in a somewhat different way, is the fondness of certain birds and animals for what is glittering. That quality has been known for some time and by such unscientific observers as picnickers who have watched helplessly while a jay carried away a silver spoon. Several other birds, crows, for example, have a penchant for shiny objects, although there is no glitter in nature except the sparkle of sun on waves or icicles (which can't be removed) and therefore shininess in itself has no survival value. Among mammals, pack rats will carry away bright objects.

Pack rats, which include the bushy-tailed wood rat, are little animals that resemble squirrels much more closely than rats, particularly as their fluffy fur covers their tails. For a long time they were regarded with something like tender admiration, for although they did steal bright articles from woodland cabins, they "always left something in return." Now it is known that they just like to collect such things for their nests, and if they are running about with one in their mouths, and come across something they like better, they leave the first. In this way a rat may take your spoon but leave "in payment" your neighbor's watch.

An amusing incident that concerns one of the rats is told by Lowell Sumner and Joseph Dixon in *Birds and Mammals of the Sierra Nevada*, a book that is an attractive combination of exact scientific information and lore with a human interest. In the days when men in the West still carried such coins, Professor W. F. Dean

put three twenty-dollar gold pieces and his gold-rimmed spectacles
in his hat beside him when he was on a camping trip with Walter
Fry in Sequoia National Park and the men went to sleep lying
on the bare ground. In the morning the money and spectacles were
gone and in their stead in his hat was a round ball of horse dung.
He accused Fry of playing a joke on him; Fry protested innocence,
and since neither man knew about pack rats then, a decided
coolness sprang up between them. They were away during the
day, but when they returned to the same campsite that night, they
saw a rat making off with one of their forks. With this clue they
searched for the animal's nest and there recovered the metal
treasures.

The enchantment with dazzle is not dysgenic; a nest decorated
with twenty-dollar gold pieces can still be a good nest, and the
appeal of glitter for some birds and animals may have some relation to pre-aesthetic impulses, a fascinating tendency — only lately
being studied — that will be discussed in the section on play.

In the case of the too large eggs, however, and the too large and
too dark female butterflies, the preference seems a total mystery.
The supernormal: young biologists mention Marilyn Monroe, and
that facetious comparison actually is interesting because Miss
Monroe's extreme attractiveness also appeared to be a dysgenic
quality. Considering the part that natural selection plays in the
destiny of all species, one can project this thought in several
provocative and perhaps disquieting human directions. Maybe the
human population explosion will correct itself in this way.

William H. Thorpe suggests that there may be another dysgenic
quality in an animal's impulse to spend all its time in play if it
is supported by human beings, either as a pet or laboratory
animal. An example was Elsa, the Adamsons' pampered lioness,
which never developed the impulse to get her own food until she
was taught to hunt by her human friends. And dogs: when they
are not fed on time, do many set about finding some mice for
themselves? Very few. Joseph Dixon, one of my wise teachers

in the techniques of field observing, told me that if I ever used food to induce birds and animals to come near, it should be the natural foods of those species (acorns, berries, and such), and they should never be given enough so that they lose the knack of their own hunting: "They can so easily be turned into mendicants." One thinks of the shorter and shorter work-weeks promised for human beings, or even workless weeks, and wonders if there is an inherent mammalian tendency to put leisure time to constructive uses; or can the ongoing, instinct-fulfilling motives deteriorate? Even the sexual instinct. It is notoriously difficult to persuade animals and birds in zoos and aviaries to mate — although of course there are other factors in that case besides the free living. One is the artificial environment.

Although we know better now, we are still inclined to consider that all kinds of change are progress. Notwithstanding, even the animals have not always continued their former headway towards more complexity and control. In some species a retrograde tendency has set in at a certain point, not taking the animals out to extinction but back to a simpler stage. One that had evolved a spinal cord and therefore an advanced type of activity has regressed so far that the cord has been lost and the animal has become little more than a mass of pulsating flesh on the tideflat of the restless sea.

The last few recent years are the only time in all history when human beings have had a chance to compare our own behavior with accurately described behavior of the animals from whom we have descended — or ascended? Until a hundred years ago that relationship with the animals was not known. When evolution did become recognized, people suddenly realized that they had almost no information about these ancestral creatures — except as food or the source of furs. How they lived, when they were seen in snatches, had been described in brief reports, sometimes by reliable naturalists like Gilbert White and Audubon and Bachman, sometimes by poets, whose truth was often as real

although differing sometimes in detail. But there was no system-
atized body of information. No one knew, actually, how much
intelligence animals have, if any, what instinct is, what emotions
they feel, how acute their senses are, or how they conduct themselves in situations similar to our own. There was very little that
anyone could take hold of, if his wish was a better understanding
of his own origins.

Curiosity was fired. In all civilized nations men of wealth en-
dowed academies to study the ways of wildlife. Biology became
one of the most popular professions. These Victorians, however,
who were the first to try to digest the thought of evolution, made
an understandable mistake. Since we have inherited animal
natures, they reasoned, animals must be much like us: they must
think as we do and have the same moral standards. Raccoons
were thieves because they stole corn from farmers; the squirrel who
ate the bread crumbs thrown out for birds was a robber; the lion
was a king; snakes were true to their Biblical reputation, the very
incarnation of evil; birds were sweet innocents, except the ones like
jays that sometimes raid other birds' nests — they were murderers.

From this thick-brown sentimentality it was inevitable that there
would be a reaction. It was led by C. Lloyd Morgan, the British
animal psychologist, who distrusted all delusions about thinking
and moralizing animals, and with his associates formulated Morgan's
Canon, or the Law of Parsimony. According to this rule an animal's
action must never be interpreted as the result of a higher psychical
faculty if it can be attributed to one that is lower in the psychological scale. The law is still considered a good one, but there is a
difficulty in the fact that a human observer, with his own psychological bent to express, still stands in the picture. The Victorians were
guilty of sentimental anthropomorphism; soon the new biologists
were indulging in anthropomorphism of another kind: they were
describing animals according to the current infatuation with machines. It was the age when automobiles, airplanes, and ever more-
complex industrial equipment were ravishing the minds of men,

and biologists like J. B. Watson and Pavlov followed along with the declaration that animals are no more than reflex mechanisms.

Earlier philosophers like Descartes lent prestige to these theories, but now they were reinforced with a whole new terminology and with new apparatus for experimentation. An animal, said these biologists, is as automatic as a system of levers: an external object or event presses a lever and the animal responds with an inevitable and predictable reaction. The existence of any innate motivations, instincts or other inward impulses, was denied. And even yet there are mechanists who lean towards the chain-of-reflexes theory, although most of them now admit that some innate tendencies are inborn. How can they do otherwise? As proof there are such examples as birds raised from hatching in soundproof rooms, where they can never have heard another bird sing and yet as adults produce the typical song of their species. What external lever, what learned behavior, that is, can account for the song pattern?

The mechanists of today do not use any such simple analogies as levers. They talk about the similarities between animal minds and computers, and they deny that there is any element in a living organism that cannot be analyzed in terms of physics and chemistry. Some of those who disagree bring up the phenomenon of "emergence": the fact that a new quality sometimes emerges when simple elements are combined. Emergence even applies to inanimate materials, for instance the crystals of salt, which are new forms that emerge from the combining of sodium and chlorine. Biologically it is said that *life* is an emergent, a novel quality not found in the original materialistic elements in whch the mechanists like to define organisms. Since life does not emerge from the combining of metals in a computer, it is claimed that it never will be possible to equate computers with living beings. Still some scientific temperaments aren't convinced. They are so fascinated by machine concepts that one can't help being reminded sometimes of the supernormal stimuli, of oystercatchers trying to hatch gigantic, inappropriate eggs.

Among the others it was a Hollander, J. A. Bierens de Haan, who cast doubt on the Law of Parsimony, thirty years after it had been adopted. He urged biologists not to try to explain an animal's behavior as simply as possible, but as correctly. By then, in the 1920's and 1930's, there was a new generation of biologists and many were ready to listen. While some of them have preferred to do their work in laboratories, others have gone out of doors, to make a real science of animal observation. They call themselves, these co-operating indoor and outdoor men, ethologists, and it is largely due to their efforts that we now have a reliable body of knowledge about our animal forebears.

For laymen ethology is probably the most interesting of the biological sciences for the very reason that it concerns animals in their normal activities and therefore, if we wish, we can assess the possible dangers and advantages in our own behavioral roots. Ethology also is interesting methodologically because it combines in new ways very scrupulous field observations with experimentation in laboratories.

The field workers have had some handicaps in winning respect for themselves. For a long time they were considered as little better than amateur animal-watchers — certainly not scientists, since their facts were not gained by experimental procedures: they could not conform to the hard-and-fast rule that a problem set up and solved by one scientist must be tested by other scientists, under identical conditions and reaching identical results. Of course many situations in the lives of animals simply cannot be rehearsed and controlled in this way. The fall flocking of wild free birds can't be, or the homing of animals over long distances, or even details of spontaneous family relationships. Since these never can be reproduced in a laboratory, are they then not worth knowing about?

The ethologists who choose field work have got themselves out of this impasse by greatly refining the techniques of observing. At the start of a project all the animals to be studied are live-trapped, marked individually, and released. Motion pictures, often in color, provide permanent records of their subsequent activities. Recording of the animals' voices by electrical sound equipment is considered essential, and the most meticulous notes are kept of all that occurs. With this material other biologists, far from the scene, later can verify the reports. Moreover, two field observers often go out together, checking each other's observations right there in the field.

Ethology, the word, is derived from the Greek *ethos*, meaning the characteristic traits or features which distinguish a group — any particular group of people or, in biology, a group of animals such as a species. Ethologists have the intention, as William H. Thorpe explains, of studying "the whole sequence of acts which constitute an animal's behavior." In abridged dictionaries ethology is sometimes defined simply as "the objective study of animal behavior," and ethologists do emphasize their wish to eliminate myths.

Perhaps the most original aspect of ethology is the way that field observation is combined with experimentation in laboratories. Although the flocking of birds cannot be studied indoors, many other significant actions of animals that are seen only infrequently in the field, or seen only as hints, may be followed up later with indoor tests. Likewise investigations made first in laboratories can be checked by observations of animals ranging free in their normal environments.

Suppose that a field man, watching marked individuals, notes that an infant animal, *a*, is nursed by a female, *B*, known not to be its mother. Later he sees other instances of such maternal generosity. Is this willingness on the female's part a case of inherited behavior, or has it been picked up as one of the social customs of the species; that is, is it *learned*? Does it mean that all the adult females of this species feel some responsibility for the young, and if so, is such a tendency innate, or could behavior like that be acquired?

Elephant mothers are among those which give milk to offspring not their own. A group of elephants cannot very well be confined in a laboratory; but if the field worker is concerned with a species of smaller animals, he can bring newborn young into captivity, raise them and mate them there, and then note the behavior of the new mothers. Since they never have seen other females nursing young, their actions will be innate, inherited. And if it does turn out that one of these females will nurse any young that come to her, it will further have to be determined whether she recognizes her own. That question too can be answered in the laboratory; it is an easy problem for an experimental psychologist. By such techniques it has been found, for example, that in the species of small brown bats called *Myotis myotis* the mothers do know their own young and likewise will nurse any hungry infant regardless of blood relationship. This maternal behavior could have been observed in a colony of animals kept for generations indoors, but since the habitat there is artificial, the only way to know whether the behavior is normal to the species was to observe it first in animals living free in their natural world. Only by such a combination of laboratory and field work can instincts and acquired characteristics be distinguished. The value of knowledge like that is so great that the wonder is why such cooperation had not developed much earlier.

Ethology as a science has so far centered around this question — with what tendencies are animals, including ourselves, born and what habits by contrast are learned? The ability to learn is a measure of intelligence, and through thousands of patient experiments those two qualities — the inherited and the acquired — are now fairly well separated and understood.

As laymen we still use the word *instinct* quite loosely. We may say, "Some instinct told me that I should sell that stock," or, "I am Irish, so instinctively I like green." Neither meaning has any relation to instinct as the biologists now define it. They recognize only about five *true* instincts, those for nourishment, reproduction (in which is included the rearing of young), sleep, care of the body surface (grooming of feathers, removal of parasites, etc.), and, according to some scientists, a social instinct which causes many animals to seek the companionship of their kind.

These instincts are innate; that is, they will come forward as pressing demands whether or not anything stimulates them externally. A male animal does not have to see a female in order to feel a sexual urge; or to see food before he feels hungry; or need any reminder to seek a place to sleep when he is tired; or to clean his skin; or, perhaps, to try to find some associates. These qualifications are not hard to grasp: that an instinct is inherited and is compulsive.

It is somewhat confusing at first to learn that there are numerous detailed ways of acting which are also inherited and yet are not basic instincts. These secondary legacies are the so-called *action patterns*, or *behavior patterns*, by which the instincts fulfill themselves. For every species there is an action pattern to carry out each separate instinct: a way, typical for that animal, to seek and find its food; a way to win a suitable mate, etc. Some of the action patterns are quite elaborate, especially those related to reproduction, where they include nest or burrow building, all the traditional ways of courtship, bearing and caring for offspring. The difference between an action pattern and the instinct itself is essentially the fact that an instinct demands fulfillment, whereas an action pattern does not cause misery in the animal if some element of it is not expressed. Also there is some flexibility in the action pattern, whereas an instinct is rigid. It is especially rigid in its final stage, the *consummatory act*. The flexibility of the action pattern is shown in the so-called *appetitive behavior*. When an instinct is impelling an animal to seek its goal, the search itself will be varied according to the external circumstances. This kind of behavior often seems desultory, aimless, but the end performance is quick and direct once the desired object is found. That last burst of activity is prompted by the *sign stimulus*, as it is now termed: the prey, the desirable mate, and so on. It also is recognized that there is an *internal releasing mechanism* which in effect says, "Yes, go ahead now." Finally, there is *learned behavior,* taught by parents or gained through social and other experience.

These few explanations make it easier to understand the recent interpretations of animal behavior, and since the theories seem to hold up very well, they probably will be accepted permanently, and therefore it is worthwhile to know the various terms. Once they are clear in our minds, much human behavior becomes illuminated: our reproductive activities, for example. Now we can distinguish between the instinctive urgency and the action patterns with which we express it. Elements of our action patterns will be inherited, such as caressing of mates and gentle handling of infants; but other forms of behavior are matters of social indoctrination and habit and those, especially, can be modified if we wish.

Two more terms are important. One is *displacement.* An animal, like ourselves, may find an instinct frustrated by external circumstances; or two instincts sometimes compete for expression. Then a tension builds up. It may be discharged through a vacillation between the action patterns of the two instincts, or by some quite irrelevant type of activity. Formerly it was thought that the "broken-wing decoy behavior" of some ground-nesting birds, in which a parent bird flutters limply off and may thus lead an enemy away from its young, was a clever and gallant act. Now the ethologists suspect that it may be due to confusion between the urge to stay with the offspring and the urge to escape by flying.

Biologists see many evidences of displacement to relieve tension in human beings. Men stroke their chins, women fuss with their hair — actions which belong to the care-of-the-body-surface instinct — when some other instinct is being denied. Smoking is often described as displacement, the instinct of sucking again being a substitution — as many smokers have recognized. Asked why she smoked, a high-school girl said, "Because it helps me relax when my love affairs are not going right."

A final term useful to know is *imprinting:* — the significant mechanism by which an infant bird or animal is inclined to identify with the first individual that gives it the suitable stimulus. Since this usually is its mother, the animal recognizes its own species by an extension of the mother figure: *creatures like that are the ones I belong with*. The outward proof that imprinting has taken place is the infant's habit of following wherever the other goes, at least for a while. The following-behavior ordinarily has a limit in time. But something profound has happened. For the infant's alignment with that first individual, and the response that the other gives him, may determine his actions months or years later in his relationship with the then-adults of his own generation. Unless he has been imprinted accidentally by a member of an alien species, he will take as a mate only one of the kind that was stamped on his early consciousness — as a mold is stamped into wax. By then, as Julian Jaynes has suggested, his youthful companions will have grown into closer likenesses of the adult who first gave him his species-pattern.

Biologists often inadvertently imprint the young animals they are working with. Human beings then become the group to which the animal sees himself as belonging. He follows the scientist everywhere that he goes if he can; and when he matures, he often courts the biologist or another human. One of Konrad Lorenz's birds, a jackdaw which imprinted to him earlier, as a love-sick adult wished to feed him caterpillars, and when the biologist was reluctant to take them in his mouth, they were stuffed in his ear. Fairly often, too, there is partial imprinting between siblings: a younger brother or sister will constantly follow an older one — a harmless development, since the original imprinter is carried in the animal's consciousness as a member of the "proper" species, not individually as the object of affection to be pursued permanently.

Imprinting has been proved conclusively as it occurs in birds, and it also has been found in some fishes and insects and more recently in various mammals. Some theories concerning imprinting in human infants will be discussed in Part II.

This interesting phenomenon has been most intensively studied by Lorenz, one of the first ethologists. Since the way he works has made possible some of his most important contributions to the new science, a little more should be told about him, and about one or two others who have been pioneers in this modern science of animals' normal behavior.

Lorenz is a man with so sympathetic a feeling for animals that even when he lived as a medical student in his parents' Vienna apartment he had a collection of wildlife about him, including a Capuchin monkey and an aquarium with rare kinds of marine organisms. Right then he had a foretaste of some of the difficulties he would encounter later and would describe for laymen in two delightful books, *King Solomon's Ring* and *Man Meets Dog.* Returning home one night, he found that the monkey had thrown a bronze table lamp into the aquarium and, unlocking a bookcase, had removed two volumes of medical textbooks, from which she had torn every leaf, stuffing the paper also into the aquarium. (Was she jealous of the attention Lorenz gave to his marine animals?) He found his "sad sea-anemones" with their tentacles clogged with the paper they had tried to digest.

It would have taken more than such a mishap to discourage Lorenz, for when he moved to a country area, he proceeded to open his house to any and all creatures that cared to enter it. Many of the creatures, including birds such as ravens, jackdaws, cockatoos, and geese, as well as lemurs and monkeys, accepted the invitation. His patient wife adjusted to this regime, making a cage to protect their baby rather than urging Lorenz to keep his animal subjects in captivity. To as great an extent as possible Lorenz has shared the environment of his animals, climbing trees for the birds' perspective and wading through swamps to feel at home in the world of ducks. Such close association with these animals has enabled Lorenz, trained in objective observation, to learn facts that could never have been discovered in the artificial environment of a laboratory.

In field work confirmed in laboratories, attempts are being

made now to test the animals in surroundings that at least simulate natural habitats. It also is true that some experiments can be carried on indoors which are not possible in the branches of trees or the mud of swamps. One scientist who has done highly productive laboratory work on animal behavior is a former student of Lorenz's, Nikolaas Tinbergen, originally from the Netherlands and now at Oxford. Early in his career he undertook an investigation, simple as he then thought, of the finger-length fish, the stickleback. He found that there was so much to be learned from these little subjects, not only about sticklebacks but about the whole subject of instincts and how they function — what impels an animal to do what it does — that he spent years in studying that small animal and became one of the world's best-known biologists because of what sticklebacks taught him. He also has done other work such as the experiments on supernormal stimuli, which he guided, and — out in the field this time — he made a detailed observation of the lives of herring gulls, the results being published in an attractive book, *The Herring Gull's World*. His chief opus, however, is a textbook, *The Study of Instinct*.

Another ethologist who has combined indoor and outdoor work with a monumental survey of all the studies of animal behavior done since the mechanistic approach began to lose ground, is William H. Thorpe of Cambridge University. His book *Learning and Instinct in Animals* (with a bibliography of 1400 titles) reviews many hundreds of important projects and thoughtfully appraises their value. Thorpe has done field work in Africa as well as western Europe, and he has lectured at various American universities. Several of his own particular studies have been made with birds, and with insects and other invertebrates. And perhaps more than any other of the modern biologists, he is interested in the significance that his subject may hold for man. While never planning a project for its direct bearing on human problems, he is philosophically aware of man's background and place in the animal kingdom. A biologist of great austerity of mind and impeccable scientific integrity, yet he often expresses a warm concern for the human condition. His small book called *Biology and the Nature of Man* helps to clarify a most confused subject.

These three ethologists are by no means the only ones who are revealing, actually for the first time, a true and realistic picture of the behavior of animals. The extent to which they and others like them are straightening out some unfortunate misconceptions is illustrated by a subject rather wildly misinterpreted at various times in the last hundred years: the songs of birds.

The music of the garden was a favorite romantic theme during the Victorian decades. The birds sang with the voices of departed loves; they sang of the inevitable departure of the listener; they sang with hope for the reluctant spring. Those were poets' conceptions. The average admirer of their songs assumed that the "father bird" was singing to his mate on the nest — expressing in his beautiful way the solidarity of family life that was so strongly emphasized by Victorian human adults.

All these subjective impressions were swept away in the period when the Law of Parsimony was denying animals any qualities except those of reflex mechanisms. Usually birds were not singled out, as some mammals like dogs were, to prove that animals are no more than automatons, but they were included in the belittling of all wildlife. And their turn for special attention came in 1920, when Henry Eliot Howard published his *Territory in Bird Life*. This report was held to prove that bird song is actually no more than a declaration of a real-estate claim; it is addressed to neighboring individuals of the same species and it says *Keep out. This piece of land is mine.*

The book was received with enthusiasm, indeed eagerness. Even Howard had somewhat qualified his statements about the function of territorial song; yet the scientists with whole hearts, and the public as their followers, assumed now that birds are no more emotional or aesthetic in their musical choruses than the arguments at meetings of local real-estate boards.

That phase as well was to pass, although not entirely. Howard's analysis is now thought to be much too restricted, for modern students of bird behavior have found many other reasons besides territory defense for birds' singing. And yet Aldous Huxley in his last book, published in 1963, used the supposed claim to property at all times, by all singing nightingales, as the pivot of his whole argument. The point is important because the book, *Literature and Science,* is an exhortation to writers, especially poets, to readjust their sensibilities so that they take into consideration all the truths announced by various branches of science. No longer can we resist or ignore those truths, Huxley says; in the life of the mind and spirit, somehow we shall have to make room for them.

He was right; we shall. But the facts we must now include in our artistic perceptions should be those of the largest proportions — and above all they should be dependable. At this stage science is proclaiming many "final" conclusions which then are revised in a few years; and the rest of us are convinced too easily by the self-confidence of the men-of-facts. Even a layman should be bold enough to question the scientists; even a layman, it is hoped, may be well enough informed so that he has at least an intuitive sense of discomfort when a scientific conclusion is incomplete, or indeed quite dubious. J. B. Watson was certain that no animal has any innate instinctual urges, and yet it took only one bird, singing in a soundproof room, to bring that great edifice of scientific theory crumbling to the ground.

Strangely, many of those who were so ready to accept on faith the 1920 explanations of bird song had evidence in their own observations to suggest that Howard's explanations are no more than partly correct, but there has been a materialistic turn of mind in this century that delights in pulling down anything that cannot be weighed or measured. Even Huxley, with his interest in far-Eastern mysticism, seemed to show it. See how he reports the nightingale's songs:

> *. . . when the cock nightingale sings, it is not in pain, not in
> passion, not in ecstasy, but simply in order to proclaim to other
> cock nightingales that he has staked out a territory and is pre-
> pared to defend it against all comers. And, what makes him
> sing at night? A passion for the moon, a Baudelairean love
> of darkness? Not at all. If he sings at intervals during the
> night, it is because, like all the other members of his species,
> he has the kind of digestive system that makes him want to
> feed every four or five hours throughout the twenty-four. Be-
> tween caterpillars, during these feeding times, he wants his
> rivals ("Jug, Jug, Jug") to keep off his private property.*

In these facetiously phrased pronouncements Aldous Huxley was
oblivious of facts that have been known to ornithologists for at
least ten years. They are summarized in Thorpe's 1961 book, *Bird-
Song*, which any bird-watcher will find as useful as an English-
French dictionary to a traveler in Paris. It is a rich source of information about the qualities of bird calls and songs, the habits
and stimuli which call them forth, the responses they induce in
other birds, and many more details, but we shall limit this report
to the occasions when songs are used.

Male birds do, of course, sing from various conspicuous posts
around the perimeters of their territories to let other birds know
that this homesite is occupied. These songs are given from such
points as the tops of trees and bushes and unobstructed fence posts
and are shrill and emphatic, meant to carry as far as possible. The
song of the nightingale that most enchants human listeners comes
mostly from within underbrush. And the bird would hardly be
interrupting a feeding session then, for his eyesight is poor in
darkness, which is therefore not the time to be seeking caterpillars.
Even owls, with their great, dark-adjusted eyes, find their prey
mostly by hearing.

Perhaps the "song of night's sweet bird," which Shelley found
so moving, is at times addressed to neighboring males. However,

nightingales are known to be among the birds in which a male sings to persuade a female to join him as mate, and then sings to her repeatedly in order to induce her final acquiescence. Songs to the female are part of the mating ritual in this species; without them it is not likely that the union would ever take place. And so the poets whom Huxley was scolding may take back their loving nightingales; they can thrill to the music and still be in accord with the facts of scientific bird observation.

It is the nightingale's song of which Thorpe writes when he says that its "elaboration of pattern seems to have gone to quite excessive lengths, unless indeed we suppose that the listening bird has something approaching aesthetic appreciation and is more stimulated by a nightingale song of high elaboration than by one that is simpler." Sound spectrographs, those electrically produced charts which show the tone qualities of bird songs and calls, indicate one reason why the nightingale's voice is so pleasing to human ears. More almost than those of any other bird its tones are very pure (that is, without scattered frequencies), and they are reinforced by strikingly definite overtones, or harmonics.

Besides singing to females, nightingales sing in the winter when territory defense is not an issue. They sing on migration. Some of the females sing. And it appears that having such lovely musical sounds in their throats, they often sing just to give them expression. More will be said on this subject when the aesthetic tendencies of birds and animals are discussed in Part V.

Concerning other birds that sing and why, here are a few more details that seem interesting:

In the songs that obviously are sung from the rims of territories and are of a public character, unmated males are inclined to sing much more than those that already have found their females. That is, the songs are lonely-heart advertisements as much as warnings to other males. An unmated pied flycatcher, for example, has been found to sing 3600 songs a day but his mated neighbor less than a third as many. And it is said that in at least one species, the brown towhee, the male ceases to sing at all once he is mated.

Songs are a means of communication between members of individual families, between mates for instance, when they are foraging. Tinbergen found that sleeping herring gulls, kittiwakes, and some terns are awakened by the voices of their mates but not by the voices of other birds in the flock.

Some female birds sing, although they almost never concern themselves with defense of the homesite: the females of twenty subspecies of song sparrows are singers. The little wren has a whisper-song that she only sings to her young. Would it be anthropomorphic to call it a lullaby? The herring gull female is one of those birds, mentioned earlier, that revert to the begging call of the newly hatched chicks during the mating ceremonies.

Most remarkable of all bird songs, it seems to me, are the duets between mates. They are heard frequently in dark rain forests and are thought possibly to be a way that the birds keep in touch with each other among the dense shadows. The greatest refinement of duetting is the antiphonal song, in which one mate sings a few notes, to be taken up by the other, the two alternating so perfectly that unless both birds are in view it is impossible to know that more than one is singing. These antiphonal performances are produced by individuals in more than twenty families of birds, according to Thorpe, who has heard some of them and testifies to the almost unbelievable accuracy of their timing.

It should be mentioned too that most of the common bird songs are much more elaborate than many listeners imagine. The songs do have somewhat regular patterns, but what we identify is often the quality of the bird's voice as much as the notes he sings. Who, without evidence, would suspect that a robin may have more than fifty songs?

Perhaps a few facts like these will help to dispel the impression created by Howard's book. That we have been so ready to give only a business connotation to the singing of birds is anthropomorphism quite as clearly as the anthropomorphism of the sentimental Victorians.

The belief that birds and animals only respond to the most materialistic stimuli dominated the work of the experimental biologists until about fifteen years ago. They have followed the theory of C. L. Hull that "Learning only proceeds when it leads to reduction of need," and as Thorpe comments, need in this context is taken to mean physiological. In the laboratories this idea has been expressed in the unquestioned assumption that animals never will take part in the investigations unless they are bribed with food. Actually there have been non-scientific indications that that is not true. Dogs that are trained for police work, it is well known, and dogs that are given obedience training learn best if they are not fed as reward for co-operating. And, incidentally, a young teacher, Allan G. Walstrom, tells me that something essential, some spontaneity and momentum, goes out of the learning process in children if they receive prizes for getting their lessons. Nevertheless, for a hundred years the biological experiments have always been set up with food as the bait for animals that perform their tasks.

The following remarks are not intended to belittle the knowledge that has been accumulated in this way. Astonishing things have been discovered about the abilities of animals, such as their time sense — rhythmic behavior so exact that bees, for instance, which discover a new patch of flowers at twenty minutes past two today will return to it at twenty minutes past two tomorrow; and the animals' number sense — some birds and perhaps squirrels can hear as many as five or six notes on a flute and translate the fiveness and sixness into visual images so that they open only such boxes as have five or six dots on the lids. A vast amount of material like this has been revealed. Some of it is described in an excellent book, *The Senses of Animals and Men*, by Lorus and Margery Milne; other details may be found in references listed at the end of this volume. Notwithstanding, when all the facts have been assembled and admired for their credibility and the precision of the research, it remains true that one entire, vast field of animal experience had not been disclosed by the method of bribing. It is the world of impressions that the creatures wish to explore, not because they will find rewards but simply because they are interested.

This gap in scientific endeavor was exposed by some of the animals themselves, in reactions that were interpreted by a perceptive biologist, Harry F. Harlow of the University of Wisconsin. In what seems to have been a sort of pure-science biology project, he gave some rhesus monkeys a mechanical puzzle — apparently just to see how they would react to it. They were not rewarded with food because there was no specific objective to be attained. What the monkeys did do was to show that they were fascinated by simply working the puzzle. They worked it again and again (an attendant would reset it each time) for twelve days, with no sign of diminishing interest. The last step in the puzzle was the lifting of a hasp that was screwed onto a board. At the end of the twelve days Harlow began putting raisins under the hasp. What happened then, and immediately was grasped as significant by Doctor Harlow, was the fact that the enjoyment the monkeys had derived from the puzzle, as such, without any reward, was then dissipated. That the raisins were there and could be secured apparently spoiled what had been so much fun. Now the puzzle was only manipulated to get the raisins and afterwards was ignored. And where does a scientist go from that discovery? Out! Out in a hundred directions.

What, besides the instinctual satisfactions like food, does interest animals? Who knew enough to say? That question never had been investigated.

From Harlow's experiment was born a whole new concept of animal inquiry, quickly embraced by ethologists: that of letting the animals make the rules for a while, of seeing where they would lead.

Harlow and his associates have pursued the idea with imagination and insight, and there have been others. One is John B. Calhoun, who fenced a large area in Maryland into which he turned a number of common Norway rats, just to see what they would do. For twenty-seven months (naturalists are patient men), he sat in a tower watching them and making notes about their activities. Rats, it might have been supposed, are known exhaustively to biologists. Thorpe estimates that 99 per cent of the psychological investigations of animals have been done with albino laboratory rats; and nearly 500 books — not articles but *books* — have been written about this one animal. And yet Calhoun was able to learn countless things never suspected about them, simply because they were living in virtually a free state and were following their own devices.

Very far from the view of animals as machines that react automatically, there has now been accepted, after dozens of studies, an absolutely new concept — that animals have an innate impulse to learn. Some biologists still define it materialistically, as no more than a practical urge to become acquainted with the environment. Others, including Thorpe, see it as something that is much more stimulating in its implications: that the urge to explore may, in the higher animals, be an impulse to enlarge consciousness, even perhaps to bring some order, some organization, into the elements that an animal can perceive.

The mechanists we shall probably always have with us, and they will continue to add welcome facts to our knowledge. Fortunately, we may always also have scientists of a more philosophical turn of mind and the flexible willingness to follow unexpected and promising possibilities.

As human beings we cannot escape decisions between right and wrong actions — called, unfashionably now, the moral problems. Usually we think of these as affecting only our species, but many philosophers and scientists do not agree. In his book *The Past and Future of Ethics,* M. A. R. Tucker admits that there is no single answer to the question of why some things are called good and others not, but he says that involved in the distinction are honor, self-respect, a sense of justice, personal responsibility, sympathy, and love; and he states his belief that all these have their roots in the lives of animals. Leonard T. Hobhouse, the sociologist, says, "If we go beyond comparative ethics to the behaviour of the higher animals . . . we shall discover a perfectly feasible line of advance."

Considering honor first, an apparent example is the well-known reaction of wolves to an adversary's surrender. When two wolves are fighting, perhaps over a territorial boundary, as soon as the loser knows he cannot win he offers his neck, his vulnerable jugular vein, to the teeth of the stronger wolf, and the victor is bound by the wolf code not to take advantage of the opportunity. An instant earlier he seemed frantic to reach that vein. Now that it is exposed, within an inch of his teeth, he suddenly is immobilized. Why? What compulsion restrains the teeth from closing into that neck? What quality overrides the assumed "blood-thirsty animal nature"?

The end of the fight is impossible to describe without implying something like honor.

Self-respect is another aspect of the wolf temperament. James Algar, producer of nature films for Walt Disney, says that his men who have worked with both dogs and wolves have been struck by a difference between them. If some offense causes friction between a friendly dog and a man, the dog is likely to come fawning around, "asking forgiveness for a fault that probably was the man's." Wolves, on the other hand, are so committed to the fine points of conduct that if a man fails in self-control, if he loses his temper to the extent of speaking harshly to the wolf or steps on a paw accidentally, with no show of malice, the wolf's previous affection is destroyed forever. No favors later bestowed on the wolf will restore his trust. He appears to feel that his confidence has been irreparably betrayed.

Many animals observe the conditions of fair play, of "equity" — that is, justice in a larger sense than our human law. It is seen in one of its simplest forms at a bird bath. Several birds often sit on the edge, one by one taking turns at enjoying the water. A time approaching one minute usually is allowed each bird to throw the bright cleansing drops over his back and wings. If he takes longer the next bird will challenge him. The bather may bluster a bit but he always leaves, and the others wait patiently until all have a chance. Taking turns at some favored activity is seen constantly in the wilderness, and far down the biological scale.

And speaking of justice, the Finnish anthropologist E. A. Westermarck made an interesting observation: that an outraged animal does not strike out blindly, venting his anger on anyone happening to be near. He is "discriminating in his retribution," punishing only the offender and sometimes waiting for a considerable length of time for that opportunity.

The great English jurist Blackstone said that our property laws are based on the concepts of ownership shown by most animals. Even spiders respect the webs of other spiders unless their own have been destroyed, and among other species the separate members of a group are allowed to keep any desirable territories they have claimed, to have their homes, their nests or burrows inviolate. The stronger birds or animals would be able to rout them, but even in species which have developed hierarchies based on dominance or leadership, the "boss" recognizes the property rights of the weaker.

Similar to this respect in regard to real estate is the respect for the relationship of sexual partners. As among human beings some birds and animals are more attractive to the opposite sex than others are. There is much rivalry during the courtship of such desirable mates, but once the bond is established the rivals retire. And monogamous mates are loyal. There is no adultery in these species, or almost never.

Responsibility for the young, at least on the mother's part, is assumed without question. Such devotion is more closely associated with innate instinct than some other forms of unselfishness, but it does go to extreme lengths. As will be told later, the care often extends to others besides one's own offspring. In a delightfully written, important paper, *Helpers at the Nest*, published in the *Auk* in 1935, A. F. Skutch reveals that many birds help their neighbors at nest-building and care of their young. These companions may be other mated pairs or often are unmated females who attach themselves like unselfish maiden aunts to young families and help raise the broods without disturbing in any way the relationship between the parents. Altruism is found among mammals too, including elephants, wolves, primates, and of course dogs. In a letter to his ten-year-old daughter William James wrote of a dog in Colorado, "He longs to do good."

Fellow-feeling has now been proved experimentally. R. M. Church working with albino laboratory rats repeatedly subjected one group to electric shocks lasting 30 seconds each time. The rats showed distress by jumping around and squealing, and other rats, after being shocked only once and for no longer than one second, were so disturbed by the evidence of suffering in their associates that their appetites dramatically declined. They were able to get all the food they wanted by depressing a lever, and the frequency with which they ate fell off significantly during their fellows' misery, continuing below normal even ten days after their own experience. A group that had not had any shocks and therefore could not recognize the cause of the jumping and squealing did not lose their appetites. The reaction of the others is described by the scientist as unquestionably "sympathetic."

Co-operation is more common in the wilderness than destructive social practices are. If that situation were not the rule, as W. C. Allee has pointed out, the animal societies would disintegrate. David Starr Jordan was one who remarked that we ourselves are composed of cells with individual lives all co-operating for the good of the community which is a human body. The biologist J. F. Conklin considers that such co-operation will have to become the general attitude, "planet-wide," in our human society.

Since morals unquestionably are found in wild nature, what *is* the difference between human beings and animals?

Too many tool-using species have now been discovered for us to be able to use those skills as a criterion of our uniqueness. Nor language — in songs, calls, animal "talk," and the dance-messages of bees it has become clear that the rudiments of communication exist in subhuman species. Other distinctions have been proposed. There is now a widespread agreement, however, that human minds differ in degree rather than kind from those of the animals.

Most philosophical biologists have concluded that human minds have evolved, just as human bodies have, from the simpler elements in simpler creatures, but that human minds have now reached a point which none of the animals seem to have attained: that of thinking abstractly — of, for example, recognizing some quality of universal good. To have achieved that ability is more than a small advance. Of course its real importance is the extent to which we put it into effect.

One of biology's liveliest questions at present is that of *purpose:* how many, if any, animals have what corresponds to a conscious intention? Can they see ahead, ever, and bend their actions to some desired goal? Although no definite proof has been found as yet that they can, it is too soon to accept any quick negatives.

How far ahead do *we* see, and what are our goals? The answers will not be found in a wilderness, but in time perhaps accurate information about the animals will give us a better understanding of ourselves and therefore some guidance in choosing our further steps.

II

ANIMAL PARENTS

That the Young May Survive

That the Young
May Survive

THE SWAN MUSSEL was not nearly as complex a creature as man, but even she had her satisfactions, and a simple nervous system with which to experience them. Scooping down with the edges of her shell, she had dug a hole, not deep, in the bottom of the pond, and most of the time she lay in this little hideaway with the two tubes of her breathing-eating apparatus extending above the silt. As she pulled the water into one tube and pushed it out through the other, she inhaled a fresh supply of oxygen for her gills and, at the same time, a stream of the tiny aquatic plants and animals that were her nourishment. No doubt she enjoyed some draughts of this living broth more than others; and on windy days when the pond was stirred, the greater amount of oxygen may have felt rather invigorating. These were not very stimulating events, but the mussel was not equipped for excitement.

A male mussel lived in a hole beside hers. Although there was no touch between them, they seemed aware of each other. Early in June eggs were formed in the lining of the female's shell, in her "mantle"; soon they moved into her gills. Now the mussel would leave her nook. She came up and out into the water of the pond, and at the same time so did the male. As he shed a cloud of his sperm into the water, the female drew these cells in through her

syphon and along the normal route to her breathing gills. In this very mild way her eggs were fertilized.

In a few weeks they had developed into minute mussels, with few of their adult organs but already with shells, which were equipped with two interlocking, sharp teeth. At that stage they became too large to remain in their mother's gill chamber. And yet they were still too small and incomplete to look after themselves. They would have to be given nourishment and protection, and in a most remarkable way those would be provided.

One morning a small fish, a bitterling, came and lingered beside the mussel. The bitterling, also, was a gravid female — two animals so unlike, and yet at this time they needed each other. The mussel opened her shell and her offspring poured out like a stream of sand. Those that were touched by the fanning fins of the bitterling, and that were brushed by her sides, instantly clamped into the fish with the teeth on their shells. They had hooked into a new kind of mother. As the flesh of the bitterling swelled from the wounds, it would entirely enclose each little mussel, which would stay, snug and well fed by the bitterling's living tissues. They would not leave these cysts until they had grown so large that they burst them, when, as maturing molluscs, they would fall out and begin their independent lives. The fish would have carried the alien young for about a month but would not suffer permanent harm. Her wounds would heal.

The bitterling seems to have been a victim, but this tiny drama actually had in it a pat element of retribution. For while the small mussels were attaching themselves to the fish, the bitterling had thrust her own eggs through a long ovipositor into the flesh of the mother mussel. There they would stay, in the gill so recently vacated, until *they* were mature enough for a free-living existence. By this extraordinary arrangement two unrelated mothers, one a mollusc and the other a vertebrate fish, had exchanged their embryonic offspring, and each would incubate the immature strangers in the nursery of her body.

The bitterling's eggs — a further touch of bizarrerie — were fertilized after they were encased in the mussel's gills, not of course by the mussel but by a male bitterling who was hovering near. Instinct apparently told him when it was his turn to take part in this elaborate performance, and he shed his sperm close to the mussel. Through her syphon she drew it in and across the bitterling eggs exactly as she had done in the case of her own embryos.

Few aquatic females give birth to living young. They lay eggs — usually in the water, although not just anywhere. Some are attached with an adhesive substance to an underwater object, often to the inconspicuous undersides of stones in a current. Those of the yellow perch are trailed in ribbons of gelatin over submerged plants. Those of a mayfly, *Tricorythus,* are suspended from plants with each egg on its own slender thread. The red salamander fixes each egg to the end of a separate gelatin stalk. And sometimes the eggs of aquatic young are carried around till they hatch by one of the parents. The water-bug mother, *Belostoma,* attaches about a hundred eggs to the back of the male. With her legs hooked under him and "starting somewhere near the middle and sidling along every little while," as described by J. R. de la Torre-Bueno, "she works her way around him as she fastens her eggs on his back by means of . . . water-proof glue." There the eggs stay, wherever their father goes, till they hatch in about ten days.

The father's willingness to assume this responsibility should surprise no one, for among the aquatic parents, it is the males more often than females that are solicitous for their offspring. The male sunfish scoops out a hollow on the bottom of his pond by swishing his fins through the sand and removing stones with his mouth. He chooses a place if possible where he can expose the roots of some water plants, a natural nest. When he is finished he lures a female to it, and they swim around in the nest together while clouds of eggs and sperm cells are discharged into the water. The female leaves as soon as fertilization has been completed.

The male of the hellbender salamander mates in much the

same way, with the difference that the mother of *his* young often wishes to stay and he drives her out. The stickleback, a small fish, makes an elaborate home for his young, a nest among water weeds. If one female does not supply him with as many eggs as he wants, he drives another and another into the nest, but none of these mothers remain. The male guards the eggs pugnaciously. When the eggs hatch, he watches over the infant fish, going after them if they stray and bringing them home in his mouth, harmlessly.

A stream where a flow of clean water runs continuously over pebbles or coarser rocks is the characteristic nursery of the eggs of salmon, whose parents make their famous journeys back from the sea, usually to the same creek where they themselves were spawned. In the case of salmon that originate in the Yukon River, it may be a migration of more than 2000 miles. When they have reached this "home," which, mysteriously, seems to them the only right place to lay their eggs, they prepare a trough in the bottom of the stream with their fins and tails, and as the eggs are dropped into it by the female they are fertilized by the male. When the mating performance is over, the parents cover the eggs with the excavated material. There they will lie, aerated and hidden from enemies, till they hatch and the young salmon start their own journey down to the sea.

A curious thing happens, then, to the parents: they suddenly seem to lose interest in living. They eat little or nothing and no longer flash about in the sparkling element that has given them pleasure for six years or more. Sometimes they listlessly let the current carry them downstream a short way, or they may move to the shallows. In either case they soon die.

In northwestern Alaska, on a tributary of the Nome River, I saw one of those spawning beds. The time was early September, and the water had sunk to a trickle. The young fish had left by then, but the mud-caked bed of the stream was covered with the dried bodies of the dead salmon parents. Though their eyeballs were gone, a trick of the slanting sun lined the sockets with round black shadows, which seemed expressive, like eyes looking out with indescribable sadness. And I was filled with melancholy, thinking of the salmon, obedient to the mute inner urge, which had come to the end of their lives in this great undertaking to give life to their species' next generation.

Of all the nurseries provided for the aquatic young, none is more fantastic than that for the tadpoles which will become the frogs called *Phyllomedusa*. When it is time for the eggs to be laid the female frog takes the male on her back and together they search for a leaf overhanging a pond or stream. When they find it, both parents seize it with their hind legs in such a way that the leaf is folded into an envelope. The female pours her eggs into this and the male his sperm. About a hundred eggs are thus fertilized, all being enclosed in a gelatin which serves to hold the edges of the leaf together when the adults have left. At the proper time as the eggs develop, they split the leaf and the tadpoles fall into the water below.

Parents like these may have been the first creatures — and are still among the most primitive — to perform selfless acts. What interests animals of still lesser development? Finding and eating food, fighting for it at times; perhaps moving about for the sheer pleasure of moving; the mating act, which for them is doubtless no more than a brief sensation. Those probably are the satisfactions of the uncounted hordes of little creatures who live and die without making any real effort to make sure that their species continue.

But now, in the aquatic animals, comes a dim, hardly conscious impulse to take better care of their eggs. At least they will seek a good place to deposit them, if only in riffles or draped over plants. Further, one may arrange a rudimentary or elaborate nest; and exert himself to keep water flowing over the eggs, for several weeks it may be, a very long time in the life of a tiny fish like a stickleback. These acts, expressing the birth of a sense of "duty," call for effort that must yield slight, if any, personal pleasure. The

young of these elementary parents will not furnish any of the
fringe benefits known to human parents — affection returned,
perpetuation of the family name, the possibility of support in old
age, and, if the young are attractive, an improved social status.
The devotion of these primitive animal parents is very innocent
and pure, and however instinctive such actions may be, the animals' little day of virtue deserves to be recognized.

None of these parents need to concern themselves about nourishment for their young, because all water contains microscopic
organisms that are an ideal baby food. For the parents of most
insects, however, that responsibility looms as enormous. Most of
the pablum for their infants will be other insects, many as difficult
to catch as a nimble grasshopper; yet the insect young, starting
life as grubs, maggots, as larvae, will have neither the skills nor
equipment to hunt. By the time they hatch, few of their parents
will still be alive to bring them food. On what will they live, grow,
and turn into bronzy beetles and those pieces of rainbows, the
butterflies?

Their parents have not neglected that problem. Eggs of most
insects are laid in nests — in the ground, in plant tissues, or
fastened to one kind of support or another, too often to doorjams
and corners of screens. The nests may be made of scrapings of
wood mixed with saliva (the paper wasps), of mud (the daubers),
or of wax or some other secretion spun out of the mother's body.
In such a cell often only one egg is laid. The rest of the space
is packed with immobilized caterpillars, beetles, spiders, grasshoppers, and such, which have been stung in their nervous systems, neatly at some spot that will paralyze the victim but will
not kill it. This food, edible and fresh and unable to fight or
escape, will be right there for the larva when it comes out of the
egg and discovers that it is hungry.

Or the egg may be laid in the living prey itself. The pimpline
insect stings a spider into brief unconsciousness, a few moments
only but long enough for the pimpline to insert an egg in the

spider's abdomen, where it cannot be reached and removed. When the egg hatches, the larva will feed on spider juice. For a while the spider seems to live normally, making webs, even laying eggs. Nevertheless, it is losing ground. It becomes duller and duller and makes poorer and poorer webs. It will live for as long as the pimpline larva requires it, and might recover, but the larva kills it with a strategic bite when it is ready to leave. Otherwise the young insect might be killed, itself, in getting away.

One group of flies, beneficial to men, arrange for their young to feed on the caterpillar stages of moths. The flies (Tachinidae) lay their eggs in the caterpillars behind their heads. When the young larva hatches it bores into the caterpillar but leaves its back end, through which it breathes, sticking out. The *Riela* mother rides around on a praying mantis until the mantis lays eggs. Then *Riela* lays *her* eggs in *its* eggs.

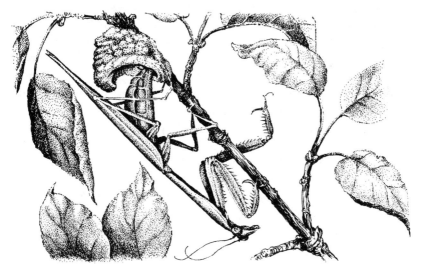

And some insects are like cowbirds and cuckoos and leave their eggs in the nests of closely related species. Among the social wasps one, the hornet, deposits her eggs in the nest of another species of wasp, whose young workers will feed her offspring along with their own. Lazy, and yet so clever that we can't help being amused by them, are some individuals of the *Chalybion* wasps. One will watch as the mud-dauber wasp, *Sceliphron*, energetically gathers mud and constructs its nest, sealing in its egg, well supplied with paralyzed spiders. When the builder has finished and gone away, *Chalybion*, bringing water, softens the hardened mud of the entrance and tucks in its own egg, for which, too, a living spider is suitable larva food.

Creatures that paralyze living victims and consume them at leisure are not very lovable by human standards. Such ultimate ruthlessness makes the sudden death administered by most predators seem almost merciful. But the cruelty is impersonal. By means that, in effect, have great foresight and ingenuity, the insect parents are only promoting the lives of their offspring. And though insects are alien to us, possibly they feel some of the same emotions that we do — even tenderness. We hardly can doubt it when we watch the small earwig mothers, which brood their eggs and, living to protect them after they hatch, fuss over them with an almost neurotic anxiety. There are even a few insect fathers that feel a paternal responsibility. Some of the male wasps of the genus *Trypoxylon* stand guard at the nest while the female is out hunting spiders; and certain male scarab beetles help the female to dig a hole in the ground, where she lays one egg. Working together then, they form a ball out of dung and roll it into the hole for the future larva to feed on.

Bees and ants and the social wasps are vegetarians. They provide communal nurseries for their young, where they will be tended by "wet nurses" who give them a food produced in their bodies, somewhat as mammals give mother's milk. The idle bee mother also is fed by these nurses, and because she must produce many eggs, she is fed more abundantly.

Perhaps we come closest to feeling some affinity with the insects when we consider that they too have weaknesses. Hornets are fond of alcohol, and if they can get it, usually from fermenting fruit, they become real drunks. They sip it until they fall into a stupor, and when they awake are so thirsty for more that they can't even be bothered to find the nest of another wasp in which to deposit their eggs.

As we zigzag along the evolutionary route, we find that the more complex creatures are usually the more dependable parents — but not always. Snakes are more highly developed than fishes; yet in contrast to the male stickleback, who gives his young such devoted care, the snake fathers ignore their offspring completely. Most of the mothers, as well, are indifferent to them. Some snakes lay eggs quite casually in the soil, in cracks among stones, or sometimes in rubbish that is fermenting and therefore warm. From then on they forget about them. Other snakes carry their young and give birth to them live, but the small snakes wriggle away as soon as they are out of their mothers' bodies. The python, however, is one reptile exception. The female of this monstrous species — she may be thirty feet long and strong enough to crush the life out of an ox — coils herself about her eggs and incubates them. She does not leave them even to eat, and during this time, curiously, her temperature rises above that of the environment, by some mechanism not understood, since all snakes had been thought to lack that adjustment. Thirty to forty of the python eggs hatch, and for a while afterward their mother continues to protect these most deadly of infants.

It is interesting to speculate why most snakes are indifferent to their offspring. One reason obviously is that the young seem pretty well able to fend for themselves. But would there be more snakes in the world if the parents were more protective? Maybe too many? Is nature keeping down the snake population so their numbers will not unbalance the life of the wilderness? Snakes do not have many enemies that would perform this function.

Birds are the world's most famous wild parents. Every child is told how the father and mother birds feed their nestlings "with worms" until they are old enough to fly; and how, then, on that

very day, the baby birds "are pushed out of the nest." Up to this
point the parents have been described as models of noble virtue,
and young listeners, I think, often suspect this tale as being partly
propaganda to win appreciation for the unselfishness of all parents.
If it is, it backfires, because our own parents show little sympathy
for the nestlings dismissed so abruptly.

And one wonders where the story arose that all baby birds are
pushed out of the nest. Was it our parents' subconscious wish, a
normal reaction to our often-exasperating behavior? The facts are
otherwise. Actually the only bird I know of that evicts an unwilling
offspring is the wandering albatross (the world's largest bird, with
a wingspread of almost twelve feet). The young one is fed on an
oily substance derived from its parents' partly digested diet of
fish, and on this nourishment the nestling — there is only one in
a season — grows hugely fat. It may be so heavy that it could not
fly if it wanted to; but it doesn't. The parents leave it, just sitting
there, for a period of four months, one hears, a period of pitiful
loneliness, during which the nestling trims down. This treatment
may arrest the young one's psychological development, for when
the parents come back, even then it is reluctant to launch from
the nest. So they drive it out. After that event the fledgling spends
some time with its father and mother, swimming around on the
ocean learning how to catch fish.

The truth about the devotion of parent birds is that most of
them spend an immense proportion of their life energy in raising
their young. In effect, many probably give their lives for them.
Many birds that have been reared in captivity, safe from natural
hazards, remain alive for ten years or more — some large birds much
longer. In the wilds the small species rarely survive for more than
a year or two. Banding records have shown that the age of the
English robins at death averages 13.3 months: they have lived
only long enough to rear one summer's young. The life span of
other birds has been studied, and none of them in the natural
environment had survived more than a fraction of its possible

years — with exceptions of course. People who provide nest boxes know that the same birds may come back on succeeding springs. This human benevolence may be one of the reasons why they do not succumb sooner. But why do so many of the rest die just after they reach maturity?

The chief reasons are weather, disease (not much of that), predators, and starvation. The toll that these take depends largely on the condition, the health, of the birds. It may be significant, then, that a large number of the lives seem to be lost near the end of the first breeding season, after an effort in raising their broods which is so great that the parents often become exhausted, even emaciated.

And no wonder! At the start of a nestling's life, when it is growing fast, it must be given considerably more than its own weight of food every day. When it is heavier the proportion of food to its weight diminishes, but during the two weeks, approximately, that an average bird stays in the nest, it receives a daily ration of half its mean weight. If there are four, five, six, or more young in the brood, the nourishment needed would seem enormous.

The infants of land birds are fed almost entirely on insects. Finding these would not be too difficult in the early weeks of the season, when most insects are slow-moving larvae like slugs and caterpillars. Later, when the larvae become insects that fly, they have less bulk, so that more of them are required to fill nestlings' stomachs.

The adult birds that normally live on insects themselves, like swifts and swallows, are skilled in catching this kind of prey, but many more birds are seed-eaters. Seeds are abundant and found in predictable places. What a change for these seed-eaters, now, to be seeking insects, which do not stay put! The parent bird, setting out in the morning, leaves a nestful of gaping, ravenous mouths, and to satisfy them requires not only continuous effort but searching — the chancy element of finding victims who themselves are foraging actively.

Tree sparrows, nesting in Canada where summer days are long, have as many as six young in one brood, and to keep them fed hunt from three o'clock in the morning till ten at night. Blue titmice, tiny birds related to chickadees, weigh only half an ounce when full-grown; yet a pair of these feathered mites have been known to carry food to their nestlings 475 times in a single day. A careful study showed that a song thrush caught 10,080 larvae and insects in one month's time, an average of 336 per day; and a pair of English robins nesting near Oxford did even better. Between dawn and dark they were seen to visit their young 29 times every hour and to bring two or three caterpillars each trip. It was estimated that in that period the parents had caught at least 1000 caterpillars.

We are talking here about parent birds with only one family of young in a summer. Some of them will have two, even three, with at least two broods being fed while their infancy overlaps. Usually the mother bird builds a new nest and lays the second clutch before the first brood are out of *their* nest. From then on the male takes responsibility for the earlier young and also helps feed the second brood when they hatch. Even then the father won't push out his nestlings. Edwin Way Teale has made an interesting suggestion: that the way baby birds flutter their wings when begging for food may lift the young suppliant almost automatically, especially after he starts to stand on the edge of the nest where the fluttering can be wider. Suddenly he is in the air — he has discovered that he can fly! After that he will rarely go back into the nest. If he would, if the nestlings all would, the father's task might be easier, for he is far from through with the task of feeding them. Parent birds of the species familiar in gardens continue to find their fledglings' food for two and a half to five weeks after they fly and are physically able to get it themselves. The reason, of course, is their need of time to learn how.

Insect-eaters like swallows and swifts feed their young in the air for a while, at first beak to beak as they hover on quivering wings. Later the morsels are dropped to them as the parent passes in flight. Soon the fledgling is catching the point as well as the tidbit and begins to acquire the speed and skill he will have to have in snapping up darting and skimming prey.

Birds that feed on the ground do not need such fine muscular control. The act of picking up is much easier and is an inborn tendency, but even the seed-eaters have to experiment: at the start they don't know what is edible. During the period of their learning the parents continue to bring them food, less every day until about the nineteenth day out of the nest in most species, when the fledgling himself will be getting about half his requirements. After that the parents' attentions fall off very fast. They still accompany their offspring, only now they swallow the food they find. The young will protest; however, parent birds don't let the fledglings make fools of them. The young have been fed so well by then that most of them weigh more than their parents do. They can stand a lean time.

They can be very mad about it. Last year the robins who raised young in our maple tree had one nestling that was much more demanding than the three others. He got more than his share and became large and fat—and spoiled. I sympathized with his parents, for I like to sit under the tree, which is near the brook, and long after that overgrown bird could look after himself, he perched in the maple and shrieked his resentment because no one came and put food in his mouth. By then his parents had left the neighborhood, rather early, and as I picked up my chair day after day and withdrew, I was sure I knew why.

By the time that they disappeared, the elder robins looked very bedraggled, surely not in the best condition to dodge an attacker or to survive a storm. Seeing them one could believe that most birds live to only a tenth of their possible lifetimes.

Biologists don't all agree on what is involved in the education of animal young. Everyone knows that some forms of behavior do not have to be learned, they are innate, but others must be acquired; and do the parents make any deliberate effort to teach? In some cases it seems undeniable that they do, even creatures as primitive as the birds.

William P. Pycraft has described some of the methods. He interprets as true teaching the way a mother grebe will take her brood out on the water and, catching a fish, will drop it in front of them. If they don't pick it up she lets the fish swim away a short distance, again demonstrates how the fish is caught, and repeats the lesson until the young see that they should *pursue* that fish. The ornithologist H. B. Macpherson watched a family of golden eagles for many weeks and has told how the nestling was taught to dismember its prey. At first he was given only the livers of hares, rabbits, and grouse that the parents brought to the nest. Later the parents, having eaten the other parts, let him pick livers out of the carcasses. One day, then, his mother put a whole rabbit's leg down in front of him. The nestling looked at it, hungry but seeming puzzled. She took it from him with signs of impatience, pulled off part of the meat and ate it herself, and flew off with the rest. The next time he was given a leg, he swallowed it bones and all. By showing him what to do and depriving him of the meat when he didn't learn, the mother finally drove home the lesson.

In some other bird species the parents appear to instruct the young. The fur-bearing mammals, however, are the ones who most often need teaching. Although the feeding of newborn young is no problem, since mother's milk solves it, the living conditions the young animal encounters as he grows older are more complex than those of most birds. The life of a mammal is less stereotyped; more unpredictable things happen, often events of too recent origin for an animal's inborn reactions to have become established. The birds' sky and trees are relatively unchanged, but a mammal's contact with civilized man, with guns and cars and bulldozers, requires adaptations that are quite new. And even in mammal habitats, that of a bear with cubs, for instance, the acceptable kinds of food are many in number compared with the food of birds. The young animal would make some discoveries — of dangers and pleasanter possibilities — by inherited impulse, but other elements of this learned behavior seem to be handed down from one generation to another. The animals have a "culture" just as human sets of habits are cultures and their culture is transmitted in much the same way — for the most part no doubt by example but there may also be purposeful guidance. All vocal animals have sounds that mean *no* and *all right* and *watch out,* and they communicate with their postures and gestures and actions. It is likely, however, that most things are learned by simply the long and close association with a mother and sometimes a father. Mammal young mature slowly. Meanwhile, it may be for years, they share the adults' world even though they can't function there yet. They learn what the social relationships are, both amicable and otherwise, and they see what is done in a great variety of situations, again and again, and a pattern of adult behavior, in all its details, is formed in their minds. Later they will live out the same patterns for their own offspring.

Some mammal young are born lacking even the most essential skills. Infant fur seals can't swim until their mothers have shown them how. The pet lioness Elsa, reared by human beings, had no instinct for catching her own prey when she was released in the wilds. She might have starved if her human friends had not taught her what she would have learned from lion parents if she had been raised normally. Actually lion young in the wilds do not learn all the tricks until after they are full-grown and have accompanied their parents on many hunts. Mammal parents may find this interminable association with offspring fatiguing — grizzly-bear mothers may nurse their cubs until they are four years old, but they don't turn them loose before they are completely familiar with what they will do as adults of their species.

What habits make up this culture packet depends largely on where an animal lives. In the ground, on it, above it, or far away from it: the conditions in each specific environment are different from any other, and the young mammal must learn how to get along best in his own surroundings.

No natural habitat is more singular than the bed of kelp which is the home of a sea otter. As the incandescent sun drops towards the rim of the ocean, touches and then moves below it, the last licks of silver light on the water fade into its molten pewter. The day has ended, and the pup in his mother's arms learns how an otter prepares for sleep. At dusk she is often idly afloat on her back among fronds of kelp, and he lies on her chest. Now she tightens her arms around him and rolls the two of them over and over until they are wrapped in strands of the giant seaweed. Just under the surface these uppermost leaves of the kelp spread out like the flat tops of trees, though more limber, with the stems — the stipes — fixed in the sand and rocks seventy-five feet below. As the wide, heavy swells of the ocean approach and pass during the night, the kelp in which they have entwined themselves will prevent the otters from drifting away. The fronds will hold them, the waves will rock them. Safely the mother and pup can sleep.

Close around them are their companions, a friendly herd of nearly a hundred sea otters who live in this kelp bed. The maze of fronds is their watery, unsubstantial island. One can swim in and out of its tangles, dive down through the foliage past the bare, rubbery stipes to the more delicate plants, like bushes, growing out of the ocean floor. The pup's mother has taken him down many times. Clasping him in one arm, she dives by backward thrusts of her strong hind feet, which are webbed. There below they find sea urchins, crabs, and clams that the pup will eat when he is no longer drinking her milk. The way she opens the shellfish when they are back on the surface is something to watch with delight as he floats in the water beside her. Whenever she brings up a shell, she also brings up a flat rock. Laying this on her chest, she lifts the shell over her head in both hands and brings it down on the rock with a crashing blow! Sometimes it takes two or three

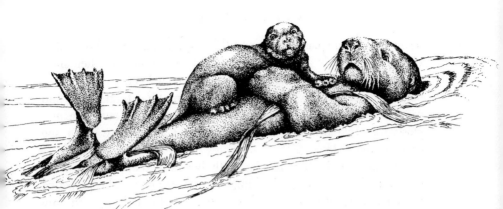

tries, but the shell breaks at last, and she takes a piece in her hands and eats out the meat within. The pup cannot do that yet, but at least he sees how it is done.

Some parts of the kelp are denser than others, and those are good hideaways. Now that the otters no longer are hunted by men, their worst enemies are the killer whales. The pup doesn't need to be taught that the killers are dangerous, but sensing his mother's fear has increased his natural caution. The whales are both watched and listened for — those lines of black whales that travel abreast, cutting up and down through the water together with a cold, rhythmic regularity which makes a pulse in the sea far ahead of the swimmers. When the whales approach, the otters all instantly stop the tumbling and splashing play that occupies much of their time and lie very still, like old drifting logs. Actually they do look like logs — a little short, being about four feet long, but with bodies quite round and fur the same nearly black color of water-soaked wood.

It would seem that a baby born in the water would know instinctively how to swim, but the otter didn't, or at least he did not want to. He could float on his back from the start. His mother would lay him up on her chest, and then, very quietly, she would let herself sink until she was entirely under the water and he would float off. She would come up a few feet away and stay near him, never making a splash or sound till he woke, maybe an hour later. He would cry for her, and she would pull him onto her chest again, and let him nurse, and clean him all over, getting every tangle out of his fur, which was the infant kind then, thick and woolly. She was very clean herself, grooming her own soft and glossy fur two or three times a day, and even more often she cleaned the baby.

She also taught him to play with her, and took him for rides out away from the kelp. Holding him on her chest, she propelled herself either with one hind foot or both, or by sculling with only her tail. He loved that, but his own swimming, properly face-downward and dipping under the waves, had to be mastered. Now when his mother put him into the water, it was face-down, and then she would swim a short distance away from him. He tried to swim after her, but he didn't go forward, his feet just made a big splash, and he was very unhappy and cried. She came back and swam around and around him, and then drew away, urging him in a soft voice to come with her. He tried again and failed and was miserable.

Many lessons were necessary before he could really swim, and even then he could not dive. He wouldn't stay *down*. In that too she encouraged him, but he didn't make progress until his back muscles strengthened so that his feet could push harder.

Meanwhile there were many more things to learn and discoveries to be made — for example, the fact that the grownups often took food from one another. One would be eating a crab, starting perhaps with its legs, when a second otter would swim up and take the rest of the crab off the chest of the first. He would not even bother to go away with it, just roll over and eat it right there. The original owner never complained; he simply dived down for another crab, if he could find one. Was the thief one of the older otters, who therefore considered himself entitled to anyone's food, not a real thief at all? One of the eldest got all of his food in this way, and no one objected. But then, he was the ruler of the herd. Two other important members were guards, who stood watch while the rest of them slept.

The male most familiar to the pup was the one who spent most of his time near his mother. This fellow didn't pay any attention to him, but didn't seem to resent him either. Perhaps he was his father.

Wherever the herd went, they went together, and sometimes they felt like traveling without going anywhere, really. There were two other kelp beds not far away, and they might spend a whole afternoon swimming from one to the other. They would all start at the same time, going along at a leisurely pace; at the second bed they would rest and then go on to the third, where they would rest somewhat longer. They could float from there back to their home bed — the tide carried them — and so they were ready to start out again immediately. They kept going around and around the triangle till the sun went down, an exercise no one might understand, but it was fun. Maybe that was its only meaning.

These are some of the things that sea-otter pups must learn. In their case the learning is especially important, because this way of life, being out in the ocean continually, is almost new to their species. Some of the habits which may become automatic in time — after thousands of years — are adaptations that sea otters only now are developing. Though men call them sea otters, they have classified them, not as marine mammals, but amphibians, like their small relatives, river otters. Until only a hundred years ago sea otters lived largely on beaches, at the northern edge of the Pacific Ocean. On the shores of the islands they found their food, slept, sunned themselves, mated and bore their young. They spent much of their time in the water, loving its motion, the freedom it gave them to dive, swirl about, splash, or float and let the waves swing them up and down. No animal that could only walk or run had as much chance to enjoy himself. But the land was another home.

Aleuts, a people very much like Eskimos, shared the otters' islands. They were not numerous. They did kill a few of the animals to make clothes of their fur, but there were so many sea otters then, hundreds of thousands, that the men were not much of a threat. Later they were discovered by white men, Russians, who considered that sea otters were the most beautiful animals in the world and organized expeditions to kill hordes of them, taking their skins back to China and Europe, where single hides sold for as much as five hundred dollars. When the United States bought Alaska in 1867, a new kind of white men killed even more wantonly (it had been a rule of the later Russians not to kill mothers and pups), until finally all the otters were gone from most islands — slaughtered. Then the men, seeing their species so nearly extinct, made a law that no one could kill a sea otter. That was in 1916, but already the last of the otters had taken steps themselves to save the few that were left: they had moved out to the kelp.

They learned how to wrap themselves in the fronds so the waves would not carry them in to shore while they slept. They learned to find all their food in the depths of the ocean. The mating act, in the watery foliage, was indeed something new, as was the birthing of young ones there — but the animals managed those things. They learned the best ways to hide. About twenty years later they found a small cove on the shore which seemed safe because a high cliff rose behind it. They began coming out there in the old ways of their kind. But some people discovered them, and on the Fourth of July from the top of the cliff threw lighted firecrackers down among them. The otters left then, for good.

Displaced animals, emigrants from the land which had been their home since immemorial time, they are making themselves a new culture. And it is interesting to wonder whether a young otter feels deprived of some deep-rootedness, having to stay forever out in the sea, whereas his ancestors, for so many centuries, went to the land. If so, does his mother's unfailing devotion help to give him a sense of belonging there in the kelp? She might well have a feeling of rootlessness too; can she nevertheless reassure her pup? The same questions can be asked about human parents and young, for we all are living in changing environments, especially those of old rural stock who have moved to the cities.

The mother otter had special problems. But so, of one kind or another, have all mothers. The life of a black bear would seem as easy as any animal's; yet she too has difficulties — arising in her cub's temperament, and somewhat in her own.

As in other years, this mother did not see her twin cubs until they were two months old. They were born early in February, in the dark of her winter den, which was a cave she had dug the previous autumn under a fallen cottonwood tree. Soon a mountainous snowdrift had covered the entrance, excluding all but one splinter of light through the tiny hole where her breath escaped. In April the snow melted abruptly under a pelting rain followed by sun, and the mother came stumbling out into the dazzle to find some food. The cubs, using their little legs for the first time, wobbled after her.

They had weighed less than a pound each when they were born. (A human cub having the same relation to its mother's weight would be but a five-ounce infant.) Though the mother bear had not seen her young ones, their soft milky scent had been in her nose, and she had felt their mouths on her nipples, pulling or letting go when, snug in her fur, they slept. And she had heard them; as they nursed they purred, a sound like the hum of bees, a lullaby in reverse.

During much of the winter she too had slept. When she roused she had licked the cubs and had felt with her tongue the way they were shaping up, had felt the change from their fine, slight fuzz to more woolly coats. By the time they came out into daylight, their fur was thick enough to give them the contours of round black balls; and they would seem like balls in the way they would roll and bounce over the ground as soon as they mastered the knack of motion.

Their mother was furiously thirsty and was muttering with impatience as she lifted her head, trying to scent some water. There were puddles left by the rain, evidently, but her nose told her that none were near enough to the den. It would not be safe to take the cubs more than a few feet away as long as they were so help-less. She led them into the den again with a stern little growl which they doubtless understood to mean *stay inside*. She found her drink in a ditch filled with runoff; then hurried back. Her stren-uous summer had started — the complex task of feeding, defending, and teaching offspring that were wayward and willful.

As yet she was hardly awake, not even alert enough to want to dig out some roots. She sat down, leaning against the cottonwood, and her head swayed from side to side with her drowsiness. Hav-ing poor eyesight, she was not peering around. She would let the scents on the spring breeze come into her consciousness; she would wait till they pulled her out of this lingering lethargy.

If any had been the scent of coyotes, she would have been awake in an instant. She herself had no enemies, but the coyotes – and there were more than a few in this valley — would keep trying to catch the cubs until they were large enough to defend themselves. Although their mother could drive one or possibly even two coy-otes away, she could not protect both twins at once unless they were out of the scene, having climbed a tree. The full-grown male bears were also a danger; however, the cubs would learn to go out to the ends of high boughs that would not support a large bear. To learn to climb trees would be their first lesson, any tree except cedars. They could climb cedars when they were small; yet the mother bear would not allow them to, for when they were heavier their claws would pull out of the shreddy bark and in time one might fall. All too soon they would find that they liked to be out on the airy sagebrush flat of the valley floor, where the breezes had such a good smell, and were cool, and dispersed the mosquitoes. The mother, as well, liked the open flat, but this being the summer when she had cubs, she must stay back in the woods.

Such constant attentiveness would seem almost impossible for an animal who appeared as dull as the drowsy bear resting against the cottonwood. She would come out of this doze, however. She had enough sense of responsibility to be one of the best mothers in any wilderness. And that in spite of the fact that she had none of the trill in her nerves that makes most of the species which hunt so keen.

Once she had watched a coyote pounce on a ground squirrel. He had stalked the squirrel, staying well back until it was pre-occupied in eating some clover. With a splendid leap, then, he came down on the squirrel with all of his four paws together — sure and quick. The squirrel did not even have time to squeal. The bear could run fast if she had to, but there wasn't that element of surprise in her motions. Squirrels often had time to dodge. What a bear did was to dig them out of their burrows, a tiresome pro-cedure, and many times the squirrels escaped through an unwatched exit. Digging, however, was a bear's way of capturing this most delectable of all prey. And digging would be the cubs' impulse, although they would have to be taught to look for the other outlets of burrows.

Ants were probably a bear's next-favorite food, best sought on the sunny days. Then the ants, indefatigable nurses, carried their eggs up out of the ground to warm them and stayed to guard them under some thin flat stone or bark on a rotting log. A bear should turn over all objects like that. If ants were found, the trick was to put a paw on them. They would swarm all over it, and one could lick them off, enjoying their acid flavor. Some cubs were born knowing enough to do that; some were not, and yet all must be shown where, in this ten-mile-square territory, ants were concen-trated.

A cub, acting only from his inherited aptitude, doubtless could teach himself how to flip a trout out of a brook, but seeing his mother do it would hasten his learning. She would show him where cray-fish hide, sometimes beneath underwater stones, sometimes at the foot of the riverbanks. Those were the questions to which a bear mother must furnish a thousand answers: how and where? Where did underground springs or moist depressions keep the grass succulent? Where were found the best roots? Where all the kinds of berries that would be welcome late in the summer, and where the acorns and other nuts in the fall? Where the most field mice and largest squirrel colonies? What did you do when you found a bee tree? The mother bear had been shown these things by *her* mother; now she must pass the knowledge on to her young ones.

And how to secure their food was only the start. They must learn the knack of a silent tread. They must learn about wallows; there they would coat themselves with mud to discourage the gnats and mosquitoes and botflies, and to help pull out the itchy old fur as the new fur was coming in. They would be shown the stumps where they would scratch their backs and the bear trees that they would bite and claw to keep their teeth and nails sharp. Even more important, perhaps, these trees were bulletin boards that told what other bears lived in the neighborhood. From them the males would discover how many females were now in their alternate breeding years; and the trees told the females about the males, how large and strong they were, for a bear always placed his marks as deep and as high on the trees as possible. On this non-mating year for the mother, they would inform her when male bears were dangerously near, for the scents were dated accurately, to the day and hour.

Some things should be avoided: shrews (which looked like mice but were bitter), snakes, porcupines — and quicksand and the widest river, which had a current so strong it had carried horses away. Bears must stay out of it. The cubs would acquire other habits, not good especially, or bad. In following a trail they would always step in the old footprints; they would walk around logs rather than climbing over them; they would walk on a log in crossing a stream, however, rather than wading through. These were just the bear ways, congenial to them but probably acquired earlier and more reliably through the mother's example. Important too was the constant exposure to an adult bear's emotional temperament, to the touchiness, the somewhat phlegmatic mood till annoyed, then the quick-flaring anger. The cubs would become well acquainted with a bear's irritability, for they often would spark it.

Right now, for instance. Here they come out of the den and, young as they are, they must start clowning. Most bear cubs have a quality found in few other animals. It is a strain of giddiness, even silliness, which shows up as soon as they enter the daylight world. They punch each other, fall down and roll over, and reel around, bumping into each other. They will run from their mother and then plop down and try to forestall her punishment by some antic which seems almost self-consciously cute. This is not merely playfulness. Play is typical of the young, but the play of small bears shows a kind of delirium which suggests instability. A mother bear knows how vulnerable they are at this time, before they can climb well and with every coyote and male bear quite aware of how easy it is to catch them. In spite of the obvious hazards, it is very difficult to instill wariness in the cubs.

The young of most mammals, of the deer tribes, for instance, are much more obedient to their mothers' warnings. A fawn will lie absolutely still until the doe gives it permission to rise. Even chicks cease their peeping if their mother's cluck commands silence. Those are inborn reactions. Bear cubs should have an equivalent impulse, and perhaps they do, but often they just feel so jolly, they fail to heed it. The sullenness of a mother bear, which is sometimes a hazard to careless tourists, may partly be due to the fact that her cubs are so hard to protect. Since she cannot control the cubs as well as she'd like she tries to control the visitors.

And yet the mother bear trains this unruliness out of her young. How does she do it? By keeping them busy, by involving them in the crowded life of an adult bear, who cannot waste very much time if she is to feed her several-hundred pounds of weight with a diet composed of tidbits like ants, crayfish, mice, and only occasionally a squirrel. To satisfy her own hunger and the increasing appetites of the young as they grow, a mother bear forages during most of her waking hours, and she keeps her cubs with her, training them gradually to take part in this effort. It seems likely that they enjoy their improving competence. This cub caught a squirrel for himself today; tomorrow his sister may get a fish. These important skills are now *theirs*. They have known the savory taste of success, and the nonsense begins to go out of them.

This type of education, of leading young animals into the adult experience of their kind, goes on in all mammal species. Most of the species have ways as uniquely their own as the bears'. Squirrels, bats, bobcats, antelopes — each of these has a particular set of habits so practical that the species survives because of them, learned as they are by each generation of young. A weasel, a very good

mother, gives her kits a complete course in where to find mice. A wolf, a very good father, teaches his pups the shrewd strategy of a co-operative hunt. He all but says it in words: you and your aunt will block the caribou on the left, and you — you help your mother harry them on the right. Your uncle will run ahead and stop them in front, and then I'll go among them and get them milling about in panic. Wolf pups do not have to be told to strike at the old and diseased and fawns without mothers. That is an inborn urge, a part of a wolf's action pattern. But containing a herd so the vulnerable will become available: that method seems to be taught.

In this type of education the mammalian young have an advantage in learning from parents who are completely mature and who give them that image. No mother bear ever acts like her giddy daughters — not after she has them. If she did, they would not be so quick to obey when she sends them up into a tree. If, in fact, wild animals hated to be grown up as much as some human animals do, their young might become as confused as some human young. For why grow up at all if you are immediately going to turn around and try to be young again? Why not just stay in this careless, immature stage? We are giddy cubs now, let's remain giddy — it's fun! If that were the pattern of bear mother and cub relationships, the young would not live to mature and before long there would be no more bears in the world. But a bear mother has no choice; she has to be what she is, an adult sobered by her responsibilities.

It is impossible to distinguish an animal parent's guarding of young from the teaching of them. The two kinds of care, protection and education, go on simultaneously and are closely related.

In most cases the eventual parting of mammal parents and young appears to be painless. The break usually is not sudden. The old bonds simply fray away, other interests coming up to take the place of the family ties. As the offspring mature they develop an urge to explore, to find mates and establish their own families, and often they start out together, their sibling attachments helping them to adjust to their independence. Meanwhile a breeding season probably has arrived for the mother. Her attention turns to her mate, whether a new one or the permanent mate for whom her attraction has gone into its more intense phase. If the young do not leave of their own accord, the male is likely to drive them away, or at least out of the foreground. Among bears, moose, and a few other animals the young may keep their distance for a brief time and then return and stay with their mother until the next young are born — or, in a few species, longer. When, however, there is only one offspring and no jealous male is around, such a close relationship may develop between a mammal mother and single child that the young one, even when grown, is reluctant to leave. Easiest for all seems to be the family with two or more siblings that leave together when their mother's time is taken up with a distracting romance. There is no clinging and no possessiveness, then, and the separation is in no sense a tearing apart.

Before leaving the subject of mothering, there is one other point to make: that the physical contact between the animal mother and newborn infant has now been shown experimentally to be of enormous importance.

Harry F. Harlow at the University of Wisconsin, with Margaret K. Harlow, has an extensive project to study the development of subhuman primates, especially the influence in their lives of love and affection. Harlow is unusual as a biologist in making a frank statement that he hopes his findings may have some relationship to the subject of human behavior.

In order to have a large colony of the monkey subjects for the investigations, ten years ago 55 infant monkeys were removed from their mothers as soon as born and were placed in a nursery where the conditions seemed so ideal — from the standpoint of feeding, supervision, and health protection — that one could wish many children might have as auspicious a start. The only thing that they lacked was contact with an adult monkey. They could play with their infant companions during certain hours, and interesting observations were made about the forms that their play took as these monkeys matured. So far they seemed quite normal.

Meanwhile another batch of monkeys, 90 of them, were similarly reared away from their own mothers but with manikin mothers that were something like large-sized dolls with terrycloth bodies artificially warmed. The bottles from which the infants were fed even had nipples which protruded from some of the manikins' breasts. The babies developed great attachment to these substitute mothers, and something was learned about the importance to infants of softness and warmth.

These so-hygienic young monkeys also appeared to thrive; more of them may have lived to grow up than would have if they had been raised under normal conditions. The fact was gratifying, since it was hoped to form them into a breeding colony, from which there would be a continuous supply of infant monkeys for further tests. To the astonishment and dismay of the scientist, the 55 motherless young never reached a stage where they wanted mature sexual relations. None of the males and only one female has ever been willing to copulate. Of the monkeys reared with the manikin mothers the record is better, but only slightly: of the 90, four have become parents. And this too is significant: of the females that did bear children, none treated her offspring well. They either ignored them or abused them so badly that the young had to be taken away from them.

There have been other surprising and sad developments as the experimental monkeys matured. They have shown many signs of extreme neuroticism and even psychosis. Most of them spend their time sitting passively staring out into space, not interested in other monkeys or anything else. Some of them tensely wind themselves into tortured positions, and others tear at their flesh with their teeth. Harlow reports that these are all symptoms found in human adults confined in institutions for the insane.

These results were totally unexpected, and even now it is difficult to explain why an early and close physical contact with mothers is so essential. Normally that kind of contact does not last very long — only a few months in rhesus monkeys. After that time the young "begin to get on the mother's nerves." And that is the stage at which impatience can lend an impetus to the start of the training program, a stage at which being treated with some irritation does not have any adverse effect on the growing monkey. It is a natural period in the animals' development, and they go on from it to mature and almost without exception to form heterosexual relationships.

In the wilds, of course, a newborn animal deprived of its mother's care would not often survive. It is not known what happens to infants that are able to live but whose mothers have given them too little attention or for too short a time. Perhaps in adult years these infants become the "lone wolves" known in many species. Men who are familiar with animals — hunters, naturalists, trappers — have long assumed that the animals' solitude when they are grown is due to a lack of mothering at some time in their youth.

In the case of monkeys like those of the Harlows', who can say whether the more important lack was the physical contact with living mothers or the failure of emotional reassurance? If warmth of feeling exists at all in these animals as adults, perhaps it cannot be expressed because they never learned the way to communicate an emotion. A social sharing precedes sexual sharing, and if there has not been a normal give-and-take between an infant and mother, the social instinct may never have been aroused. In the results of the Harlows' experiments some animal psychologists see a similarity to the hundreds of known situations in which human children have failed to develop normal social attitudes when they were deprived of maternal care, or had inadequate maternal affection, during some of their early months. When those children did not actually die, as many did, they, like the Harlows' animals, have become withdrawn, sometimes antisocial, or have failed to establish families of their own in their adult life. Now the possibility is proposed: that a deficiency in the mother-child relationship actually means that no "imprinting" process occurred.

As explained previously, a bird or animal shows that imprinting has taken place when it consistently follows its mother. A frequent exchange of vocal sounds also has been called a sign of imprinting by some biologists. The human child, not yet able to propel himself, cannot follow, but it is said that he may have an equivalent approach to his mother by smiling. The baby smiles; the mother, if she is there and has normal maternal emotions, smiles back at him; he coos and she talks to him. Through such an interchange he is forming a social bond with his human species which carries on, usually, for as long as he lives.

Just as in birds and animals, for a child too there may be a definite and quite limited time in which fellow feeling can be established. In the human infant it is thought by some experts to extend from about the sixth week through the sixth month. If, during that period, he makes his bid for affection and there is no response, something — trust? — dies in the small heart which, according to the child psychologist Dr. William Goldfarb, probably never can be revived. The theory that a failure to *imprint* is the damaging cause of the later troubles has been proposed by Dr. Philip H. Gray, for one. (Unloved human infants often develop another surprising side effect: a lack or deficiency in their time sense. The reason might be that their first outgoing gesture — a smile — did not meet with the normal reaction, and so the usual sequence in time, of cause and effect, did not register on the still-impressionable "wax" of the baby's mind.)

The suggestion that there is a crucial period, sometimes short, when — and only when — a behavior pattern can develop was proposed as long ago as 1892 by William James in his *Textbook of Psychology*. That concept is now very widely accepted and, among other behavior patterns, applies to the carry-over from an infant's imprinting by the mother to the choosing of a mate of similar character. The fact that birds reared by foster parents probably will court members of the foster group many months later has been proved for numerous species, among them owls, ravens, ducks, geese, a bittern, and a domestic turkey. And "similar forces will, of course, operate on the parent-offspring relation in groups other than birds," as R. A. Hinde has written. By this time that phenomenon has been demonstrated in a great variety of animals, among whom, Hinde is convinced, human children doubtless should be included.

He speaks of the "evidence that the various behaviour patterns which contribute to the relationship [between mother and offspring and subsequently between offspring and other adults] each have a sensitive period of their own which may be limited in the manner described in James' 'Law of the transitoriness of instincts.'" It is an inescapable conclusion from that concept that, as Hinde says, "Proximity to the mother-figure for much of the time is of great importance to the human child from an early age until three to five years."

Hinde's remarks quoted here are in a section titled "Studies of Problems Common to the Psychology of Animals and Men" in a volume edited by W. H. Thorpe and H. L. Zangwill: *Current Problems in Animal Behaviour.*

A further thought: those who are inclined to follow Freud and interpret most human celibacy as deviant should give serious attention to the Harlows' motherless monkeys. In those subhuman primates, at least, the failure to mate has not been a diverted sexual impulse but, rather, no impulse at all.

A happier situation in the rearing of wild-animal young is the part played by adults who do not have offspring themselves but in many cases apparently feel as responsible for the young of the species as parents do. Ptarmigan mothers baby-sit for each other. On the arctic tundra I once flushed a female ptarmigan that was shepherding fifteen fledglings. The average brood is but four to seven, and so she may have been doing duty for two other mothers. In birds that have two broods a season, the first family of young often help to feed the second. That is especially true of house martins, swallows, and water hens (gallinules). Among pelicans the *younger* brood help to feed the older, but perhaps in that case they are trying to ingratiate themselves, for the older nestlings sometimes devour the younger — the only bird species in which that is known to occur.

There are many records of wild birds that are not parents giving food to the fledglings of others — enough to have caused Goethe to comment, "If it were a fact that this feeding of strangers were a universal law of nature, it would unravel many enigmas."

Bison (buffaloes) furnish one of the most impressive examples of impersonal protectiveness among mammals. There aren't many bison left, a few controlled herds in the western states and a few more, transplanted, free-ranging herds in Alaska. The "thundering" millions were such a spectacular part of the western scene in the days when that country was being explored, however, that there are many authentic accounts of their habits. Among bartered buffalo robes, the woolly hides of the bison valued for warmth by Indians and white hunters, occasionally there was a rare skin, "not more than one in ten thousand," on which the fur was fine, smooth, and light. The Indians explained that those were the hides of motherless calves, orphans which became pets of the whole band and were licked by all its adult members. Such licking of the young is typical of many furred animals. The offspring is thus kept clean and the habit is also believed to be a kind of petting, comforting, as a human mother will pat her baby. It was apparently through such more-than-normal "fondling" that an orphaned bison calf acquired its beautiful shiny coat.

The vast herds of bison on the plains were composed of small bands, fifty to a hundred, usually led by a wise old female. Such family bands, into which the great herds split up in the summer, were very clannish and very affectionate. Sometimes when a cow was killed, all the others stayed and allowed themselves to be slaughtered rather than leave her body. As they moved about, grazing, resting, or going to rivers and springs to drink, the old leader walked at the head of the line, with the dozen or more of the bulls guarding the mothers and offspring.

Generally such bands were accompanied by a few wolves, which foraged for smaller game but always hoped to secure a straying calf or wounded or ailing adult bison. They were especially alert during the birth of the calves. For her labor a bison mother goes apart from the band, but only a little way. The calf is not strong on its feet for three or four days; meanwhile the mother stays close to it. If the wolves move nearer, she stands over the calf and bellows for help. Immediately the bulls hasten to her and form a ring about her and the calf, with their heads facing outward and horns lowered in threat. If a calf becomes separated from the band in the later months when it moves with the others, the wolves know—and so do the bulls and at once circle around it. The calf is the son of one of these bulls, but since bison do not live in individual family groups, no one bull has the possessive sense that this calf is his. The calf is a bison: reason enough for the bulls to act selflessly.

The usual wolf pack is composed of a mated pair, their latest litter of pups and perhaps one or more of a previous litter, and, attached to this family, several other adults which may be uncles and aunts of the pups or may be outside wolves, unmated and unrelated. All help to rear the pups. Often one of the unattached females stays at the den to protect them, giving their mother a chance to hunt with the others; and all the adults bring food to

the pups. Sometimes the food is carried to them in the hunter's own stomach and is disgorged in a state as unchanged, apparently, as when it was swallowed. No one knows how a wolf can stop its digestive process for the meal intended for the young and yet let it proceed at its regular pace if the wolf himself is to be nourished by it.

Adolph Murie has described a fight that he witnessed between a grizzly bear and her three lusty yearlings that made an attack on a den with young wolves. To her surprise perhaps, four adult wolves were at home at the time, and in defending the pups, all were as ferocious as the little wolves' father. The next day the four grizzlies came back and found five adult wolves at the den. The scene was one of furious action, as the bears kept moving in to try to drive off the wolves. The wolves could not risk a close combat with the strong bears, but they kept dashing at them for nips and bites, while the bears lashed out at them with both teeth and paws. The wolves finally drove away the bears.

All the wolves apparently had an equal concern for the pups' safety, and is it possible that actually the father felt not much more involved than the others? Could it be that he did not realize that he *was* a father? How would he have known? Among mammals there is great diversity in the roles played by fathers: the males' attitudes towards their young range from hostility, as in bears, to the concern of fox fathers, who will risk death for their pups. More fathers than not are nowhere around when the young are born and probably never realize that they have sired them. And do *any* animal fathers?

It is not necessary to think so. There are too many cases in which male, as well as female, animals feel responsibility for the immature. The young need protection and so it is given, not because the infants are "mine" but — a mute impulse — because they carry the seeds of the future. Among primitive human tribes often the male's role in procreation has not been understood. Superstitions about what has caused the birth of children have included the influence of the sun, the rain, the rivers, and trees on the mothers. In India barren women walked around trees in order that they might be fertilized by the tree spirit. When human minds were quite late in understanding what now seems an obvious situation, can we suppose that pre-human minds know any better?

Ira Progoff, psychologist and philosopher, says that animals strive to maintain their own lives and also are ready to surrender those lives "in the service of a larger life continuity." Pointing out that there are many examples of this sort of sacrifice in nature, he says that an animal's true instinct "is not for *self*-preservation but for *life*-preservation."

In the care of the young this devotion to life above self is clearly seen. There is a moving story told by Victor Cahalane of an adult elk, a female, who was resting slightly apart from her herd when a coyote's baying rang through the clear, cold, wintery air. A louder, more distinct call proved to the elk that the enemy had come nearer. In her confused scramble to safety she dashed straight up a snow-covered slope and was followed by four young fawns. They could not all have been hers, since an elk bears only one, rarely two, offspring. The fawns tried with all their strength to continue climbing the hill through the drifts, but the attempt was beyond them. All gave up, mired in the snow. The fleeing elk, possibly hearing them whimper, looked around and discovered their plight. She turned and went back, into the danger, to rescue them. By pushing and hoisting them one by one with her forefeet, she got them out of the drifts and then took a longer route with them up the mountain, on an easier, slower course.

Under what animal "drive" is such a heroic act to be classified? No matter — enough to recognize what a compelling urge the cow elk was feeling, that the young of her species, at least the *young*, must survive.

III

SEX

The Silenced Bell

The
Silenced
Bell

By the time that young animals reach maturity, most of them have absorbed from their parents' teaching, or from sharing adult activities, all they will need to know for their everyday living. But nothing has helped to prepare them for finding a mate. For each of the many animal species the mating customs are different. They are of dazzling variety and in some species extremely elaborate. Dances, calls and songs, special displays of fur, feathers, or pigmented skin: each detail is traditional, each step of a dance, note of a song, or seductive movement has been decreed. Even more strict are the prohibitions, especially as to timing. The growing animal soon will perform all these rites, and yet no one will tell him what he must do and must not do. No elder will give him advice, no companions share sexual secrets.

In a way he is fortunate. He has inherited no religious taboos, and he won't have his natural way confused by fashions in loving — fashions temporary and artificial, which are a pressure exerted on young human animals by movies, television, advertising, popular songs, and books. A wild creature does not have to reconcile such conflicting notions of love as Casanova's and Romeo's, or con-

flicting live models that he might want to copy. And no psychiatrist analyzes any animal's sexual difficulties, reducing to the small, precise dimensions of words what the lover probably feels as amorphous — and dark and immense. Strictly, completely on their own are all animals, male and female, when sex overtakes them.

Yet they do have a guide, the one within: instinct. It does not shout, and some animals have to learn how to listen. The more complex, highly evolved mammals may do more than a little fumbling in their approach to first mates. We often assume that the coupling of animals is abrupt, brief, and fully effective from the beginning. That is not always true. The late Robert M. Yerkes of Yale University, writing with J. H. Elder of the mating of chimpanzees, said that "prior to sexual maturation, the female chimpanzee . . . learns from social contacts all that is necessary to enable her to behave wholly appropriately and effectively in the mating situation . . . By contrast, and this seems strange indeed, the recently matured male who is inexperienced in mating with a mature and receptive female commonly acts initially as does the sexually immature male, somewhat playfully, puzzled, and as if at a loss how to meet the situation. Even if, with the cooperation of the female, he attempts to copulate, he usually fails." Biologists have described other animals whose first mating is far from automatically assured.

And many of them go through a preliminary anguish that would seem familiar to the parents of adolescents. A human father or mother would recognize the irritability, tensions, and tantrums; the strange eating habits, fasting one day and stuffing the next; the benumbed attachment to one individual who may appear even less prepossessing than others. ("It is a curious fact that the morphological or psychological traits of certain males make them clearly preferred by certain females," writes the French ecologist François Bourlière of chimpanzees. Is the preference as curious as the fact that biologists consider it so?) As some animals enter their breeding cycle, they show these signs of disturbed emotions. Nevertheless they develop a responsiveness to the prompting of instinct that is almost incomprehensible to a human being. We who are human have lost the ear for those signals — to such an extent that the peak of the average civilized woman's receptiveness does not even come, now, at the time when she could conceive. Hers is a deafness that would have caused any other species to have become extinct. Let us watch a porcupine, one of the mammals who is most sensitive to the sound of her bell. She is necessarily so alert because her internal program allows her only a very brief time to mate.

This one is rather young, having had but one previous pregnancy. Now in July she is her normal self and could be described as a happy little creature, with a considerable talent for amusing herself. She lives on a farm in New Hampshire, one abandoned these many years by its human owners. Here a company of a dozen porcupines have established several dens, in the cellar of the old house, in the barn, and in two or three rock piles. Although there are no close companions among them, the porcupines treat one another with tolerance, and they have flexible social habits. On one night a group of six or eight may sleep in one of the dens together; on the following night three or four. Some like to sleep alone. Our female prefers a crevice among the rocks into which, she has found, she just fits. But when the weather is stormy she may cuddle in with some others.

Food is no problem; the leaves and bark of the trees in the woodlot, and now in summer the soft green meadow plants, keep the colony nourished with only the effort of chewing the fibers up. And the porcupines fear no enemies. Dogs come around sometimes; if they could get to the porcupine flesh they know by its scent they would find it delicious, but the porcupines have an easy defense. They just back up to a dog, raise their quills, flip a barbed tail in his face, and he runs away howling. The male porcupines enjoy wrestling, but they are careful to remain facing each other, there being no quills in the fine, soft fur of their bellies. They like to challenge the females, but when they do, they make sure that the game is welcome.

The one that concerns us will not often wrestle. She prefers other ways to let her energy boil up in play. Now in the moonlight she lies on her back at the edge of the meadow, and with all four feet in the air she fools with a stick. She bats it around, tugs it, gnaws it, and throws it away. Next she pretends to defeat an enemy: this old stump — couldn't it be a dog? She backs up to it, raises her quills and thrashes her tail against it, enjoying the rattling, a warning, made by the quills.

This is one of the better nights. She will go and gnaw on an old rusty oil drum beside the drive. It makes a splendid loud clanging and, like all porcupines, this one delights in any resonant sound. She likes something else: rhythm. She stands upright and marks time with her hind feet, swaying from side to side and giving her own particular twist to the dance — a turn of one wrist and the other in time with her steps. Two of the porcupine colony join her. One keeps reaching down, also in time with his steps, as though he were lifting things. Another male walks past the dancers. He acts as if he were not seeing them; then he wheels suddenly, seizes the female and holds her and bites her neck — gently, for this is not sex play, not in July. She wriggles away from him. Sensing that she is not angry, he chases her in a little game, like pups playing tag, but more cautiously, never ignoring those quills.

A free season, now with her young one looking after himself and the new mating program not yet beginning: a sweet season, but short.

By the middle of August the porcupine is becoming nervous. The ease, the lightness are lost from her mood. She still goes through some of the motions of playing, but now it is with an urgency. Even when she is well fed, she bites into sticks and the bark of trees, often impatiently. She climbs the trees for no reason, going up and coming right down again. She and the other porcupines do their dance several times a day, and faster. They do everything faster. A new whining sound often is heard in the woodlot and meadow, a complaining about the mate-hunger that

grows within them. The female whines are subdued, the males' are more shrill and louder.

The hunger is generalized at first, a diffuse restlessness. The males fight rather frequently, with each other, not ever now with the female. She won't stand for much. By the end of September the hunger is starting to be a torment. It is more localized; our porcupine tries to get some relief by touching herself to the rocks, to the stump, to the ground. After she puts her scent on the ground, one of the males is likely to come by and pick up that bit of earth in his forepaw and smell it. But no male pursues her. They will leave her alone until she has given a sign that some one of them is acceptable.

Still the tension continues, the hunger increases. The porcupine has a new trick for relief. She goes around riding a stick, walking upright and dragging one end of the stick on the ground, between

her hind legs, holding the other end in a forepaw. The males have similar, solitary diversions.

Why are the sexes so slow to approach each other? Are they stupid? No, they are very smart, exquisitely sensitive to the inner instructions. However difficult waiting is, they will delay till the final bell, which will ring for the female when her physical preparations are quite complete.

She now enters a different phase. She becomes very quiet, seeming unnaturally subdued. She stops eating. She "mopes," as one observer described her. It almost seems as if she has suffered some grief, but the explanation is otherwise: she has become still in order to let her emotions gather for one brief and explosive release.

It is November. Among the males in the colony she has made her choice. She spends most of the time sitting near him. But not for much longer.

At last the moment for coupling arrives — almost inevitably, for it seems that there are few frigid porcupines. The female takes the initiative, as she must since she is the one whose internal event sets the time. Rather suddenly she comes out of her waiting mood. She sniffs the male in significant ways. He responds. They touch noses, retreat a few steps, rise on their hind feet, walk towards each other and, standing upright, touch noses again. This touch is the trigger. With the speed of a fire storm the female is down and the male is atop her.

With his mate armed so awesomely, he is brave indeed. She is co-operative. She has flattened her quills and has drawn her tail over her back so that he partly lies on its soft underside. Nevertheless this is one time when the female, as Ernest Thompson Seton remarked, "has complete control of the situation." The male does not try to restrain her, as the males of some species do, by grasping the female's sides with their forelegs and taking the fur of her neck in their teeth. The porcupine female may end this embrace whenever she wishes . . . but she isn't impatient. It may last for as long as five minutes and be repeated, but only during a span of three to five hours. Then the female is through. She will no longer receive this male, or any other, until a year from now. So perfectly has she timed the coupling, however, that her pregnancy almost certainly is assured.

After sixteen weeks she will give birth to a single young one, unusually precocious. His quills, soft while he is being born, will harden after the first few hours, and already he will know how to back up to an enemy and lash out with his small deadly tail. He will even start foraging for soft vegetation at once. Although he will be nursed, too, for several weeks, he is a very capable baby, and therefore his mother will have comparative freedom until she begins to feel restless again. She will lie on her back and fool with a stick. She will gnaw on the oil drum. She will dance, to express pleasure, not tension. She will play tag. She will be herself, for her reproductive instinct will make no demands. This quiescent interlude will last for about two months — less time than the build-up for a new mating will take.

What seems most remarkable about porcupines is not the long emotional preparation for accepting the male, but the female's alertness which finally tells her that this is the day. For there will be only one day in all the year when receiving the male will result in a pregnancy. She has, in fact, less than a day in which to note the signal, reveal her willingness to the male, carry out with him their brief mating ritual, and then come together. Yesterday would have been too soon; tomorrow would be too late. Only today will do, but there is little chance that she will make a mistake.

The reason why the timing must be so exact is the fact that only one egg cell a year is released from a porcupine's ovary. And that ovum can only be fertilized for fewer than twenty-four hours. Twelve hours is probably the maximum time, and if the male's sperm should reach the egg near the end of that period, there is the possibility of a disaster that nature can't often permit. How attentively, then, a female porcupine listens.

Even if the coupling takes place immediately after ovulation, there will be a delay while the sperm cells are traveling up through her reproductive tract. The egg will be fertilized at the top of the oviduct, the tube which leads to the uterus; the fertilization must occur there. The first of the sperm to reach the area do not unite with the egg — their function is different. They release an enzyme which helps to make the egg ready. When the second wave of sperm cells arrive, one will penetrate the egg, and from the joining will come the new individual. The biologists Lorus and Margery Milne have a quaint phrase for this last happening, quaint especially if there has been any courtship between a male and a female. They call it the final conquest of the egg by the sperm.

In having only one period of heat, one oestrus, in her whole breeding season, the porcupine is like a number of other animals but is exceptional in the shortness of its duration. Females of some of the other species accept a male's attentions for three to five days preceding that pinpoint of time when the egg leaves the ovary. After the ovulation the couplings cease within hours. For all of this group of mammals precision is quite essential, however, for if the female should miss conceiving during her single oestrus, she will not have another chance for approximately twelve months.

More leeway is given those females who can produce more than one egg cell per breeding season. The "breeding season" is a rather elastic period which, in their case, may even last two or three months and make it possible for the females of these species to come into oestrus, that is, form a new ovum, several times if the first union is not successful. These periods of heat are separated by a few weeks: the female receives the male during one day or a few days, and if no pregnancy results, there is a little recess while another ovum matures. With such an extended breeding season a mating pair may form a closer bond of companionship than the porcupine could — as we shall see presently in the case of elephants.

First it should be said again that during any one oestrus the short life of the egg cell is an inescapable limitation. This very close timing has been discovered only in recent years. In experiments done with various species of mammals, a startling fact has been learned: that too long a delay between the release of the ovum and its penetration by the male's sperm will result in either a loss of the embryo ("spontaneous abortion") or, worse, the birth of a monster. Some sperm, in most mammal species, will remain alive and motile in the reproductive tract of the female for twenty-two or a few more hours. The *number* of sperm cells will decline, but any that are still able to make their way into the egg will not have degenerated. The situation regarding the egg cell is different: it degenerates very rapidly and yet, in some cases, it may be fertilized even after it has deteriorated. It will produce offspring of the best quality only if the union of sperm and egg occurs very soon after the ovum leaves the ovary. Half a day later the union may still take place, but the fertilized egg may not succeed in becoming attached to the wall of the uterus and will therefore be lost. Or it may be implanted there and start to grow but then fail, with the result of a spontaneous abortion or a premature birth. If the egg is close to the end of the crucial period when the sperm joins it, the embryo may be born at full term but it is likely to be a deformed individual. Given another hour, the full-term embryo is not "likely" to be a monster — it is almost certain to be.

"Monster" is a fearsome word; technically it only means a newborn or embryo animal that is greatly malformed. Those that are less so are called abnormalities, and there is no sharp distinction between them. Both words refer to deviations that occur in the development of the embryo.

Such malformations have several causes. As we know, they may result from drugs in the bloodstream of the pregnant mother. There are also hereditary causes; and experimentally the development of an embryo has been altered by the temperature of the environment where it is growing, the chemical composition, and the amount of available space for the organism. This error of timing here being described is a new discovery, made not by the medical profession but by the biologists who study animals. Its effects are so sure in the case of subhuman mammals, however, that it seems to warrant more attention than it has had in its application to human beings.

Dr. Colin R. Austin, author of *The Mammalian Egg*, states definitively, "The eggs of most mammals can wait for little more than 12 hr if fertilization and development are to occur in a normal manner." Twelve hours is an average. The limit for the ovum of the mare and cow is twenty hours, the same length of time for the guinea pig, only six hours for the rabbit, and for a woman probably no more than eight hours. According to Dr. Edmond J. Farris, ovulation in the human female usually takes place in the afternoon. If intercourse occurs more than eight hours later, it seldom results in conception; but if it does, there is little chance to escape a birth accident.

Early miscarriages will prevent many of these from being detected; but not all. F. P. Mall, who did much of the early work on birth abnormalities, estimated that 80 out of 100 human pregnancies result in the birth of normal infants. Seven, he said, are aborted as ova with recognizable changes of a pathological nature. In 12 embryos and fetuses, when recovered, are found, "especially in the younger specimens, minor changes which must be viewed as forerunners to real monsters." About one pregnancy, he said, will produce a monster at term. All the embryos leave their epitaphs in the reproductive tract of the mother, and these can be counted during surgical operations. Some embryologists put the percentages of miscarriages even higher than Mall. Thus physicians confirm an old wives' tale that miscarriages are fortunate, for in many of these cases the child would have been defective.

Abnormalities in the offspring of domestic animals and animals bred in laboratories are common (two-headed calves and double-hoofed horses on farms, etc.), but in such instances nature's subtle timing of instinct has been interfered with by the man who is breeding the animals. Biologists who study animals in their normal habitat have remarked that they never or almost never see monstrous young. No doubt they occur occasionally, because instinct is not infallible. However they are not nearly as frequent as in the barnyard . . . or as often as in the human species, whose ideal sexual timing may be disturbed by many sorts of irrelevant happenings — traffic jams, theater dates, malfunctioning freezers, croupy children, fatigue: all the civilized factors which can postpone husband-and-wife embraces. To say nothing of the strange shift in women's peak of receptivity from her oestrus period to the prevalent time, now, of just before or just after menstruation.

The reliability of wild animals' timing may suggest that their physical organization is almost mechanical. Certain scents or sights or sounds send their impulses to the creature's pituitary gland, which releases hormones that go to work in the reproductive tract, where they set in motion other, even more complex physical changes. When biologists first began to analyze glands, they believed that this sequence was quite predictable and that they could control it very precisely. They learned otherwise. The central nervous system, which takes into account an animal's wishes, turned out to have an important effect on the mating behavior. The environment was a factor. Some animals aren't inclined to mate during storms; on the other hand wind, whipping the sea into white caps, is sexually very stimulating to sea otters. In the end other biologists had to admit the truth of what Sir Julian Huxley has said regarding evolution, that *"mind* [his italics] has thus been the sieve through which variation in courtship characters must pass" — mind, the animal's mind, both choosing one mate instead of another and either resisting or giving in to desire at the suitable moment.

That fact being true, it is not anthropomorphic to recognize that various species may give psychological and emotional tone to their male-female relationships. Not much is possible to a creature, such as a porcupine, who associates intimately with a mate for so short a time. But see what occurs among elephants: true "friendship," which has a chance to develop because of the female's long breeding season. Admittedly, too, elephants have a quite-high degree of intelligence, a delicacy of manner, and even something like altruism. An appreciative spokesman for elephants, Richard Carrington, says of them, "Elephants are creatures of affection, and perhaps none of the so-called lower animals enriches the purely mechanical processes of reproduction with a nicer sensibility."

It is fall when we find this female. Her life, if not stimulating lately, at least has been busy. She has been raising a calf of her own and helping to care for the smaller calf of another mother. Both females nursed both of the young (the calves fed from the sides of their mouths, pushing the breasts with their short little trunks to help swell the flow of milk); but the chief need for the double solicitude had been, until now, the danger of tigers' attacks. For several weeks after an elephant calf is born, tigers are ravenous for it. Two adult females, therefore, always keep a calf between them wherever they browse. Both of these calves, however, were large enough to defend themselves. They still needed guidance but not continual guarding by both of the mothers.

The herd had come down from the higher slopes, here in Burma, where they had spent the monsoon season, feeding up there on bamboo. Now they were in a foothill swamp of *kaing,* tall "elephant grass," in the bend of the river. The grass was tender and succulent, and the calves were munching along quietly. One mother stayed near them; the other grazed here and there, seeming not satisfied with the luscious fodder.

A number of males were attached to this herd of adult females, calves, and adolescents of both the sexes. The males moved with the others on their migrations; when they stopped the males kept to themselves on the edge of the group but depended upon the females in several ways. If a male elephant should be sick or injured, one or several females would come to his aid. A weak elephant was in terror of lying down, since he could not raise his huge weight off the ground again with diminished strength. If he did go down, the cow elephants, and it might be a bull, too, one on each side and behind, would lift him onto his feet again. Another thing: the cows' wisdom was reassuring. Almost always it was a sensible elderly female who decided the time when the herd should move to a new feeding place, and the route. Besides relying upon the cows in such practical ways, there was always the chance that one might accept a closer companionship.

The mother's grazing had taken her near the edge of the swamp, towards the open grove that surrounded it. One of the males was pushing over a tree with his forehead against the trunk. A smaller tree breaks; this one came up by the roots in a cloud of dust. The male had wanted the tender leaves at the top. An elephant always is willing to share a tree he has felled, but now, as this one started to browse on the upper twigs, the swing of his tail and a certain friendliness in the way he was watching the female made it appear that he wished she, especially, would eat his leaves too.

He was quite a magnificent beast — he weighed seven tons, a ton more than the female, and he had one very fine, long, white tusk. The other tusk had been broken off in a fight with another male. It was not a fight between sexual rivals, which does at times happen: both of the elephants then were "on musth," as men describe a male's periodic attacks of madness. A sign of musth is a brown discharge from a gland near the elephant's eye. A male's hostility can be gauged by the amount of secretion, and a guess has been made that it is this acrid fluid, draining into his mouth, which enrages the animal. Most of them act at the time, however, as if they were more than irritable, indeed literally insane. The attack of musth lasts for about two weeks, during which he is a danger to all living things, including the females of his own species. Otherwise there is a gentleness in the elephant's disposition which is not surpassed by many wild animals. This female, who could observe that the male was not now on musth, had no reason to fear him.

He removes a twig, and see how he does it: the two rounded

knobs at the end of his trunk close like fingers around the stem and with the least possible force pull it off. The branch hardly stirs. A vine is encircling this bough. He unwinds it, again with a fine and precise, always patient touch. After eating the vine and more leaves, he has an appetite for a root. The tip of his trunk pushes away some of the loosened soil and curls itself under the root, which comes free with earth clinging to it. He knocks the dirt off on his foot and, coiling his trunk, puts the root in his mouth. There is no hurry about this foraging. He will need about three hundred pounds of food today, but the food is everywhere, and by working steadily, even slowly, he will get all he wants.

He doesn't eat flesh. In fact, if he should find a small, helpless animal on the elephant trail, he will carefully pick it up with his trunk and lay it off at one side. The yapping dogs of a hunter would bother him, and he would hurl rocks at them, swiftly and very accurately: throwing, a motion only possible to the most intelligent animals and somehow seeming less ugly than more direct kinds of attack.

He throws with his trunk, through which he breathes and drinks and with which he feeds himself — but it has a more subtle capacity. The female, now eating grass, has not strayed very far, and after he chews and swallows the root, the male stands still for a moment, watching her. Is he moved by her soft ways? Perhaps. He comes forward and gently runs the tip of his trunk down her back. She lifts her head, meets his eyes, and with the tip of her own trunk she touches his neck. That is all that will happen today. The two will resume their feeding, and when she returns to the swamp he will go with her. He is willing to take his time, but something momentous has started this afternoon.

From now on they spend all their days together, and their nearness seems almost enough. There are, however, more and more frequent caresses, a fondling which seems as yet to express no more than affection. The male's trunk will brush her side, a touch that she almost always returns. Or the forehead of one will give a little

push on the side of the other. They nibble each other's cheeks—
the play is growing a bit more stimulating. Tails swing and ears
flip, and the pair are communicating with sounds. In the male's
throat is often a murmur of satisfaction, and she answers with a
soft chirping, surprisingly light for one of her size.

Weeks will pass with such expressions of tenderness but no
real excitement. When a more sensual stage is reached, their
trunks show their true versatility. They are often entwined. They
are tied in lovers' knots over the elephants' heads. The tips are put
into each other's mouths, an elephant's kiss.

The dalliance becomes more intense. Her motions are more
inviting—so provocative that female elephants have been called
the most sophisticated of all wild animals in their courtship. And
finally they play with their trunks erotically. They tease. But
when the climax is reached, even then in the male's embrace there
is no coercion.

With his forelegs along her back, he half kneels behind her. Smoothly he rises. There is no other visible motion (though the male organ itself is motile), and during the union no sound. At the end he is almost upright, with his forefeet resting lightly upon her hips. Only a short time has passed, not even a minute. When it is over, he walks away a few steps, noiselessly. For this is the hour when mysteriously the jungle becomes utterly silent. Even the insects are still. The female, making no sound herself, stays where she is, but a brief little movement shows her excitement.

In the next day the pair will unite again, perhaps several times, and then the female's sexual cycle will go into a quieter phase. But her breeding season is not at an end. If conception has not taken place during this oestrus, and it often does not, there will be other occasions a few weeks apart. Meanwhile the two elephants are inseparable. Great and slow and gray they move through the jungle shadows and, all quietly trusting time to wait, they love each other — possibly very much.

For this mated pair obviously are joined by more than the simple physical urge which subsides as soon as it has been satisfied. Reports vary as to the length of time that elephant mates associate; up to four months says one observer, up to ten says another. No one knows whether it ever continues after pregnancy has begun. But finally the female starts breaking away, showing a wish to rejoin the herd. She will stay with the herd during her pregnancy, which will last twenty-two months, and when the birth takes place, the other females will surround her with their protection. While she is in labor they will stand close about and trumpet loudly, with the purpose, it is believed, of warning tigers and hunters away.

The female will carry no torch. Some flexibility in her temperament seems to let her replace the companionship of her mate with that of the herd, and later the daily association with the one friend who will help to defend her calf. The male has given her up reluctantly. He has tried to hold her but, since he could not, he will seek a new female. The male elephants go through a succession of deep, if not permanently enduring affairs until they are fifty years old or more. After that age they join with one or two other elderly males, aloof from the herd and perhaps missing what they have had, for their tempers are apt to become quite short.

Although altruism, a psychological trait, affects the quality of the elephants' male-female relationships, the physical cycle determines how long the pairs stay together. The male's fertility and desire are continuous; yet the female, absorbed with maternal cares, removes herself from his company for three years at a time. Such an arrangement doesn't offer much hope for monogamy. Monogamy among animals requires a different physiological pattern. It is possible to a number of species and always is interesting, but before we consider it, there is another sexual system too widespread to ignore: that of the male with a harem.

I suppose that anyone who writes about animals (or anything else) should confess a personal bias. The pronghorn antelopes, holding their heads so high, throwing their pretty heels in the air with exuberance; the pronghorns with great black inquisitive eyes and with white rosettes on their rumps which, as Seton says, flash like bright new tin pans in the sun, are one of my favorite species. That kind of preference is frowned on by the scientists who try to eliminate all emotion from their observing. Yet a certain amount of subjective interest can call intuition into play, and intuition can furnish leads to more understanding. Something I learned concerning the sex play of pronghorns would not have come to light but for the special circumstance that one of my earliest loves was a dappled-gray wooden horse on a merry-go-round.

He was named, by me, Gray Beauty, and he galloped around a steel pole at Luna Park outside Cleveland, Ohio. He did gallop. Some of the carousel horses just pumped up and down; *small* children rode those, and babies in arms were held in the chariots. But Gray Beauty, due to the mechanism under his legs, pitched about as if he might bolt away any minute, and part of my pleasure was to imagine the clustered thumps of his hoofs.

It was to hear John Philip Sousa that my parents went out to the park. To be free of a squirming child, they would give me a fistful of nickels and then sit with their feet in the tanbark listening to the band while I, having appropriated my Beauty, rode around and around interminably in the line of their watchful sight. No one knew what a soul-satisfying rapport there was between me and the little horse. The experience could have been dreamlike, but it wasn't because of the crowd of small boys who were always there, dressed up in white shirts to come to the park but acting as wild as they ever did on school playgrounds. They were never content just to ride around but must change horses constantly, stand in the stirrups and lash the wooden necks of their steeds with the reins, and even jump on and off the circling platform of the merry-go-round itself, disregarding the rules.

"Why d'you always ride *that* horse?"

"I just like him."

"It isn't a him, it's a her. They're all girl horses here. They're silly. They're girls."

But Gray Beauty was not a girl, he was a male for the sufficient reason that I had willed it so.

The musical program always seemed to include the *William Tell* overture, and for that number a backdrop of canvas mountains was used. They had snowy summits, over which moving gelatin lights painted a lurid sunrise. As each of the circular trips reached a certain point, I could see that scene, and I tried to imagine that Gray Beauty and I could ride away out of Luna Park and gallop on and on till we found the white mountains. But the fantasy never reached that goal. The rowdy boys always interrupted it.

Later I learned of the Viennese dancing horses, who often prance two and two in circles around the Hofburg Opera House, keeping time to a Chopin waltz. Were they the prototypes of Gray Beauty, and did merry-go-rounds, which were made first in

Austria, originate in the ancient art of those wheeling, real horses? And what gave the Lippizan horses their start? Listen to this, from William P. Pycraft's *The Courtship of Animals:* "The old naturalist and traveller Schweinfurth tells how he once encountered a herd of Hartebeest which were apparently effervescing with animal spirits, for they kept running around in couples, like horses in a circus, using a clump of trees as a pivot. Others, in groups of three or four, stood by, interested spectators. After a time these, in turn, took their places and ran around, two at a time, in their own circuit and in the same fashion. Their evolutions, he says, were so regular as to suggest the guidance of some invisible ringmaster. These gyrations may be regarded as an erotic dance."

Roe deer have a tendency to follow a circular course in their sexual game of tag, and it is customary in other antelopes besides hartebeest. In roan and sable antelopes and the Cape eland the male circles around the desired female; and the impalas of the Congo have their own variation — troops of about twenty males run in circles around the assembled females and young. In the pronghorns (who are believed to have deer as well as antelope ancestry), the usual route appears to be that of a single pair at a time, who circle out from the herd and back.

Horses and antelopes are, of course, somewhat related; and did the first builders of carousels know that connection? Wooden antelopes sometimes were used among horses on merry-go-rounds.

I did finally find mountains not painted on canvas, in northwestern Wyoming, and on a high, level plain below them, the pronghorns. They are fairly numerous there in the Great Divide Basin, which is a vastly wide bowl in the sky, rimmed with snow-covered peaks. The antelopes live on the lower slopes in the summer, in family parties usually, a buck guarding his several does and twin fawns. Winters are spent in larger herds down in the shallow coulées, protected from blizzards. In the early fall the pronghorns are out on the valley floor, where the herds come together after their several months spent apart.

That was the season when I discovered them, one day while I was sitting under a willow, watching for grouse, and became conscious of continuing flashes, as if someone were signaling with a mirror far out near the horizon: the pronghorns, signaling, actually, among themselves with the white rosettes they make by raising the fur on their rumps. They were not near enough for me to see them well, but knowing about their keen eyesight and great curiosity, I tried waving a handkerchief on a stick. Once Joseph Dixon drew antelopes to him by lying down on his back and kicking his feet in the air. Would a handkerchief be as interesting?

The pronghorns came, streaming across the flat as lightly as if the breeze carried them. At a moderate distance the one in the lead and then all the other animals paused. The handkerchief no longer waved. They watched a while, tensed for flight, and peered sharply over the sunlit sage. In the clarity of the air at this height, an object a hundred yards away seems as close as a touch. And is that a movement, a finger adjusting binoculars? The proud heads come up even higher, the huge dark eyes all converge on the willow . . . The pronghorns wait . . . Possibly, after all, nothing dangerous? The chest under the loose poplin jacket does not visibly rise and fall. The new object is strange but somehow not very threatening. Maybe something wild too. Anyway antelopes can run faster than any other animal on the continent. They can always escape — anything but a bullet. And no bullets are being fired.

Two of the fawns break away from the herd and race off a short distance. A doe follows them, not at an anxious pace. A few of the older animals drop their heads and begin to graze. Their confidence seems contagious. The herd loosens its stiffly attentive formation, and one by one they go back to their normal affairs.

Their normal affairs at this season, early September, were lively and playful. The fawns, by then three months old, seemed obsessed with the fun of *running*. Their slim little legs could go nearly as fast as the grownups' — so fast that a human eye sees them only as blurs. The fawns would run out from the herd and often a buck ran out with them in what apparently was a game.

All the adults were doing a good deal of running about. One buck, especially, raced around and around in a way that might have appeared demented except that so obviously he was expressing high spirits. And now the real thing: a doe has gone speeding away with a buck in pursuit.

Off they dash, flying over the plain, the two of them pinwheels of motion — always, it seems, an equal distance apart. She circles around and he close behind her; then, to make the game more exciting perhaps, she begins to dodge, in and out of the herd, away on the plain and back and around, and still, surprisingly, she and the buck run in unison. She does not need to be caught; she can run as fast as her follower — faster, say hunters well acquainted with antelopes. If this buck had not been the one of her choice, she could have escaped from him. Most likely, in fact, she belongs to his harem, and she knew at the start of the chase that she would agree to be captured. When she has run long enough for this time, she comes back to the herd, comes with her buck and willingly, not subdued.

In like fashion each buck wins his four or five does again every year. In September the does are in oestrus, but not on the same days necessarily. The buck's fertile period will last longer than any one doe's, and if he is lucky his mates will be able to stagger their peaks of affection. The surplus males are the ones out of luck. They keep trying to steal the does, and the lord of the harem battles them — not too viciously. These are not often fights to the death. If the harem system is unfair to the bachelors, it tends to keep the quality of the offspring high, since only a buck who can defeat his rivals will father young.

September is therefore a month of many excitements, of lovemaking and dueling and with the does often running away, a pretense, a chance to go racing around with the buck, who goes after them. An animated and frolicsome time — a carnival, with the frequent rearing of one of the beautiful heads high above the others, an antelope momentarily riding an antelope: a merry-go-round!

There was even a backdrop of mountains, gilded white in the sun; and the pronghorns' bugling and stomping didn't obscure the soft whine of the wind whipping, eddying through the sagebrush, a sound not totally unlike a calliope distant in space or time.

The pronghorn harem is an interesting family arrangement, so smoothly efficient — with the does taking turns watching the fawns and the buck giving his little group loyal protection — that it seems almost a step towards monogamy. Wolves, coyotes, and foxes are believed to be truly and permanently monogamous. After their breeding season the sexual need of the mates for each other recedes in both, but the bond between them does not dissolve. The pairs live in the same den, and at the time when the young are born, the male brings food to the mother. Later he helps to guard, teach, and feed the young. Beavers too are monogamous; also chinchillas and probably others among the wild mammals. Swans, Canada geese, and some other birds mate for life, and so, surprisingly, do a few fish.

Of most significance to a human being is the mating of other primates besides ourselves. None of the monkeys and apes that exist today are direct ancestors of ours, with the partial exception of one (to be described later), but we have received some of the same physical and psychological traits from a common relative further back on the primate line. One of our functional similarities is the female's oestrus cycle, which comes about once a month in most of the primates, and another is the uninterrupted fertility of the male. These conditions, allowing the sexes to attract each other more or less continuously, have presented the primates with new emotional opportunities — and new problems. In the primate sexuality, will the constant association of males and females make it easier for them to live harmoniously, or otherwise? Will it mean simply more of the same kind of sex other animals know, or will it be different? Will monogamy become more, or less, prevalent? Human cynics often declare that women are "naturally" monogamous and men polygamous: is this the situation with monkeys and apes? And, most important from nature's own standpoint, what becomes of the female's instinctive caution to restrict conception to the hours that produce maximum quality in the offspring?

Since the relationships between sexes will be quite different now, here is a quick backward survey of the situation among pre-primate mammals:

For most of them sex is a sometime thing, very intense while it lasts, but when it subsides the whole business seems to go out of mind. During the recess many male animals find their companionship with other males (not often in homosexual relationships, although those do exist in some species: the house mouse, some bats, rhesus monkeys in males; the brown rat and some others in females). Together or singly the males forage, build shelters against winter storms, wander about, and do a certain amount of mild battling with other males to determine which is the stronger. After a while they start to get ready for the new sexual encounters, sometimes by growing natural weapons such as the antlers of deer and moose, with which they will fight off rivals. And some of their masculine energy is consumed in just being, and in becoming, splendid fellows, so that they may appeal to the females when *they* have become ready.

There is not much sociability between males and females during this time, though they live in the same areas and of course they meet often. Between them there is no animosity. A female would never, conceivably, attack a male, and the males have some built-in hesitation about attacking a female. An example of this reluctance is familiar to anyone who has lived in an apartment house with a dog. The elevator stops at your floor, where you wait with your pet on a leash. If the opening door reveals another owner and dog inside, you ask, "Female?" If it is, you and your male dog go in with no possibility of a fight. Should the inside dog be another male, both owners tighten their leashes and pull back on the growling opponents. Two male dogs would have had to decide by a show of antagonism, or actual combat, which one was dominant. A male and a female are always interested in each other, but not as contestants.

At the time of their mating the pre-primate sexes seek out each other, in most cases still in only the friendliest spirit. In a few species — some squirrels, weasels, shrews, and members of the cat family — there is a last-minute fracas, often so noisy that it attracts attention (those alley-cat fights on the fence), and has caused a widespread impression that mating among all wild animals is accompanied by these skirmishes. That is not true; and in even the species which seem so antagonistic, the male does not become really aggressive until the female indicates that she is ready. Often she starts the whole thing and, whatever her size or strength, she determines the outcome. For without her co-operation no union takes combative species mentioned above, the scramble provides a stimplace. In most animals ovulation precedes the coupling, but in the ulation which apparently is required to release the egg from the ovary — a sequence of events that biologists call induced ovulation. Incidentally, it is now believed that intercourse may occasionally cause a woman to ovulate outside the time when normally she would be fertile. (That is the situation, as much as irregularity in a woman's cycle, which may make it impossible for the rhythm method of contraception ever to be dependable.)

As soon as the female animal has become pregnant, she ceases to be receptive and she often parts company with the male. Her associates during the rest of the year may be other females or, more likely, the young she bore in a previous litter. In either case she is very much her own woman. She catches her own mice and digs her own roots. She goes and comes as she pleases. If the day is windy and bright, and she wants to bound over the hills, animated and free, she does. If she wants to rest in the sun, she does that, and no male would assume that he had a right to object. In the case of monogamous pairs with joint households, the male probably takes the initiative in any effort that concerns both of them, and his mate assists voluntarily. If a relay pursuit is the best way to bring down a deer, the male wolf or coyote leads and his mate cooperates in his strategy; if a beaver dam needs repair, the mother and young help the father, who seems to direct the work — but no male "bosses" his mate. If she wishes, and ordinarily she does, she carries half, at least, of their common load of responsibility, but not because any demands are made except those of her own nature.

It is not a male's world that she lives in, nor a female's world. It is just the world, and the male and female are two self-reliant creatures who share it. They may be together permanently, or very infrequently, but in neither case are they competitors or, of course, enemies. There is room for both in their habitat and enough food for both. They will need each other from time to time, and neither will try to prove himself, or herself, by outstripping or by subduing the other.

Into that Eden — of innocence because there all the animals obey nature's laws — entered not the serpent but an emerging brain, one that could ask, why should I not have more of what I enjoy? No one knows just when it happened, but obviously at some stage the developing mind of the primate glimpsed the momentous idea that he need not wait to be moved by instinct. He could take initiative, reach for the things that delighted him. He could grasp them whether instinct propelled him or not. "Idea" is too sophisticated a word; "a new kind of impulse" would be more accurate. It did originate in his recently evolved higher nerve centers, however, and what an immense step, then, the primate took. It may have been the first exercising of a somewhat-conscious purposive will.

Perhaps food was his inspiration, more food than he needed, because now he had come to recognize that flavor might give him pleasure — the flavor of a banana for instance, more bananas and more and more, whether or not his hunger was satisfied. Mammals below the primates stop eating when they have consumed all they need. They do not, of course, "use restraint"; instinct simply alerts them to turn away from their food before they are satiated, and as a result they remain lean and lithe, in fit condition to hunt or escape a hunter. But many monkeys and apes have learned to gorge themselves on fruits, which are abundant in their tropical habitats. Some of them have developed great paunchy abdomens, even at times have become grossly fat, with such an obsessive fondness for food that they hoard what is left when they cannot possibly eat any more. A strong baboon often clutches every last morsel, refusing to part with any that he can hold, even though comrades, including the young, may be starving.

And sex: why wait for the inner signals? Should creatures as smart as monkeys and apes deny themselves what could so easily be obtained? At some stage in their evolution, the males of some primate species began to adopt a demanding attitude. It was no longer enough that she, the smaller, the weaker, never would challenge his strength. Now she must bend to his will. Here, finally, she comes, a choice little morsel herself. She had taken her infant down to the river and she has stayed too long. Anyway, she is not very receptive today; a male would not know why. He'll cuff her, he'll teach her not to leave him alone like this. There, she is down on the ground, very quiet; and so is the baby. Why does she not get up? He'll cuff her again. In some way she seems too still. Maybe she never *will* get up. Too bad, but she shouldn't have made him wait.

The statement often is made in biology textbooks that true rape is unknown among any animals except the human. The reason is anatomical: in the pre-human pairs the back-to-front position in copulation allows the female to move away. When human beings began to walk upright, a forward shift in the feminine genitalia made face-to-face mating convenient — convenient, but it renders the female helpless, at the mercy of any male. Speaking solely of physical force, it may be accurate to say that rape is only possible to the human species, although some pre-human primates found that rape could be accomplished by intimidation. The male would threaten and attack a female in various non-sexual ways till she learned to submit to his will because of her fear of him. Actually the intimidation might not have been necessary because the female, too, had discovered that she wanted more sex. He often attacked her anyway. Perhaps he enjoyed exercising his new sense of power.

No biologist was there to observe and report the steps by which the new regime came about. Nevertheless, we see in the rhesus monkeys what happened (not in all species of primates) when instinctive controls had been lost and sufficient intelligence had not yet evolved to supplant it. These monkeys belong to the Old World group found in southern Asia and Africa. The various species arrange their sex life somewhat differently, most, however, treating their mates in ways that may have given rise to our adjectives "brutish" and "bestial." Sometimes the words are applied to all animals, but I don't know of any they properly fit except Old World monkeys.

The rhesus monkeys have nothing that even approximates family life. They live in large bands (sometimes as many as 85 animals) consisting of one dominant male, subordinate males, and females and young. All the females are accessible to all males except that the dominant male has first choice. As among animals below primates, the female indicates when her oestrus has come, although the males would know anyway because her sitting pads then become scarlet. They attack her when the arrival of her receptive period leads her to seek one of them; when the relationship has become established, the male partner attacks her if she turns to another, even though he himself may have become depleted; as her oestrus wanes and fatigue overtakes her, she is attacked again. In 45 copulations of free-ranging rhesus monkeys observed by C. R. Carpenter, the females were attacked in 22 cases. In 16 they were injured, twice seriously.

One wonders why a female goes through with all this. The answer may be that in spite of the danger she is so desirous during her fertile period that she solicits attention anyway. She may have developed a masochistic tendency that keeps pace with the sadism of the males. In any case all these monkeys seem to be hypersexed. In the same group that Carpenter watched, one male had consort relations with 55 females in a period of two months. Homosexuality is common among them, especially among the males, the subordinates often soliciting, sometimes for favors and sometimes for protection against other males, for the males attack one another, as well as the females, almost constantly.

The baboons also are Old World monkeys. They live in Africa and a few in Arabia. In intelligence they are more advanced than the rhesus monkeys and have developed a family life of the harem pattern. A family includes a despotic male, several females, the young, and on the fringe of this company, one or several bachelors. The peripheral males have no chance to mate unless they can steal a moment with one of the overlord's wives, who usually are willing. If he discovers them, he may attack them or take out his rage by attacking an infant or one of his other mates. It is reported that the disloyal female often is killed by the now-released lust of the bachelors.

In his relationship with his females, the dominant male always determines the time of copulation. His mates most attract him during their oestrus periods and, having several of them, the male can hope there will always be one at the peak of desirability. Except when they are in oestrus the females do not seek a close relationship with the male, but he often demands compliance at other times. Frank A. Beach writes that the female's response in such situations "has the appearance of submissive acquiescence to a potential enemy." (The rather prevalent idea that human males are polygamous may have arisen from the monkey and ape arrangement in which a dominant male has more than one partner. The situation is not quite comparable, however, for responsiveness is not constant in the mates of most pre-human males. It still is true at the monkey level that the females have a lingering reluctance to copulate except at the time when sound offspring can be conceived.)

Increasing control in these sexual matters is found in the chimpanzees, who, being apes, are further advanced than monkeys. They are quite various in their individual temperaments. Some are cruel and belligerent, others form friendly and loyal attachments, and their good will includes some protectiveness of their companions. In mechanical aptitude chimpanzees "have a gift approaching genius," wrote Robert M. Yerkes, who spent a lifetime studying these apes in captivity and was fervent in their defense. L. Heck, who observed them in Germany, wrote: "The chimpanzee is not merely curious, but is eager to know . . . He understands how to draw conclusions, to follow from one thing to another, to carry over certain experiences purposefully to relations new to him." Heck adds, "He is sly, crafty, self-willed, but not stubborn."

He is an unstable animal, as W. T. Hornaday describes him: "Except when quite young either nervous or hysterical . . . rough, domineering, and dangerous." When the apes reach maturity, they are masterfully strong and "quickly become conscious of their strength . . . The male is given to shouting, yelling, shrieking, and roaring and when angry rages like a demon." It is not surprising then that, at least in captivity, a male chimpanzee sometimes threatens a female into submission.

Yerkes described the approach of chimpanzee mates to each other: "In sexual play and pre-mating activity the male . . . may stand erect, sometimes with hair rising and arms swinging. He may strut about, stamping, with shoulders back and chest expanded. Often he shouts, rushes about, jumps, strikes or pounds objects within reach, or even his female companion . . . Sometimes she marches about with him . . . and at other times she avoids him as if fearful of violence. In general, his postures and actions are roughly and menacingly demonstrative, strongly self-assertive, and expressive of physical strength, while hers are relatively gentle, self-effacing, ingratiating, and self-protective."

There is more than meets the eye in those adjectives which describe the female. For the chimpanzee reasoning powers, as well as the craftiness, are in the head of the female as well as the male. If the male can attempt to rule her through fear, she can understand that desire as strong as his gives her a weapon. She can use her attractiveness to get her own way and win special concessions from him — and she constantly does. For illustration, when she is in oestrus, he often lets her have first chance if any especially delicious food is available. At other times he tries to prevent her from getting anything, except occasionally scraps that he doesn't want, such as banana peel. Then, however, she frequently offers herself and, with his attention diverted, slips in for a stolen bit. This manoeuvre is very typical. Yerkes found that the female chimpanzee in oestrus indicated her willingness first 85 per cent of the times there were copulations, and even during the infertile periods of her cycle, she made the advances 65 per cent of the times, usually to secure some advantage. Thus prostitution entered the primate scene. But the male chimpanzee often demands that the female be acquiescent, even against her wishes.

Since these are descriptions of chimpanzees in captivity, their behavior is probably not quite as it would be if they were free. But with such numerous matings — at least 545 — observed in the Yale Laboratories of Primate Biology, it seems likely that the chimpanzees revealed characteristic traits to the scientists. Chimpanzees have not been studied thoroughly in their African wilderness.* What reports there have been indicate that their family life is the harem type.

In the species of primates so far described, it is evident that the male-female relationships have deteriorated as the animals climbed the ladder of evolution. The male has become a bully, the female in many cases has become coy and foxy and ever willing

* Such a study is now being made.

to trade on her sex. Actually, unless she has learned how to trick her mate, she is a pitiful creature, timid and cowed and forced to violate her most important feminine instinct. It is impossible not to remark on the contrast between this poor animal and the free and spontaneous female in sub-primate species, where, as the great British zoologist Sir Solly Zuckerman emphasizes, she determines that matings must take place at the wisest time.

If this is the best that primates can do in their personal lives as their brains become more complex, it can be questioned whether they really are making progress. This, however, is not the best they have done. These monkeys and apes represent only one way that primate sexuality has developed. Among other primates there are different sorts of relationship between males and females, which allow the two sexes to take continuous pleasure and comfort in the companionship of each other. The contrast is great, so striking as to cause wonder that the two groups of animals both belong to the primate order.

In South and Central America live several species of monkeys which are similar in structure and mental development to those of the Old World, and yet the males are completely without the aggressive, despotic qualities that make sex in the Asian and African monkeys so full of stress. The aversion of the American monkeys to fighting is interestingly shown by the way that adult males will separate two young animals when their play becomes rough enough so that one might get hurt. At times there are controversies between neighboring clans, but they are settled by shouting, not by hand-to-hand fights.

Their peaceable temperament is expressed too in their sex life. They mate promiscuously for the most part, and no male of an American species considers himself to have any "rights" and therefore shows no hostility towards another male who is engaged with a female. The male usually, although not always, takes the initiative in the pairing. The female sometimes exhausts more than one male during her oestrus period, and then if she wants to turn to another, she is quite free to go. As Beach comments, the New World female monkey "does not employ sex as a social device to avoid injury by a male." She would have no reason to do so, since it is not the custom for males to threaten her.

Also typical of a gentle relationship between primate sexes is that of gorillas. Gorillas are more intelligent animals than the New World monkeys and no more belligerent. These were the least known of the apes until they were studied a few years ago in their African habitat by the astute young biologist George B. Schaller, who has described them in great detail in his book *The Mountain Gorilla.*

For nearly two years Schaller literally lived with one group or another of these enormous animals (males weigh up to 450 pounds) that hitherto had been thought to be fearfully vicious. He found them most amiable; associating with them so closely that he slept at times within 30 feet of a clan, yet he never was threatened seriously. When he inquired of the local African natives, he learned that gorillas rarely if ever attack a man unless the man is attacking them, and even then they do not seem to have any desire to kill. A gorilla retreats after one punitive bite, which may be fatal although usually it is not.

The same tolerant disposition is typical of their relationships with one another. Gorillas live in small companies consisting of one dominant male, subordinate males, a few females who "belong" to no male in particular, and the youngsters. Except for the leader the hierarchy is rather loose and its organization appears to depend more on the personality of the individuals than on size or strength.

Dominance is shown chiefly by preceding the others on trails or by demanding the better place to sit, such as one protected from rain. If the subordinate animal does not quickly give up his advantage, he is often reminded with a light slap from the back of the hand. Schaller once saw a female appropriate a dry spot that was occupied by a juvenile and then lose it to the dominant male, who pushed her out into the rain herself. Though not chivalrous, he was not angry. When excited by some strange situation, conceivably dangerous, all the gorillas make the defensive gesture of beating their chests and shouting. The dominant male does this loudest and longest, one of several ways he expresses his sense of responsibility for protecting the group. At most times he seems to be rather aloof, but one is impressed by the amount of affection his followers show him. The little ones play around him and on him (Schaller once saw an infant go to the resting male and lay his head on the big outspread hand and thus drop off to sleep); the females generally sit or sleep near him, sometimes leaning against his body, and even the other males may sometimes move closer. The dominant male is, in the true sense, a leader, no despot. When he gets up to go on to a new feeding place, the rest fall into line behind him immediately; they stop when he stops, and usually they go to sleep in their separate nests and awaken when he does. Yet he does not restrict the activities of his companions. Schaller observed two instances in which females were copulating with other males only a few feet from the leader, and he showed no jealousy or

other sign of objecting. Obviously he is not the lord of a harem in the way of the dominant male baboon.

And there seems to be no more duplicity in the female gorilla than there is in the females of New World monkeys, for the female gorilla is not attacked either; she has nothing to dread. The dominant male expects deference from all the other animals in his clan, but he shows in nature the same disposition that a well-treated gorilla shows in a laboratory: "He is very stable emotionally, a constructive animal." He has been described in the scientific literature as "deeply attached to gorilla companions."

Schaller's observations are based on a study of eleven separate gorilla groups, or clans. A group seldom included more than sixteen animals, of both adults and young, though its size was subject to change. The group might be joined by one or more outside individuals and insiders might leave, but there was always one dominant male, a gorilla apparently in his prime.

The social life of these apes is especially interesting because gorillas do not confuse sex and dominance. Though they arrange themselves in a hierarchy, layered according to something like strength of will, and, among females, the age of the youngest child, their sexual acts do not express mastery of one animal over another. As in most of the pre-primate species, the mates come together simply for mutual pleasure. Sex with gorillas is therefore easier, more spontaneous, than it is with the chimpanzees, for example. One can wonder if this difference has anything to do with the tendency of chimpanzees to be "hysterical" and gorillas "stable." In chimpanzees the struggle of wills between sexual partners must often produce a tension that gorillas escape.

The sexual chaos of rhesus monkeys, the amiable polygamy of the New World monkeys, the frequent viciousness in the baboon harems, the armed truce of the chimpanzee males and females, and the permissive paternalism of the gorillas: this is strangely diverse behavior for animals who all belong to the same primate order. None of these monkeys and apes have adopted the monogamous state to which most human beings aspire; but there is one other primate not yet discussed — the gibbon.

We have very reliable information about these small apes. Gibbons have fascinated travelers to Southeast Asia for centuries, and there is now the excellent and detailed report of the biologist, C. R. Carpenter, who spent hundreds of hours observing 21 gibbon families in Thailand. Although gibbons stay most of the time in the upper boughs of tall trees, Carpenter was able to watch them intimately, for he found, in a wildlife reserve surrounding a Buddhist temple, cliffs which rose steeply out of the forest. Some of the time the animals were only thirty feet from the biologist, sitting up on a cliff with his binoculars and recording equipment.

In Thailand, as everywhere, dawn came first to the treetops. The frothy green plumes were in sunlight while the river below in the canyon still was a vein of the night. Grades of gloom hung in the mists above it; knots of shade were caught in the festoons of mosses. Moisture from heavy dew dripped from the giant ferns. But the day was already a bloom on the tips of the tallest trees, and the gibbons were there to proclaim it. They had slept on the middle boughs, but today, as on all days, they had climbed to the highest branches as soon as the sun had touched them. Perched there, with knees under their chins and long arms grasping the boughs for support, the gibbons began their dawn chorus.

They sent their songs ringing across the dark canyons, and from opposite ridges came the answers of neighboring gibbon families. A third and fourth group joined the musical conversation. How splendid to start the day with a call to neighbors and hear them reply; splendid to be a gibbon up in the freshly washed light while the rest of the world was dark!

From the infants with thin piping voices to adult males, whose vocal volume is said to surpass any man's, the gibbons all sang the same tune. A real tune it was, begun in the key of E and rising by halftone steps to exactly the height of an octave, where the voices trilled with great flexibility. Each tone was introduced with a grace note, the keynote E, and the whole up-flung roulade had the effect of expressing trimphant joy. At the top, during the trill, the gibbons quivered through all their bodies. Finally they let the song ease away in a few diminishing quarter tones.

The gibbons have a whole repertory of calls and cries, all somewhat musical, but this morning performance is considered a marvel. For these apes are the only animals below man who can sing true tones, with voices organized like the human voice. They don't, of course, have more than an ape's range of thought and emotion to put into music, but "they are the only mammals who truly sing."

In this family the adult female, the mother, apparently was the one who enjoyed the performance most. She kept the others there singing for nearly two hours (too long, said some of the human beings below). When she finally had had enough, she took the initiative in leading the family down to the ground, where she and her mate and three of their young ones darted about for a while, catching grasshoppers.

All of them, including the one-year-old infant, ran on their hind feet, balancing with their extended arms. Seen thus on the ground, they looked extraordinarily human, though small, rather like very thin children. (In size gibbons are between monkeys and the "great apes." It is thought that they may have been larger once and evolved towards less weight, an advantage in swinging about in trees.) They had no tails. The skin of their faces was dark and was rimmed with a neat ruff of white fur. The rest of their fur, silky and rather short, was black or dark gray. Their faces were shaped much like ours, with large eyes, small noses, and mobile lips, which sometimes curved up in smiles (called real smiles by even the most scientific observers), although much of the time the mouths drooped a little, with an expression both proud and wistful. The gibbons' hands were in some ways their most remarkable feature. With abnormally long fingers, but with nails shaped like a human's and with opposable thumbs, they had such a delicacy of touch, they seemed to be made for nothing more harsh than tracing the pattern in butterflies' wings or brushing droplets of dew from flowers. When the gibbons climbed back up their lodge-tree, they circled the trunk with their arms and "walked" up, with legs nearly straight.

This family included a nearly grown daughter, two younger sons, the infant, and a relative who was senile and so knotted up with arthritis that he was unable to leave this tree. He was dependent for food on what the others would bring to him, and they gave him good care. The female had saved the last insects she caught for him.

It was the family's habit to go about through their territory of thirty-five acres or so each day, stopping in whatever trees the fruits, leaves, and young growing tips were at their most tempting stage. Meanwhile they would make sure that no neighboring gibbons were trespassing. On such trips the family went out together, but this was a morning when they would separate. The daughter, absorbed in a romance, had left as soon as the singing ended; she would spend the day with a young male from another family. The mother was temporarily handicapped by the infant, too heavy now to be carried easily and too small to have learned all of a gibbon's skill in swinging about through the trees. They parted, the father and sons looping away on an aerial path, with the tolerant father letting one of the sons take the lead.

In their moving about there was no hard and fast rule of precedence. While the young ones were inexperienced, either the father or mother went first; thus the immature gibbons learned what jumps were safe and how to make their swings so that, from a high start, they could stretch out their elevation as far as possible before landing on boughs so low that they had to climb up the trunk of a tree again. They came to know various routes through their trees very well, although, as the trees grew, new routes were constantly opening up. Jumps from tree to tree that had been too great became possible when the branches were longer.

As the family roamed, each one made the jumps that were set by the leader. This was the first time the father had let the younger son go ahead. From the lodge-tree he launched himself into the air spread out flat, like a flying squirrel. With his left hand he caught a branch thirty feet away, without checking his speed leapt away to another bough, which he caught with his right hand, and on to another caught again with his left. Thus he flew, facing one way and then the opposite, and so swiftly, he seemed only to touch the branches he passed. Once when a bird crossed the father's route through the air, he caught it with one hand while aiming accurately for the next bough with the other hand. He would not eat the bird — this appeared to be only a bit of play, or possibly an unconscious exercise in dexterity.

The youths and their father each had his preferences as to food. The one leading liked nuts and took the others first into a betel palm. They went on to eat the bright, spiny red fruit of a rambutan tree, acid tamarind pods, huge plantain bananas, and mangosteens, whose thick rind had to be peeled before the gibbons could bite into the juicy pulp. The animals were fastidious in their eating, removing skins and seeds of fruits and any bruised spots with their teeth and fingers, and chewing slowly, as if they savored the taste.

Hearing a chattering up ahead, the father, leading, took off abruptly. What he suspected was true: a family of neighbors were climbing into his fig tree, whose fruits were just then becoming deliciously ripe. Swinging in through the air, the father shrilled out a protest. The trespassing gibbons paused. Standing upright on a thick low branch of the fig tree, the father warned them away in a voice like an attack. The other family yelled back and, since there were six of them, their noise could overwhelm his. The sons joined in the father's bellowing, and the other gibbons reluctantly went down the tree. The father and sons followed them to the ground and on to the boundary of the properties. Once more in their own territory, the six stood and hurled taunts. As he answered, the father's voice was becoming more mild, not forgiving yet but no longer outraged. He had won, and before many minutes he might exchange friendly calls with these neighbors, for a gibbon's anger is quick to subside.

At no point had he made any threatening gestures. In most cases these little apes replace rage, which so easily becomes slaughter, with indignation expressed in sounds rather than blows. They do have a strong sense of justice however, and if someone imposes on them in a manner that can be punished only with action, their bites are swift and effective. Most often the boundary disputes are settled by shouting.

The father had not seen his daughter all day, although several times he had heard her voice. She had found her playmate. First they had swung about through the trees in a breath-taking game of tag. Like brothers and sisters who often challenge each other in daring, these two seemed to be proving how strong and graceful they were. When the competition went out of their game, they just wandered about, eating some fruit and enjoying their easy companionship. They went down to the ground and caught some ants and drank at the spring, by dipping their hands in the water and licking it off the fur. They found a bear's nest and curled up in it for a rest and groomed each other a little, but their play didn't go on to completion — not yet. They had been spending their days together for four or five weeks, but like all gibbon courtships, this one would be rather long. Gibbons are somewhat reticent about taking their partners. Any tendency to be domineering or cruel or demanding, in either the male or female, could make the other quite desolate. Apparently such mistakes seldom are made. The tenderness in the mutual feeling of this young pair was growing; before many days it would become more compelling, and then they would disappear from this part of the forest and from their families. They would explore till they found an unoccupied group of trees they could claim as their own.

Back on the lodge-tree the mother had watched her mate and

the sons as long as they were in sight. After that there came into her manner a slight suggestion of loss or uncertainty, though of course it could have been no more than loneliness. The gibbons' way of life is precarious, and they have the tentative way of some human beings whose happiness is especially fragile.

The female rested awhile, with her eyes on the distant trees and her head turned to one side, the better to listen for voices. Later she nursed her infant, stopping the process several times to tip back the baby's face and look into it with a seemingly loving smile. Then she groomed its fur. This ritual, practiced also by other apes but not with fingers that have a gibbon's exquisite touch, consists in parting the hair of the other animal, taking off any bits of dirt or dried skin, taking out any tangles, and smoothing the hair back in place. No parasites ever establish themselves in a gibbon's fur, and when this baby's fur had been groomed, she was as clean as a human child. On a nearby branch the old one was grooming himself as well as he could, but his back was out of his crippled reach. When she was through with the baby, the mother also groomed him. Mutual grooming is done between all the members of gibbon families, and the elderly gibbon was treated like one of them.

The female was clearly unhappy by midafternoon. She huddled up in a soft fur ball, looking as though her life were suspended until her mate should come back.

His return was heralded by the clang of the bamboo stalks through which he was traveling. As he would swing out on one and then let it go, the stalk would spring back and, striking others, make a sound that was almost metallic. The female heard it and, bright with joy, she ran out a few steps on the branch where she had been resting.

Here he came — no bird and yet flying as swiftly. It was a long jump to the lodge-tree, but the male caught the branch just above the one where his mate stood and waited. He came to a swinging stop and let his feet down on her bough and walked towards her. Theirs was the greeting of all affectionate gibbons, but its being familiar did not diminish its grace. As the pair advanced, with each step more slow, both of them smiled, each uttered a soft cry, and their arms folded around each other.

In this way they came together whenever they had been separated. Today, however, they realized that they wanted more. Again the male caught the branch above and swung in past his mate. When he was behind her, still with most of his weight hung from the bough overhead, she stooped for him and their union completed itself with the male swinging forward and back like a pendulum . . . forward and back until finally he became quiet as, reaching around with one arm, his mate held him close to her.

The pair left the middle boughs of the tree and the rest of the family. They climbed to a crotch between higher branches and there settled down to a time of grooming each other. For a while

she lay on the branch in front of him while he parted the fur all over her body and sought for any minute speck of dust. They reversed their roles and she did the grooming. The process went on for some time after the fur of both was immaculate, and the harmony in the way they adjusted positions was itself like a form of love, a sign of a deeper harmony in their emotions.

These, then, are the gibbons. The details of their family life have not been idealized; all are found in reports that are considered reliable. It is true that a good deal of warmth creeps into the accounts of most observers:

"With what elegance and gentleness it takes with its delicate taper fingers whatever is offered to it!"

"A cry of fright, pain, or distress from one gibbon would bring all the others at once to the complainer, and they would then condole with him and fold him in their arms."

"It made use of its two arms as we do; its face was fashioned almost exactly like those of the savages at the Cape of Good Hope; . . . its cry was exactly like that of a child."

"They seemed to be above all of a very tender disposition, and to show their affection toward those whom they knew and loved, they embraced . . . them."

The comments about the morning song of the gibbons is condensed from an analysis by George Robert Waterhouse, who transcribed the song into musical notation. He summarized: "It appeared to me that, in ascending and descending the scale, the intervals were always exactly half-tones; and I am sure that the highest note was the exact octave to the lowest . . . The quality of the notes is very musical." The conclusions of Waterhouse have been confirmed by later biologists who have recorded the voices. Gibbons make numerous other sounds. Louis Boutan described one as "sweet and plaintive — to call attention of a friendly person. 'I am here.'" Boutan spelled the sound *Thwiiwwg!*

In his long report on the social activities of free-living gibbons

Carpenter writes: "There is little competition for food and little aggressive dominant behavior. Even in a cage a dominant animal never takes food away from a subordinate . . . Association during feeding, play, rest . . . grooming, mutual assistance, cooperative guarding and defense, all strengthen the family structure . . . The female's continuous receptivity would seem to compensate for the lack of more than one female for each male and support the family type of grouping."

Female gibbons are the only females below human beings who are continuously "receptive," but Carpenter's own description of the female's frequent initiative in love-making seems to indicate more than a waiting for the male to express desire. Biologists have some difficulty in finding the words to convey just what does happen when female animals make the first approaches. The term they most often use is "aggression," but the females are never aggressive in ways that the males are. They don't — they can't, of course — make demands. They reveal a readiness and perhaps a wish, many times no more than a question implied by a posture or gesture, *Now?* Or they say *Now?* with a flirtatiousness which is the very essence of femininity. The males do not show any sign of being alarmed. Usually they respond with eagerness, but if they aren't interested, they don't react with hostility or dismissal — except in the species whose males are bullies.

Among all monkeys and apes the females follow the rule of the pre-primate females: even after the sense of acute timing has been lost, they still have an instinct to make the advances. Among the hypersexed species, the rhesus monkeys, baboons, and chimpanzees, these approaches can seem very insistent, though they never involve threats or any suggestion of force. Among gibbons, gorillas, and New World monkeys neither males nor females are much absorbed with sexual activities. Many biologists speak of the milder species as having "a weak sexual drive" — a comment which may reflect the civilized modern attitude that there hardly can be too much sex. But "moderate sex drive" would seem more accurate, for these animals have no difficulty in maintaining their populations; they are among the primate species that are given the best chance of surviving and perhaps of continuing to evolve.

The contentment the gibbon sexes know with each other seems to be an extension of the fellow feeling they express in numerous other ways. They appear to have an extraordinary tenderness and ability to convey it. They even convey it to human beings. People who have had gibbons as pets tell many anecdotes about the animals offering sympathy. I have a word of testimony myself. I had gone to spend an hour playing with a captive gibbon and had taken an orange to her. She ate it daintily, first removing the rind and later, after she'd chewed the pulp, removing the white skin from her mouth and laying it on a shelf. She handled the orange so much as a civilized person would that I remembered poignantly how closely related we are, how, as many anthropologists believe, gibbons and human beings left the primate stem together in a common relative, *Pithecanthropus*. Knowing how long ago that separation took place (estimates are in hundreds of thousands of years), and how very much longer had been required to produce even that gibbon-man, I was stricken to realize that all this achievement might come to an end in our generation. The threat of nuclear armaments seemed, as never before, a shattering tragedy. All the time I had been with the gibbon, she had watched my face with grave, gentle eyes, and at the thought of the bomb I suppose I showed my distress. She suddenly reached out her hand and took mine, not understanding my sadness but in effect giving comfort. She *was* comforting, a little soul seeming to offer reassurance that was selfless, without words, but a sharing. Since a gibbon may feel sympathy on so mundane an occasion, and communicate something like it so well, it is not surprising that a strong bond of mutual dependence forms between mates, a bond that apparently always is permanent.

Those evolving males who found that they liked to intimidate mates were responsible for putting their females on the defensive;

they were responsible for replacing joy and freedom in sex with fear and deviousness. But their aggressiveness was not the sole reason why nature's bell became silent. The risk of blighting one's species by bearing cripples was taken by other primates besides the despotic males. Many monkey and ape defectives are born, animals which have abnormalities of the spinal column and ribs, misshapen skulls, deformed limbs, in some cases the incomplete formation of an entire limb — these in the New World monkeys, gorillas, and gibbons as well as in species whose males demand submission at off-cycle times. With increasing intelligence, obviously, the sexes became aware of each other more consciously, and then warmth of feeling may have become a motive as strong as the coldness of lust.

Would it not be amazing if the Fall, that mythical event which has so troubled mankind with a sense of guilt, were no more than this: that the primate's evolving mind began to overrule nature's restrictions? In many cultures and many religions there is a clouded memory of a lost Eden. In the Golden Age in all of those golden worlds there were no women. It was the coming of women that was believed to have destroyed innocence. Sex itself does not appear to have been the source of the guilt; homosexuality, sometimes prevalent in simpler societies, did not seem to arouse the anxiety, but rather the sexual experience of males *with females.*

The locales where the myths originated are too widespread for all of them to have been influenced by Hebrew sources. In many it was the eating of certain forbidden plants, or despoiling of flowers, that was the unforgivable act assumed to have loaded a sense of sin, forever, on all the sons of the transgressor. Food is one of the most familiar symbols in the myths of primitive peoples. It stands, of course, for sexual intercourse between men and women; and the plucking of prohibited plants was a taboo among natives as scattered as those of Mexico and Australia, Madagascar and Tibet, and of Greece (the Golden Apples, stolen by Heracles; and even the serpent was there in the person of the hundred-headed dragon).

One can appreciate the French lamentation, *Tant de bruit pour une pomme!*

But it was more than an apple. The psychological burden called in Christianity "Original Sin" becomes easy to understand if one believes that the real violation was the seeking of intercourse during nature's forbidden time.

IV

AGGRESSIVENESS

How Red the Tooth and Claw?

How Red
the Tooth and Claw?

I T WAS WARFARE in miniature, and the opponents in this case were plants. On one side were the aggressors; on the other side those that were doomed — a very menacing species when they were in a stimulating environment, but just then they were resting, warm enough and well-enough nourished to reproduce themselves, although rather sluggishly. They were like an army asleep in a vulnerable position.

No one could have predicted the slaughter that was about to take place, but it happened suddenly that the aggressive plants, reproducing explosively, advanced towards the idle ones. They did not kill them by trapping them, as some plants will trap flies; they simply released a substance that was deadly poisonous to the victims nearest them. Those a bit farther away had their reproductive capacity paralyzed. It all happened very silently, though quite quickly — and it was a victory as famous as any battle between human enemies in this most warlike century. For that victory was the conquest of the bacteria *Staphylococcus* by a spreading mold, *penicillin*. It took place on a glass slide in the laboratory of the bacteriologist Arthur Fleming, who was soon to be Sir Arthur Fleming, honored because he had seen that battle and a flash of insight had told him the significance of the fact that a mold can destroy a microbe.

The antagonism between the two minute organisms is but one

instance of a situation which exists throughout nature. Plants destroy other plants, usually by taking over their living space when the seeds of a stronger species fall among those that are weaker; animals eat plants; animals also eat other animals. The first discovery of this arrangement can be a profound disillusionment. It can be such a shock that the compensating factors are never glimpsed. The relation between living things is seen as universally one of malice, a view which can furnish the basis for lifelong cynicism.

For many a child the knowledge of nature's food chains comes early, when he learns that in real life the dear little woodfolk of his storybooks *eat* one another. The tales that he later reads for himself may deepen the shock, for some of them will have been written by men who delight in gore. The older child hears, until he may come to loathe the phrase, Tennyson's comment that nature "is red in tooth and claw," and he may absorb the idea that every wild animal lives in terror of instant death. Illustrations for stories like these may be even more vivid than the blood-relishing words. In my own memory are two pictures I saw when too young to be critical of them. In one a wolf was attacking a deer. The deer leaps in the air, her whole body convulsed with fear and her eyes frantic. The wolf springs for her throat. His fangs are bared in a snarl one can almost hear, foam drips from his mouth, his mane is bristling, and his eyes glitter with what the artist probably would have called blood-lust. In the second picture an eagle is perched on a cliff, standing actually on the body of a rabbit with his bloody talons deep in the rabbit's torn breast. The rabbit must have been dead by then, but the artist had painted its eyes as more consciously desperate than a rabbit's eyes ever are in even its moments of most intense life. The rabbit *knew* that it had been killed, and the experience had been agony. The eyes of the eagle, focused on some far horizon, were proud and cruel.

Like most children I partly repressed the horror those pictures aroused, but a sense of pervading evil remained. It was there and it had its effect in nightmares—until I was old enough to go out into the woods and see nature's world for myself.

In the first fatal encounter I watched, a fox was the hunter. Tawny-coated, he was enjoying himself in the limber green grass of a meadow. Rather idly he seemed to be looking for food, since he sniffed the ground here and there and sniffed the breeze; but his mood was light, and his movements suggested that he was taking pleasure in his own grace. He heard the click of a tree squirrel's claws and raced towards the oak, barking, although he must have known he could not reach the squirrel. A brown towhee was scratching under a bush, jumping forward and back on parallel feet. The fox bounded towards it, not so fast but that the bird had a chance to fly up and away. As the fox returned to the meadow, a dragonfly, conspicuous with the sunlight stitched into its wings, skimmed over his head. He leapt for it but not eagerly—that too was only a bit of play. Very suddenly, then, the fox became still, listening, with his eyes on the ground and his motionless head slightly cocked. With brilliant speed he springs into the air and comes down with all his feet clustered into a grasping unit. He has caught his prey, a young ground squirrel, perhaps. I could not see what it was, but it was more than a mouse, for it went down in several bites. Meanwhile the fox, as he chewed, seemed strangely casual, almost uninterested. Here was a revelation: that fox didn't hate his victim any more than I hate the lamb when I watch a butcher wrap up some chops.

Let Adolph Murie describe a few incidents. He has observed the large carnivores, leading their normal lives, as intimately as any living biologist.

Of wolves, which feed almost entirely on caribou in some parts of the North:

"Generally, the caribou seem not to be worried much by wolves unless chased. I frequently noted caribou bands watching the wolves when they could have been moving away to a more secure position. . . . All day the caribou had been in the vicinity of the [wolves'] den, but the resting wolves did not molest them. . . . The large black-mantled [wolf] was in the lead, trotting gaily and briskly with tail waving. Once he dashed at a band [of caribou] then stopped to watch . . . Once the black male galloped hard after a herd but stopped to watch when he was near it." On another occasion the same black wolf "ran in such a way as to drive all the caribou off the grass-covered flat toward the gravel bar. He did not try to catch any of them."

The kills are made "quickly," many times with a bite on the neck. The victims are almost invariably the young animals, the diseased, or those too old to make a speedy escape. "A calf dropped behind the others. This seemed to encourage the wolf to put on added speed, and in less than a quarter of a mile he overtook the calf, knocking it over as he closed in." The wolf was hungry and fed for about half an hour. "This calf was captured more readily than usual."

Murie describes a grizzly bear watching two newborn moose calves, the bear apparently waiting for a lapse in the moose mother's protection: "The bear was lying on its side, its huge head resting on one paw . . . I saw the bear lift its head and look briefly down at the moose, and then go back to sleep . . . The bear later moved up the ridge four or five yards and stretched out on its side again. About half an hour after I had started my observations, the bear galloped across two or three shallow draws as it circled to one side of the moose, coughing two or three times as it galloped." A grizzly bear coughs or tears at the turf with its forepaws when it is contemplating attack. Many other animals understand these signs and take them as warnings, and therefore the grizzly's behavior is strangely inconsistent with an animal often accused of being "a killer."

Grizzlies have been known to attack human beings and maul them. As a species they have been hunted so much, their fury so often has been aroused by the smell of men with guns, that human beings may simply be identified in their minds as predators (see page 172). Polar bears do have the unfortunate habit of eating human flesh. Most often that would be Eskimo flesh, and one may wonder whether the bears believe those men to be seals. Since Eskimos often wear sealskin parkis, eat a great deal of seal meat, and cleanse themselves with seal oil, the bears may confuse those familiar-scented small men with the bears' customary prey. However, the polar bears have even more reason than grizzlies to hate human beings, for white men hunt them in airplanes illegally, running them back and forth till the bears are exhausted; only then does the "sportsman" land, and, quite safe himself, shoot his bear.

If the incidents described by Murie indicate blood-lust, that appetite hardly should be described as voracious. Many modern biologists, who don't get their impressions from myths but from patient watching of animals living free in the wilds, contradict the idea that the predators hunt with sadistic cruelty. Animals do have very effective weapons, and they can use them with speed and skill — but in their food-seeking with little if any malice.

In his book *Animal Behavior*, John Paul Scott has presented the more recent scientific knowledge about predation:

> *Fifty years ago it was the fashion to picture the life of animals in nature as a constant battle for survival, with intense individual competition for food and hungry predators waiting around every corner, ready to snap up the unfit. We have since found that highly competitive situations occur very rarely except in populations which have become disorganized as the result of overcrowding or a disturbed social situation . . . As for predators, they often lead lives which are the opposite of the bloody, slavering animals of fiction. We can watch the behavior of coyotes for days without ever seeing them kill a single living thing, and when their stomachs are examined it is evident that a coyote has to eat almost anything that it can get hold of: carrion from animals which have died of disease, garbage, old scraps of leather, and even berries. They do*

occasionally capture small rodents and sometimes are able to find an unprotected newborn fawn. One of the few cases in which coyotes have actually killed an adult deer is so remarkable that it has been written up as a special scientific paper.

The preceding arguments should not be taken as an attempt to prove that animals do not kill for food. The carnivores hunt, of course, but in most cases not in a spirit that could be described accurately as vicious. Desperate hunger can make the slaughter seem more obsessive, and two situations are quoted often as evidence that some animals kill wantonly, for the pleasure of it.

One is the habit of shrikes of catching small birds and mice and impaling their bodies on thorns. That is the way the situation is always described: "impaling their bodies on thorns," and the shrike's bad reputation may be due to our shrinking from that detail of a thorn piercing a heart. But a thorn will stop a heart, thereby cutting off pain, as efficiently as a talon will. Shrikes are more clever than cruel. Although they are born to be eaters of meat, they do not have the strong feet of the raptorial birds, which hold their prey in their claws while bites are being torn off. The weak-footed shrikes therefore have learned to make their prey fast on thorns or to wedge it in crotches of trees while they eat it. Even when shrikes kill more prey than they eat at once, they may be air-drying the others, only provident as the squirrels are when burying acorns, or the foxes and wolves which store dead mice for lean winter times.

The second situation cited often to prove animals' cruelty is the way that cats and some other species play with a victim, letting it go and catching it over and over again. We decide that this is a sadistic practice because we identify with the mouse — but can the cat do that? Does the cat have imagination which tells it that the mouse is suffering prolonged fright? The possibility is extremely doubtful. My Husky dog recently caught a young rabbit. His first pounce broke its neck and so it was dead at once, and the dog, Tuno, was obviously disappointed. (The rabbit's nearly closed eyes seemed the most dead thing about it, lacking the slightest hint of the terror so graphically shown in the picture that haunted my childhood sleep.) Tuno put the limp rabbit down on the ground. Clearly he wished it would bound away. He nudged it. Nothing happened. He backed away a step, watching the rabbit intently. He flipped his tail and urged the rabbit with several little barks. When Tuno is given a dog biscuit, he plays with it, tossing it up and catching it as it comes down: how much more fun to play with a dodging rabbit! Before eating his prey, Tuno carried it around for many minutes, quite gently, and when he finally bit into it, his mood seemed dejected. There was no slightest hint that he had wished to torture the rabbit; the swing of his tail, his facial expression and, most, the jaunty way that he frisked about while he still thought his prey was alive were dependable signs that he merely wanted to play. In the last few years careful studies of animal play by German biologists indicate that the cat-and-mouse game is indeed only that — a game till the hunter is ready to eat his catch, when he kills it abruptly. Leopard seals similarly tease penguins, Richard S. Peterson tells me, but only when they are not hungry, it seems.

Many deaths in the natural food chains occur so fast that there must be no time for the victims to sense fear or pain. A peregrine falcon dives out of the sky at speeds up to 150 miles an hour: what chance has the bird that he captures to panic? Owls, which can appear as motionless as the trees in which they are sitting, are not always thought of as making lightning attacks, but their swiftness was illustrated by a great gray owl in Wyoming, whose care I inherited from a naturalist. The owl was not caged; he led his own life in the forest, being fed several mice every afternoon near the cabin. When the naturalist went away in the fall, I was given this fascinating task.

One bright frosty morning I was out of doors collecting stones to make a vivarium for some captive frogs, stones that were small, mostly round and gray, the size and color of mice. I had not seen the owl that day and did not know he was near as I crouched on my heels, picking up the stones. At a moment when there were three in my hand, the owl struck. One instant I held the stones, the next instant the owl was perched on a branch of a bush about eight feet away, and he had the stones in his claws and I had a gash on my empty hand to prove he had taken them. A great gray owl is a huge bird. It has a wingspread of nearly five feet, and yet I had not seen him approach, or come down in front of my eyes, or take the stones, or fly to the bush with them. Human eyes and minds simply don't register motion this fast, and surely a mouse, whose life would have been squeezed out as the owl closed its claws, would never have known what happened.

It is said that an animal's eyes do not adjust to movement more rapid than the speed at which it can run. The reason is obvious: if the prey cannot dart to safety, there is no usefulness in faster perception. Few human beings can run more than ten miles an hour, and when a car comes racing out of a side street at sixty miles an hour, and the motorist who hits it says "I didn't see it," he is telling the truth. At that speed and at very close range, he *couldn't* see it, at least not effectively. As long as an approaching object is farther away, its speed *relative to our eyes* is slower, of course.

When I came out to feed the owl every afternoon, he would be waiting in a spruce tree about two hundred yards away. As I held out my wrist, immediately he would sweep forward — so large that a branch of the tree seemed to be detaching itself — and at first I could see him clearly. Then, when he was near enough for his great speed to be evident, my view of him seemed to blank out. He was no longer there — but he is, he is on my wrist, where he has alighted with infinite softness. Since many animals do not have vision beyond a fairly near foreground, the entire approach of such a predator may be invisible to them. When the prey can run nearly as fast as the hunter, for as long as the chase continues the prey may feel terror.

One must spend many months in a wilderness to see even a few attacks. They take place without warning and usually are over so quickly that dependable observations are hard to make. Finally, after watching enough of them, the neutral quality of the pursuits becomes evident. Perhaps it is not really important whether one dies between murderous, vicious jaws or jaws that are merely hungry; yet to me it was a moment of great relief when I realized that man's expression "blood-lust" means no more than the literal ache of an empty stomach. During a youthful and idealistic period I wished passionately that all animals might be vegetarians. It appeared clear a bit later that perhaps justice should be done also to plants. As far as we know plants have no sentient life, but there is an impulse in all protoplasm to bring itself to completion, and a buttercup eaten by a rabbit has been denied its maturity just as much as the rabbit has when it is eaten by a hawk. The mutuality of plants and animals became obvious when, in high school, I saw plant cells die under a microscope. As the life of a plant cell departed, that too was a death. All living things on this planet prey upon one another. But the fact can be stated another way: that we all sustain one another.

Our primate relatives are vegetarians, except for a few that eat insects, and we can wonder what gave the human species its original taste for meat and therefore the habit of killing prey. The best explanation seems to be that as we evolved, as intelligence and ambition grew, we came to feel that it took too much time and effort to gather roots, leaves, and fruits. We were losing our own furry covering, we had to have some new kind of protection against weather and killed other animals for their pelts. Either before or after we began to wear hides, we learned that the carcasses could be food, more concentrated nourishment than plants are. If we ate them, some of our energies were released for other activities besides filling our stomachs. And so we became hunters.

We began to raise our own cattle at a time now estimated as about 10,000 years ago. The killing of them became less and less personal. By then, however, the chase itself had become a quickening pleasure and one that is slow to die out of the human consciousness — though there does seem to be a conflict in emotions when a man who is engaged in benign activities most of the year yet finds it a thrilling satisfaction to shoot game in the fall. The hunters sometimes express admiration and even a sort of affection for a deer they have felled, as Indians and Eskimos also do for their victims. The evidence seems to suggest that animals hunting for food are equally free of hate.

Men use guns on other occasions, of course: in personal feuds and in war, and it is then that the charge behind the bullets is liable to be anger. So too it is with animals. They have their own fearsome weapons and they use them with vengeance when some situation arouses their rage. Why they kill at those times, and what the situations are, is revealing about what animals value most highly.

It is well at the start to distinguish between the fighting of males and of females. "The female of the species is more deadly than the male," wrote Kipling in a line repeated by many men who never read a poem voluntarily, especially not one published originally in *The Ladies' Home Journal*. Kipling was right in his main assumption and right too when he recognized that those deadly females fight only in desperate situations: when they are defending their young or are trying to preserve a relationship with a mate (a situation which is also defense of young, but at one remove). Female animals do not fight very often for homesites. Except in captivity they seldom fight to maintain social status and certainly never merely to prove that they are stronger than an opponent. Males fight for all those reasons and a few others that females do not appear to take seriously enough to do battle. But once a female animal does join a fight, Kipling's comment is true: she does not stop until she or the enemy is soaking into the bloody ground.

Anyone who is familiar with wilderness customs is careful not to approach a mother animal who is accompanied by her offspring. The mother will not wait to see whether the human being is friendly. She will lead the young ones away from him secretly if she can, but if the intruder has cut her off from those young, instantly and ferociously she may attack. Her precaution does not apply only to human beings. Since the flesh of the very young is relished by many animals, the males of some species endanger even their own pups and cubs. (It should be remembered that the males may not realize they are the fathers.) The mother is wary of such a male, as well as traditional foes, and she need not be larger or stronger than the attacker to save her brood. From fury so overpowering he usually retreats.

Females sometimes fight other females when necessary to preserve their relationship with a mate, but these battles are not so frequent as those in which they defend their young, and for the significant reason that mate relationships are respected by most animal spinsters. When we reach animal harems we might expect to find animosity between females sharing a mate. That is not often the case. Even among groups of pronghorns, where all of a buck's does seem devoted to him, the does apparently do not feel jealousy. Instead they show signs of enjoying each other's company, for during the summer, when the buck stays somewhat apart on a higher point of the mountain slope from which he can guard his composite family, by preference the does graze and rest together, sharing responsibility for the fawns.

In the baboon harem there is a definite hierarchy among the females but still slight antagonism. The top honors rotate. The females not at the moment in breeding condition always give way to the one who is in oestrus. The same situation holds true among chimpanzees. Gorilla females have a different system of social rank: the most respect goes to the one with the youngest infant — but the gorilla family is not properly speaking a harem, since the male leader does not restrict the females' choice of mate to himself. Incidentally, gorillas have more tactful ways of asserting rank than some other animals do. A gorilla, male or female, who wants a subordinate to give way will tap his arm lightly with hand or fingers or, if more urging is needed, may push with both hands or with the chest. Gorillas are not impatient. The one with the prior rights may wait for the other animal to decide he must step aside.

The more closely the male-female relationships approach monogamy, the more antagonism there is likely to be between females competing for the same male. Sometimes, however, there is adjustment to a triangular situation — occasionally among lions, and grizzly bears. Adolph Murie observed a male grizzly with two consorts and reports that the females paid no attention to each other. But Lois Crisler, who with her photographer husband tamed eight free-ranging wolves, writes in *Arctic Wild* about a wolf tragedy due to feminine jealousy.

The first two wolves the Crislers acquired, from Eskimos, were siblings, Trigger and Lady. As they matured they treated each other with generous, touching affection, and when five orphaned wolf puppies were introduced into their lives, they fed and protected them with as much devotion as if they had been their own. Among domestic animals and wild animals in captivity incestuous matings are of course common. It is not known how frequently they occur in nature, and therefore it would have been interesting to see whether a sexual relationship would develop between this wolf brother and sister. Female wolves do not breed, however, until they are two years old, and before Lady reached that age a strange wolf appeared from the tundra. Named Silvermane by the Crislers, she never learned to accept human companionship, but she stayed near their cabin and soon began to court Trigger. He was slow in responding, and was his fondness for Lady the reason? And did Silvermane, with her wild intuition, feel that she had more authentic right to Trigger than Lady had? After several days, during which the ill feeling between Lady and Silvermane became more and more intense, the newcomer killed Lady. And Trigger left, deserting the puppies that he had cared for so earnestly, to go back to the wild with Silvermane.

The most extreme case of female jealousy among animals may be that found in gibbons. In these permanently monogamous pairs, the partners so literally "mean everything to each other" that they have no social relationships outside the immediate family. The male is watchful to see that his mate has no chance to become fond of another male, and she is even more on the alert: she quickly and very effectively attacks any female who shows signs of becoming a rival. Even to her own daughters as they mature she apparently makes it clear that they are no longer welcome at home. It is probable that no other pairs in the animal kingdom express, and therefore may feel, such tenderness for each other as gibbons do. They apparently have a real talent for conjugal love, but perhaps they pay a price for it. Among human beings a diversity of social relationships is believed to promote the highest degree of mental health and, among the subhuman primates, the New World monkeys and the gorillas, who have great variety in their social mingling, seem to be the most stable. On the other hand gibbons are high-strung and mercurial — a penalty for so possessively concentrating their attention on one individual?

For male animals, too, sex is a powerful — the most powerful — cause of fighting. Now comes a difference, however: males do not fight to kill a rival but in most cases only to make him depart. And he does go. The moment both know how the battle will end, the weaker male turns aside and retreats. Although animals have much pride they are not so foolish that they will die for it. More-over, killing in this situation would not be according to nature's program. Nature is always concerned for the future of the species, and those vanquished bulls, bucks, rams, cocks, and other males still will be needed to father young.

From time to time two rattlesnakes will engage in the beautiful exercise until recently called a mating dance. Anchoring them-selves with the rear two-thirds of their bodies flat on the ground, the two snakes raise their heads and the forward third of their length and begin a sinuous weaving together. Sometimes they are entwined, sometimes they draw apart and form lyre-shapes.

The motions seem ritualistic, and if one snake loses its balance, the "dance" starts all over again. The grace of this action is very appealing, but as herpetologist Charles E. Shaw at the San Diego Zoo observed it, it seemed to him that the dance was really a contest of strength, and he noted that it ended with one snake's head down on the floor and pinned there by a coil of the other snake's body. He examined the pairs more closely then, and found that they were, always of the same sex — males — and further investigation proved that wrestling snakes such as these were rivals. Other herpetologists had been thrown off by the fact that the wrestling snakes do not injure each other; neither uses his poison fangs as a rattler does, for example, when he fights a king snake. The pair of rival snakes fight in earnest, but the objective is merely to assert superiority, not to kill.

One of the most ferocious-appearing attacks made by one male animal on a rival is that of a fur seal upon a neighbor who tries to steal one of the cows in the first male's harem. In the spring when these animals come to their breeding grounds on the Pribilof Islands, the older males arrive first. They are huge animals weighing up to 600 pounds. Among rocks they establish adjacent territories, each with as much space as a bull feels he will need for his densely packed harem. As the cows haul out of the sea several weeks later, the bulls push and herd them into the territories. The more lucky males sometimes accumulate harems numbering eighty cows or more.

The cow seals are about to give birth to the annual crop of pups, and no mating takes place until after the birthing is over. Meanwhile each bull guards his living treasure and tries to increase it if possible. Eighty cows aren't enough, ninety are not enough if a bull can steal others. The cows are gregarious and they tend to stay with the home group, but if the lord of the harem sees one of them being snatched away, he rushes after her, catches her by the neck, and hurls her back.

More challenging to the established family, so outrageously unbalanced in numbers, are the thousands of bachelors, deprived of mates by the greedy oldsters. The lonely bulls prowl around the edges of breeding groups, hoping to snatch a little illicit pleasure, and with them the battles are frequent. One would expect tubfuls of blood to be spilled, but let Dr. Kaare Rodahl tell what actually happens, as described in his vividly written book about Eskimos, *The Last of the Few:* "With raised head, wide-open throat and flaming eyes, with gleaming teeth and steaming nostrils, the owner charges, roaring with an echo that thunders among the rocks. He . . . jumps straight up on all four flippers so that his entire body flies through the air. Like a fighting cock, he strikes at the neck of his opponent . . . and shakes him violently. Then both contestants roar and hiss a few times, turn around and gallop [away] on their short clumsy flippers."

To an inexperienced onlooker the battles appear violent and vicious. But Richard S. Peterson, who has spent most of three years in observing the fur seals, says that actually the contestants only make passes at one another. An interloper is bitten if he will not leave, but the attack ends as soon as he is pushed over the boundary line. Killing is not in the plan.

Perhaps this is the place to explain that it is possible to provoke fights between animals that are ordinarily peaceful, and at times this is done to create drama for moving pictures and television programs. The artificial aggressiveness is produced in several ways. One is to have an off-scene stranger, often the cameraman, stampede the animals into crossing into each other's territories. The borders are invisible to a human being, but to a fur seal bull, for example, an intruding bull, who may only be trying to escape from a cameraman, seems more of a threat than the man is. The bull who is defending his homesite therefore attacks his neighbor, and the neighbor, caught between dangers, puts up his best fight. Battles between Husky dogs can be instigated by feeding one and depriving another, or by taking a bitch away from her mate and tying her near a different male.

The same false suggestion that animals are blood-thirsty killers is used as a staple of outdoor stories, in both books and magazines, but it seems especially mischievous in the case of pictures, because the average person, who has no experience with which to judge their accuracy, sees the blood flowing "with his own eyes" and is led to believe that "animals fight all the time." Something dark can happen then in the mind of a viewer contemplating his own mammalian ancestry.

Males of the species with horns and antlers are the ones who appear to have the most deadly weapons. To see a mule deer or white-tailed buck, an elk or moose stride through the forest with more than a dozen spears in his crown is to wonder how any of them survive their traditional fighting. According to legend, conflicts between the bucks are more stimulating to them than their mating activities are. It is the season for contests, and is there not a slain buck after every battle?

One year, doing field work in Wyoming, I was camped at the foot of Mount Moran during the period of the rut. Moose and elk were all about and I was sure I would see at least several of the clashes. About dusk one afternoon the wilderness quiet was broken by a sound which I could only visualize as caused by tin cans hurled violently against rocks. What maniac had found his way here, five miles from the nearest road? Cautiously I peered out — and found a strange sight: a moose fighting a tree. He was not rubbing the velvet off his antlers; they were clean and polished, and very resonant. But he was attacking the tree from all sides. He would back away and then, with lowered head, he would lunge forward into the branches. He struck again and again, until the tines finally would engage with the boughs, when, with a twist of his powerful neck, he would break off the boughs. Not until he had stripped the trunk bare did he stop. Then he moved away, doubtless to hunt for a foe who would fight back.

A day or two later he found a mate, after she'd called with what one of the cowboys described as "an unhopeful groan." I saw the

pair every day and kept expecting some other bull to come by and give this one a chance to defend his rights, but none ever did. The courtship was doomed to be peaceful.

During the same weeks a bull elk was bugling each moonlight night and a few times at dawn. The call is a challenge to rivals, although it is hard to understand how a sound so thrilling and pure — like gold, like the morning sun on the mountain snows — could provoke even another bull to anger. Towards the end of the time one young, smaller bull did come and he and the big bull had a pushing contest. With their heads together and hind ends swinging about, they measured strength, and the lord of the harem drove back his unworthy opponent. When the younger bull tired, he simply ran off. The larger bull did not pursue him and there was no sign that he had been injured in any way.

All hunters have listened to tales about the big fights, and some must have seen them. Others have probably heard them, like Ernest Thompson Seton, who wrote of elk, "I have tried many times to see a real Wapiti [elk] duel. I have heard them in the woods more than once, but never actually saw one." Were they in fact duels with trees? He says of moose: "In these combats the weaker generally saves himself by flight; yet . . . the battle sometimes had a doubly fatal termination through the locking of the horns." Of mule deer: "The antlers themselves are developed along lines that prevent the bucks hurting each other, rather than as deadly weapons, and in most cases the battle is little more than a pushing bout." And of white-tailed deer: "Strange to tell, in battles with his own kind his antlers prove almost wholly weapons of defense. Desperate effort and trifling bloodshed seems to be a fair summary of the usual fight between two bucks." A recent observer, Professor Heini Hediger, noting that the antlered animals fight off predators with their *hoofs* — predators rather than rivals — believes that the fragility of the antlers, dropped after each mating season, probably means that they are not meant to be weapons to kill with. They do appear formidable, and perhaps that somewhat false impression is actually their purpose.

For, as the great Oxford behaviorist Professor Tinbergen has written: "It is a very striking and important fact that 'fighting' in animals usually consists of threatening or bluff. Considering the fact that sexual fighting takes such an enormous amount of the time [in the breeding season] of so many species, it is certainly astonishing that real fighting, in the sense of a physical struggle, is so seldom observed." As in the case of German duels, some wounds may be permissible, a slash through the skin of the neck, perhaps, or a nick in an ear, but most of the battles between male animals are indeed really bluffing contests and partly are battles of wits. No one doubts that wits are shown in a poker game when a player so far overbids a poor hand that he intimidates his opponents, and anyone understanding how easily antlers are broken must suspect that the great bulls are essentially doing the same thing when they lower their heads and advance, making themselves look invincible. They are mighty in something that surpasses brute strength — in cunning, and perhaps in a capacity for amusement, for some biologists consider these male contests mainly a form of play.

One explanation for the mock quality of the sexual fights might be that the males do not really consider the females worth dying for, but as we shall see, bluffing is characteristic of most other male combats too. Males, as Kipling wrote, are willing to compromise issues, to negotiate. A female can't compromise if the life of her young one or the relationship with a mate is at stake; but the female temperament does occasionally defeat its purpose by taking a situation too seriously.

Next to mates a homesite is the possession that male birds and animals are most quick to defend. Usually the two can't be separated. One biologist says that a male bird probably would describe a mate as "the other bird that lives here," and when he defends her, inevitably he is defending the nest. Unmated creatures also defend their homes at times. If they have them, they all seem to resent intruders.

When human beings go out in the woods they are usually on vacation. They have a new sense of freedom — what a grand, spacious way to live, here where there are no rigid patterns of streets, no road signs or traffic rules, no fences. What an enviable life the animals lead, able to go anywhere they wish, any time, with no feeling of being restricted! The fences are there, however. They just are not obvious because they are made of such deceiving materials as brush, trees, stones; of wallows and rubbing rocks; of burrow holes or mere depressions in earth or grass; and especially of signs we are not often able to be aware of — scent stations, that is, clods of earth, stumps, bushes, trunks of trees, where the owners of the adjacent homesites have deposited urine or scent from special glands to announce to trespassers that this property is already occupied. A map of any wilderness area, showing the plots owned by animals and birds, would be covered with such a network of boundary lines that one might wonder if the creatures have any freedom of movement at all. Some of them do have, but many will not allow any other members of their own species to invade the spaces that they have claimed.

In most cases the homesites are willingly shared with other, different species. A meadow is peacefully occupied by a single family of foxes, one of badgers, and (more warily on their part) of ground squirrels. In the surrounding trees will be nesting various kinds of birds. All these and many more species tolerate one another but would not let more foxes come in, or badgers, or squirrels, or related bird families. Human beings feel much the same way. Usually we do not object to sharing our yards with birds, squirrels, chipmunks, any animals that do not damage our property. Let us come home and find a strange member of our own species on the porch, though; we expect a satisfactory explanation or we call the police.

Some of the very simplest creatures have homes to which they are devoted — limpets, for instance, those little molluscs that creep around in their conical shells for such food as lichens. Each limpet returns to the same small depression in the tide-rocks, where he snuggles down, always facing in the same direction, so that his shell grows to fit the stony edge of that niche exactly. A limpet, at least, does not have to expel any intruding neighbors because no others would match his space.

Some other quite primitive animals, toads, lizards, and turtles, establish territories and attack any males who trespass. It is suspected lately, however, that what they will fight for is the mate, "the other animal that lives here," more than the piece of property. But a fish: there's your possessive home-owner! Since many male fish build their nests, tend the eggs, and protect and rear their young alone, a "mate" is not really that; she is only a very brief and casual acquaintance whom the male has induced to enter his nest and deposit some eggs, and he couldn't fight for her if he would because she does not stay with him. Even before she has come, when the fish has only the territory he claims and perhaps the start of a nest, he will fight any other male who challenges his ownership.

The so-called fighting fish of Java very earnestly try to kill each other. Theirs is no bluffing contest, and the outcome is so definite, so complete, that the Javanese people bet on fights between the fish kept in tanks. But these fighting fish are exceptional. More characteristic are the sticklebacks, whose antagonism can seem so ferocious, and yet serious injuries almost never occur.

A stickleback is about three inches long. Its nest is somewhat less than an inch in diameter, a beautiful little piece of architecture, in one species a globe shape made of the finest shreds of aquatic plants stuck together with a cement which the fish secretes, and carefully smoothed on the surface with his mouth and with pressure from the sides of his body. The nest has two entrances so that water can flow through, and after the eggs have been laid in it, the male will stay at one entrance, fanning fresh water across them until they hatch. That fanning motion is one of the marvels of animal behavior, for ordinarily the fanning by the fins would move the male fish ahead, but an accompanying reverse motion of his tail keeps him stationary, all these movements being most perfectly, rhythmically synchronized. If the supply of oxygen in the water decreases, the father fans faster.

That activity lies in the future, however. At about the time that a male stickleback is finishing his nest, he begins to glow. He glows literally, like a small neon figure of a fish, lit by his satisfaction with his achievement. From a dull, blackish-olive color, suddenly he is transformed. His throat and belly become brilliant red, his back a luminous blue-green, and his eyes emerald. These colors will help to attract a female, and the red of his belly will also inflame the anger of any other male stickleback who is in breeding condition. The crudest lump of a dummy stickleback will incite a male if only its "belly" is painted red. (Even a red mail truck that used to stop outside the window would enrage one of Tinbergen's sticklebacks.)

He and his neighbor may enjoy their disputes over their boundary line, they continue them for so long. Either may trespass and the owner will chase him out, pursuing until he is near the neighbor's nest, when the chase is reversed. Each little fish is most ferocious when he is on his own property; as he nears the other's nest his sense that he is invincible seems to flag, whereas the owner becomes mighty with indignation. Back and forth go the routs. The two fish nip at each other and they raise their wicked-looking spines, which once were believed to be deadly weapons. It is now known that the spines cannot puncture the tough skin of the small opponents. At the boundary line, exactly, there is a curious, mutual behavior: the fish both stand on their heads and nibble the sand, believed to be a displacement reaction, though the bristling spines tell plainly that angry feelings have not been appeased. All the time the two glowingly advertise their intense emotion, but nothing more comes of it than this fine display. Let a female swim by, however, choosing one nest or the other, and the fight is forgotten, for now she must be induced to lay her eggs by nudging her rear with a quivering motion. And then will begin the long process of aerating the eggs and raising the young. The bluffing contest is over.

Many fish that "fight," indeed, do not even pretend to strike each other. They merely beat their tails in such a way that each sends a jet of water against the sensitive lateral line of the other fish. With both opponents thus thrusting currents rather than blows at the adversary, the engagement appears to an onlooker more like a dance of exceptional grace.

One animal, the mollusc called the swan mussel, is, itself, a territory. As described on pages 52–53, a pair of small bitterlings lay and fertilize their eggs within the shell of this mollusc. She is their "territory" for as long as the eggs need this protection, and the fish who is the father will not allow any other bitterling to come near.

The creatures that, in general, are most active in asserting their rights to individual properties are the birds. It has now become well known that their defense of their little plots is one of the reasons why the rest of us have the pleasure of hearing bird song.

The discovery that birds claim and defend territories is often thought of as a twentieth-century achievement because that behavior has only been understood in detail since H. Eliot Howard published his *Territory in Bird Life* in 1920. Actually, Aristotle made some observations on bird economics. In *Historia animalium* he wrote, "The fact is that a pair of eagles demands an extensive space for its maintenance, and consequently cannot allow other birds to quarter themselves in close neighborhood." He described the same situation for ravens. In the third century B.C., Zenodotus wrote, "One bush does not shelter two robins." Also of robins Konrad von Gesner said in 1555, *"Erithacus avis est solitaria,"* and G. P. Olina in 1622, "It has a peculiarity that it cannot abide a companion in the place where it lives and will attack with all its strength any who dispute this claim." These European robins are belligerent birds but they do not often "attack with all their strength." Buffon was more accurate when he wrote in the eighteenth century that the male robin "chases all the birds of his own species, and drives them from his little settlement." Buffon wrote of nightingales that they "are also very solitary . . . they select certain tracts, and oppose the encroachments of others in their territory. But this conduct is not occasioned by rivalship, as some have supposed; it is suggested by solicitude for the maintenance of their young, and regulated by the extent of ground necessary to afford sufficient food." Gilbert White thought that sexual rivalry was behind the formation of territories: "During the amorous season, such a jealousy prevails between the male birds that they can scarcely bear to be together in the same hedge or field . . . and it is to this spirit of jealousy that I chiefly attribute the equal dispersion of birds in the spring over the face of the country." We know now that the territories are defended because they are the homesites where family life is carried on, and that the limits are often defined by the food requirements. Most of the songbirds, whose young will be hatched in outside nests, need enough feeding space near the nest so that the tiny offspring will never be left very long by their parents. The nestlings must have comparatively enormous quantities of nourishment, very frequently, or their energy drops, they become chilled, then cease to accept the food that is brought to them, and soon die. Birds that nest in holes in trees are less exposed and keep warmer, and therefore the parents can forage farther afield. The territory of those parents may be only the tree itself.

If a bird is returning to last-year's nesting site, he knows exactly what shape and size he wants his territory to be, and he doesn't waste even an hour before taking up his position on various points on his borders, singing to announce that he is the owner of all the land enclosed by these stations. In the case of most birds it is more than one tree but not often more than an acre. If he is a new, young bird, it may take him two days, rarely longer, to look over the ground and decide how much space he will defend. Meanwhile his neighbors are deciding what *they* will defend, and disagreements are settled by the birds singing at each other — very much as two gold miners, each wishing to claim a certain promising piece of ground, might argue the matter in court. Beautiful as the bird songs are, some of them, too, are arguments, and it speaks well for the birds' reasonableness that the controversies almost always are settled without physical combat. (It is no longer considered true that all birds' songs have this business significance, as explained in Part I and later in the description of animal play.)

A robin will value a nice stretch of lawn which promises a good harvest of worms; finches will want crops of seeds; warblers and swallows an abundance of insects. These special needs have a bearing on the kind of territory a bird will try to establish, of course. Suppose that a bird makes a miscalculation? There is a fine tree for a nest in the area that the robin selects, but the lawn below may not be kept sprinkled; it may dry out and then there won't be enough worms. Or the expected seeds in a field of wild grasses may not mature because the field is plowed up as a homesite for human beings. Or unseasonable frost may kill many insects on a low patch of ground. For some unforeseen reason a bird's territory may prove not to be adequate. And all the surrounding country is held by other members of one's own species — what then does a bird do for food?

He trespasses, and usually the owners of the land where he doesn't belong are lenient. As the season progresses, there is a good deal of this crossing of fence lines. Sometimes the theft of the food is not discovered, for the intruding bird always goes onto a neighbor's property inconspicuously. He stays under the bushes, moves quietly, and of course does not chirp or sing. Even if he is found there, the owner may sing to tell him that he had better go home but will seldom attack and may not even try to bluff the intruder into retreating. Earlier, at the time the nesting activities were just getting under way, the trespasser would have been chased out indignantly. Occasionally, not often, such disputes result in fatalities. David Lack, the British ornithologist, has reported a count of 110 robin deaths in which the causes were known: four were attributed to attack by other robins (44 by cats; 24 robins were caught in mouse traps, 11 were killed on roads, etc.). But if slaughter is rare among birds, many species are among the world's best bluffers. Who has not seen the head feathers rise, the body level down, and the open beak make a jab? A threatening bird can look as formidable as a tiny dragon.

Sometimes a whole flock of birds holds and defends a certain area, and this area may be further divided among the individual birds. In flocks of seabirds that nest on shore, the single territory may be only so large that one individual, sitting on eggs, cannot peck the next neighbor; but that square yard of space, or less, is known unerringly to its owner and to the other birds, who respect it. Of the birds that migrate, many scatter when they reach their southern wintering grounds, fitting themselves in among the local bird population. Since the migrants are mostly different species, they are not treated belligerently. Nevertheless, a few of the species which nest and defend territories in the Northern Hemisphere also claim homesites in their vacationing winter quarters and drive out their fellow travelers.

Occasionally mated female birds help to defend the homesite, but usually they leave that responsibility to the males. Unmated female birds seldom establish territories. Some, not all, unmated males announce boundary lines around plots which they claim as exclusively theirs. Actually, if there were more suitable spaces, many more birds might form family relationships. There have been estimates that in some bird populations as many as 40 per cent are not mated. Their single status is not due in all cases to lack of facilities. Among birds — and mammals too — there are individuals that simply appear to have no wish to mate. When tested they have proved to be physically sound, with a normal hormonal balance, and therefore the reasons for their reluctance are assumed to be psychological. But many others, among birds especially, seem to remain unmated because they fail in the competition for a share of the naturally limited space. This limitation is considered desirable, for the food supply probably would not support a larger number of bird families, and the territorial system is therefore a check on a population explosion of birds. The limitation is considered desirable, that is, by people — not by the spinster and bachelor birds, for whenever one of a mated pair meets disaster, a single bird moves into its place at once, and except in those species like trumpeter swans that mate for life, the new one usually is accepted. Sometimes a single bird is so aggressive that he ousts a rightful owner from home and spouse. That does not often happen, however. Once a family arrangement is established, it seldom is challenged.

Most of the larger mammals and some of the smaller have territories which they defend. That of a grizzly bear is said to have a diameter of about nine miles, of a family of wolves at least as large and perhaps several times wider. Mammals that live in herds do not seem to feel possessive about their part of the landscape. Those that wander from lower to higher altitudes in the summer, as mule deer and elk do, usually return to the same region; they could be said to have two seasonal homes. White-tailed deer are by nature so attached to the place where they are born that most of them spend their lives within half a mile of it. If the vegetation becomes overbrowsed and the deer are moved somewhere else, they are apt to drift back.

The competition for living space is intense, but in normal times animals work out the division of it so that, on any given day, they have reached a fair state of equilibrium. Each evening (each morning for the nocturnal species), all over the landscape countless birds and animals go to sleep; they relax their alertness in the precarious safety of nests and burrows. That is a sentimental thought which would have appealed to Victorian nature-lovers, but nevertheless it is valid. An animal's home gives it more than its sense of rootedness and the comfort of familiarity. In most cases it is so constructed that it provides some protection from weather and enemies. It is a little fortress, within which the creature can put aside briefly the tensions of being wild. If he did not defend it, his indifference would be the surprise.

A food supply is an essential part of most territories. What animals want, actually, are "farms," real-estate holdings which provide for them, and especially their young, not only homesites but dependable sources of nourishment. On any single occasion, however, they may be less possessive about their food than one might

expect. When an animal first starts to eat, he will not allow others to share his catch, especially if he is very hungry. A dog, the well-fed domestic pet, lives in an atmosphere of artificial antagonisms and usually will make a great show of anger if another dog tries to take his bone. His growling, bristling of fur, and showing of teeth are the well-known bluff, and in most cases they are enough to prevent a fight. In wild nature too bluffing is used to defend one's meal, but with this difference: usually the hungry onlooker knows he can afford to wait, for once the original owner's stomach is full, he generally is willing to let others finish his catch. Wolves and bears may half-heartedly, shallowly, bury the surplus, but as often as not they are too sleepy after a good feed to do even that, and they turn away knowing quite well that neighbors of various species will start immediately to eat the rest.

This sharing of spoils is common. African lions indirectly feed a host of birds and small animals with their leavings; incidentally, they will let a jackal snatch a bite even while they themselves are eating, but a hyena may not approach. A polar bear supports an arctic fox, who is always allowed to finish the parts of a captured seal that the bear does not want. The fox tags along with the bear everywhere, all over the frozen sea, to secure this bounty, and the bear does not seem to mind. Perhaps he finds some satisfaction in the companionship of the small fox. A few seagulls, too, are permanent members of the company.

Adolph Murie describes a wolf which had brought down a caribou and was having a feast for himself when a wolverine came along. Wolverines are such surly creatures that most other animals give way to them. There are records of two black bears giving up their cow carcass because a wolverine wanted to feed on it; three coyotes in one instance and two mountain lions in another departed from their spoils when a wolverine approached — simply to avoid unpleasantness, Dr. Murie believes, since all of these animals are much larger than a wolverine and certainly could have killed one of them, fighter though he is, if the food had been worth it. In the situation that Murie tells about, the wolf withdrew until the wolverine had eaten all that he wanted. When he had lumbered away, the wolf went back to his carcass. Waiting too was a red fox, who had to be patient longer, for the wolf would not let the fox come to the bounty until he was through. And perched on the overhead branch of a tree was a raven, he also waiting, and presumably he would not have a chance at the meat until after the fox. Would the caribou feed so many? Probably; for, though old, it had been a large animal. And all these creatures would take their turns without any of the bloodshed so often considered to be a frequent wilderness happening.

Some sharing of food is involuntary. Mice dig up the nuts buried by chipmunks and squirrels; blue jays make off with the mushrooms that tree squirrels dry on branches. These thefts are often discovered, and the rightful owners are fearsome in their protesting. But no one is killed. In the case of most animals food does not seem to be property in the sense that a homesite is. The hazards of hunger are faced anew every day, and so food may be lost without making a big emotional production out of one's anger. Perhaps only creatures as truly secure as some human beings are feel violent indignation at being robbed.

It should be said again that when two male animals confront each other, over any issue at all, they are measuring strength, and they know very quickly which would win in a fight. They do not seem to enjoy fighting for its own sake (except during the rut) in the way that some men do. (They don't enjoy watching fights, either. During any real fray other animals often show great distress.) And since the one destined to be the loser does not relish the chance to take ineffectual jabs at the winner, why should he enter a battle? In their adjustments to one another, animals seem to act with exquisite logic.

Most disputes are between only two. There is one creature — only one in all the animal kingdom — that does as man does: makes war in a group upon another group of the same species. Those are the harvester ants, which live in regions where the seeds on which they subsist are not always plentiful. The ants gather and store them in "warehouses," and sometimes other colonies of those ants make raids on the ones that have a supply of the seeds, kill the owners, and carry away the crop. This behavior is defined specifically as warfare by the biologists, who point out the many times when wars between men, also group affairs, have been waged for a food supply.

Although war is so nearly non-existent in wilderness populations, it must be admitted that there is one exception to the rule of bluff-rather-than-fight between individual males. In this situation a male, including those of some of the simpler creatures, attacks instantly and with clear intent to kill when a strange member of his own species appears suddenly on his home grounds. A stranger is recognized as such, for most birds and animals know who their neighbors are. (Many distinguish between human beings and even in some cases between human sexes, in which case they nearly always show a preference for men or for women.) The habits of the familiar neighbors are dependable, and once the local population have got their fence lines agreed upon, those in adjacent territories are largely ignored. But let a stranger of one's own species appear: that is a menace too serious to be trifled with.

If the stranger had his own mate and homesite and food supply, he would not be here. No doubt he would like to establish himself, and in the eyes of the resident his own situation is likely to appear enviable. The stranger, therefore, is a threat: an outsider, a foreigner, a potential competitor — definitely unwelcome. At the first, quick sign of hostility the stranger often retreats. If he doesn't, he nearly always loses the battle. For any intruder, fighting on ground that belongs to another, seems to lose courage. In order to win, most animals act as if they need to feel that their cause is right.

The reason why it is only the stranger of one's own species who is treated so violently probably is the situation described by the biological theory that no two species on earth occupy exactly identical niches. By "niches" in this sense is not meant hidey-holes but the whole sum of an animal's external circumstances: its preferred type of homesite; food; sunning, resting, and watering places; family and neighbor relationships; and all the other living conditions. No two species want precisely the same things and therefore, it is thought, no two species are really competitive in a given area. It is a nice distinction, since two species of sparrows, for instance, differ but slightly in what they need; yet if the species are truly distinct, they tolerate each other in the same habitat.

From the animals' point of view perhaps the key factor in this tolerance is the sexual one, for the single condition that divides one species from another is, crudely defined, that they do not mate and produce fertile young. The assurance that a male of a slightly different species will not covet the resident's mate is reason enough to permit him to come into one's territory and settle there. The conception of a niche, in men's minds, includes much more, but in the animals' minds, or at least emotions, it may be related chiefly to the barring of sexual rivals.

It might be interesting to mention the way that animals handle the "racial problem." Among the wild creatures, as among human beings, races are *sub*species. They may differ in external features such as color — in animals and birds the color of fur or feathers; they may even differ somewhat in superficial structures and slightly in behavior. Such differences are enough to cause the taxonomists to class two groups as separate races, but the two are still considered to be the same species as long as they interbreed.

In some circumstances the two races may be the forerunners of distinct and separate species. By the time they have evolved further in their different directions, their males and females no longer will accept each other, and two species instead of one then will exist.

A neat example of the way this development can occur was described in 1952 by Van T. Harris. It concerns the attractive little field mouse called the deer mouse or white-footed mouse, *Peromyscus maniculatus.* There is good reason to believe that two groups of this species migrated in different directions not very long ago. Starting at the northeastern end of the Great Lakes one group advanced westward along the Canadian shores, where they became adapted to living in forests of tall trees with dense shade. The other group spread along the southern shores of the lakes, where they found grasslands and dunes. Eventually the mice proceeded so far that they met again. By then there were two races, *gracilis* and *bairdii,* so conditioned by their experience that when they are put together in a laboratory now, the northern group take refuge under paper trees, and the southern among artificial grasses. More important: their behavior, as well as choice of vegetation have changed so much that the two races no longer interbreed in the wild where their latest habitats overlap. No doubt these two groups soon will be classed scientifically not as separate races but separate species.

The fact that a population of animals of the same species can divide and go their separate ways is very interesting to biologists at the present time as a possible process by which evolution might be facilitated. It has long been held that new species develop only when some random gene mutation produces an animal which is better able to survive in his given environment, and through natural selection this advantage is perpetuated in offspring. Now let us say that the "given environment" is a new one into which he has moved. In the old habitat the gene mutation might not have been beneficial; in this one it is, and it therefore is incorporated in his racial stock. By this means an environment may have an indirect effect, favorable or not, on genetic inheritance and on the emergence of a new species.

The biologists are calling this process geographical or ecological speciation, and through experiment they hope to learn much more about it.

When the now separated groups of birds or animals change to such an extent that their males and females no longer accept each other, they are said to be sexually isolated, and this sometimes happens before a separation into two distinct species becomes complete. As explained earlier, the mating rituals between a male and female animal are far more complex than appears by casual observation. All the preliminaries during courtship must be correlated exactly. Voices play a part, also the choice of time and of place, and during coition, the performance of both the partners. If a population of birds or animals divides — the two groups moving into separate regions and, in adapting to their changed habitats, becoming somewhat diverse in their behavior — it is obvious that their males and females may no longer be able to get together, even though they may encounter each other later.

The only racial problems that might occur in a wilderness, then, are probably those that arise between two races which are in the process of becoming different species. There must be a stage at which their division is not final, and the question must have to be

answered: to breed or not to breed? If their food habits have
changed in the new locations, their body odor may have become
altered, and body odor is thought to be one of the crucial factors
in animal matings. Also, aside from the question of accepting each
other as mates, at some stage there could be a question of whether
to let an individual share one's territory. If he is now a member
of a species that already has become alien, he can live here; if he
is still only of a different race, he may be a sexual rival and therefore he must be treated like all other members of one's own species
— restricted to the status of a neighbor, not allowed to come near
one's family or nest.

If the above description sounds as though animals were always
pulling apart from one another to form new races and species, that
impression is unintentional. There also are races which are inter-
breeding more and more frequently, so that apparently they are
tending to form a homogeneous mixture. The familiar small birds,
juncos, are an example. There are several species of juncos, each
species composed of several races. But juncos have a sociable tendency to interbreed, to such a degree that almost everywhere there
are hybrids. With little expectation that most bird-watchers can
keep them separate, one ornithologist recommends that we "just
call them all juncos."

As for a definition, then, of how birds and animals treat the
members of other races: they treat them as if they were all one's
own kind, unless the races are in the process of drawing apart
geographically and therefore perhaps in structure and habits.

The impression that nature is red in tooth and claw was derived
chiefly from hunters, because, for a very long time, hunters were
the only ones who penetrated the wildest areas. It is a cliché that
hunters, subconsciously or otherwise, tell about their experiences
in terms as exciting and horrendous as possible. Hunters are often
dramatic men. They dream of fearlessness and valor — of stopping

charging elephants, lions, and grizzly bears with well-placed bullets. And if the animals would seldom attack unless greatly provoked? Is that a depressing thought? A library copy of a recent scientific book on animal behavior includes a paragraph which explains that the weapons of antlered species are generally used only for bluffing and harmless pushing contests. That paragraph has been crossed out with a heavy — angered? — pen. What had affronted the previous reader? What had been lost in reading it? The stimulant of danger? But wildness itself, not vicious wildness but the marvelous, elementary force in animal natures, is quite as stimulating if one is exposed to it long and closely enough. (Besides, there are other wilderness challenges, if not the assaults of crashing animal foes.)

Now, since carefully trained, scientific observers like Adolph Murie, C. R. Carpenter, and George Schaller are going out and actually living among the animals, often for months and sometimes for years at a time, we know that blood flows much less freely among the wild ones than the early hunters assumed. Another reason why the biologists see the animals in a different light is the fact that they themselves do not arouse the same aggressive impulses in animals that hunters almost invariably do. The late Joseph Dixon, West Coast naturalist of the National Park Service, usually had a few protégés whom he was introducing to the wild world, and he advised them never to go armed into the habitats of the more formidable species. "Most wild animals now know the odor of guns and ammunition," he said. "They know guns are used for slaughter, and when they smell them, all their fighting tendencies are aroused. But even more important, if you go unarmed into their world — and it *is* their world, where we are outsiders — you go humbly. You give way to them, you are the one who gets off the path when you meet, as you should. Your manner will help to protect you then, for humility is the best defense with an animal."

I was one of Mr. Dixon's fortunate students, and I did go out and live, unarmed, among animals potentially dangerous, and I wrote about them as I saw them: that is, as seldom angry and, with me, surprisingly friendly. To most readers my reports, which were as true as I could make them, were convincing, but occasionally letters arrived, all much the same and going something like this: "What you say about animals isn't true. I know differently because I have been a hunter for twenty years." I have not been offended; those hunters do know one aspect of animal behavior, the defensiveness against deadly enemies. But it would be sad never to have a strange deer come up confidently and put his muzzle into one's hands, never to see him off guard, wandering around at his ease, showing such delicacy of movement that he avoids stepping on flowers.

There is one more type of conflict between animals to consider, although it seldom or never breaks out in bloody violence. It is the psychological discord — mental anguish, really — that results from a condition with which human beings are all too familiar, overcrowding.

The very suggestion of overcrowding in a wilderness seems to contradict a favorite belief of nature-lovers: that nature manages her own world so well that prey and predators always balance each other; that the hunting species weed out, as the saying is, the old and unfit and take enough of the young to prevent population explosions; that the normally smaller families of predators prevent the possibility of any one species of prey ever becoming exterminated completely. Nature's balance — we hear much about it, and it is a system of awesome efficiency. It is not perfect, however.

Some species over-produce quite consistently. Their numbers increase and then abruptly decline, in fairly regular cycles. Perhaps it simply takes about the same period for the populations to reach their peak every time; but it also is thought that the fluctuations may have some relation to extraterrestrial influences. The cycle of snowshoe hares, for example, is said to correspond to the eleven-year cycle of sunspots. During their times of superabundance the hares die by thousands from a disease which seems to result from stress and to be due to their overcrowded living conditions. Experiments with other species of animals show that the single factor of too many individuals in a given space, with no other privation whatever, sometimes causes symptoms such as enlarged adrenal glands. Heart disease also may result from crowding, as announced late in 1963 by scientists at the Penrose Laboratory of the Philadelphia Zoo. Herbert L. Ratcliffe, working with chickens, and Robert L. Snyder, observing captive wild woodchucks, found that caging too many animals within one enclosure can cause a drastic increase in fatal heart attacks. Physical contact is not necessary; even an excess of stimulation by voices can be disastrous. Heart disease has increased among other animals in the zoo, such as antelopes, deer, monkeys, and apes, since the practice began of displaying them in groups because the public likes to watch them that way.

Some animals cope with crowding in other ways besides dying. One of the most provocative, in view of the growing human urge to be on the move, is the method used by the small arctic rodents, the lemmings. Their population, like the hares', explodes periodically, the lemmings' reaching a peak every three or four years. At that time the lemmings are producing not only more litters but larger litters than usual. The cause of their abnormal fertility is not known, but whatever the explanation, the lemmings become extremely nervous during their months of excessive crowding. They run about frantically in the upper latitudes where they live, and some of them race away in their famous hordes, generally downhill on a course which brings them eventually to the sea, and they enter it, probably thinking it only a very wide river (they are good swimmers), and drown. As their populations rise, many also are killed by their natural enemies, snowy owls, jaegers, foxes, and wolves. These species increase in numbers then — not due to undefined influences, only because they have found an abundance of easily captured prey. When the lemming population crashes, many of the predators also die, apparently from starvation rather than from the effects of overcrowding.

Since the pathological consequences of overcrowding have been understood, few biologists believe, as many once did, that the lemmings make their migrations and are impelled farther and farther because they have exhausted the vegetation on which they feed. When in 1953 a migration of lemmings came to the sea at Barrow, America's northernmost point of land, I arrived two days later and walked a long distance back on the tundra over which they had passed. The plants seemed of normal size. As described by the Eskimos and white members of the hospital staff, the lemming horde reached the shore on a front that would be nearly as wide as two city blocks, with the little animals running about eighteen inches apart. They were accompanied by their usual predators, and at Barrow the sled dogs were turned loose and caught many of the lemmings before they had reached the water.

During several previous years, at a location in Northern Alaska, I had had a captive colony of the lemmings (*Lemmus alascensis*) and had made a small, casual study of my own of the effects of crowding on the lemmings' temperament. They are extremely interesting creatures. Although rodents and only slightly larger than house-mouse size (but with long, silky fur), they are much more vocal than mice, more individual in their reactions, and more inventive in their play. To speak quite unscientifically, they give an observer the impression that they are enjoying life. They were supplied at all times with water and an abundance of food, including the arctic vegetation to which they were accustomed; they had moist earth to dig in, pieces of driftwood to climb and run on and chew (as they did, apparently, for the salt content); and they had nesting materials. As nearly as could be judged, they lacked none of the necessities of their normal living conditions.

They were confined in three enclosures of different sizes, and when the lemmings were distributed with sufficient space for each group, they thrived. Experimentally, then, I began putting more of them into one or another of the enclosures. They still had everything they needed and plenty of it — except elbow room, and elbow room proved to be an essential. Up to a certain limit of numbers a group would get along well together, with such signs of friendliness as little games and frolics and the habit of sleeping three or four cuddled up in one nest. Up to a maximum number, different for the various-sized enclosures, all went well, but the addition of only a few more lemmings — sometimes only one — was an intolerable too many. With such crowding they all began to show irritability. Instead of amiable pushing contests, nose to nose, they would stand on their hind feet and box, trying to reach each other's throats, with their tiny fangs bared. When I removed the lemmings that were the surplus population, the anger subsided, and I concluded that the pressure of too many individuals in a given area was such a strain that the lemmings had been trying to correct the situation in their own way — not analytically, of course, but smaller numbers would have been the final effect of their fighting.

Other animals, whose populations do not show the extreme variation of hares' and lemmings', here and there and at one time or another find themselves living in habitats which are more restricted than they would like. When they do, a significant change takes

place in their social relationships. They develop a type of social order based on dominance, called in the new biological terminology prostasia (from the Greek *prostates,* "one who stands before"). With it goes an increase in aggressiveness — not to the extent of mass slaughter, but certainly of mass unpleasantness. Protasia is found in many groups of domestic animals and also in those in zoos and laboratories, where evidence of it has been seen in mammals, birds, reptiles, and fish.

As the crowded creatures begin to get on each other's nerves, they arrange themselves in hierarchies, the same that have long been called the peck order, also the nip order and the chase order, although the causative factor, the restricted living space, has not always been understood. The peck order, first described by the Norwegian Schjelderup-Ebbe in 1922, is well known in its general outlines: how the most domineering hen in a domestic flock pecks all the others and never is pecked in return. She is called the Alpha hen. The *B* hen takes this abuse from *A* but pecks all the others; *C* is pecked by both *A* and *B* but is dominant to the rest. There are some interesting details: occasionally a flock is ruled by three dominants of superior but equal rank, who peck one another and all the rest but never are pecked by anyone else; a hen tyrant may have a favorite who is low in the scale of subordinates and will give her advantages in a number of ways; the lowest hens learn that they may avoid the unwelcome mistreatment if they move very slowly and quietly and are silent. In flocks composed of both hens and cocks, the males are inclined to ignore the more dominant females and choose mates from among the lowly. Among jackdaws, as reported by Konrad Lorenz, a female who has been one of the humblest rank becomes one of the highest if mated with a dominant male.

These arrangements are hauntingly familiar.

In our aggressive society it may be easy to sense the satisfactions of the top hen; her prestige and her personal power are objectives that we are encouraged in a thousand ways to try to attain. A little effort of the imagination will show what it is like to be the hen in the lowest position. She meets active animosity everywhere that she turns. Every one of her fellow beings is an unmistakable enemy. She can only avoid injury by muting all of her own desires. Many times, for no more tangible reason, she dies. And degrees of misery must exist all through the group. Sir Solly Zuckerman defined a dominance order as a series of reactions conditioned by fear and pain. Enduring these may be better, at that, than dying from heart attacks.

To a small extent dominance orders exist in wild nature, though in times when populations are in equilibrium, a wilderness society is usually composed of members democratically equal in rank, or of an outstanding leader with voluntary followers. The followers often show evidence of affection for their guide; and the situation could not often be otherwise, for in nature mistreated subordinates can just go away — the fences are not all that high. A true leader may be very helpful and usually seems to be recognized as the animal or bird who is most alert in detecting the approach of predators, most canny in finding food, watering places, and salt licks, most wise in choosing migration routes. In some species, such as elk, the leader is usually one of the older females. Perhaps her concern for repeated litters of young has given her a habitually keen sense of caution and possibly even some sense of responsibility.

No one knows, although many have wondered, what is the quality that allows one bird or animal in a dominance order to humiliate others. Is it inherited or acquired? For a while it was expected that that much of the puzzle might be solved by the Dionne quintuplets, for one of them showed very early a greater facility in her relationship with the others. The five sisters are known to have the same genetic inheritance — identical germ-cell structure — and therefore any differences that they developed in behavior or otherwise might in their case be attributed to what happened to them after birth. Not quite literally; it was recognized that their positions, interactions, in the crowded uterus of the mother would have been an environmental factor too, but they were as good subjects as could be found for the study of the nature-nurture problem.

The environment in which they were raised during their early years under control of the Canadian government was almost identical for all five. Therefore few, if any, differences in behavior were expected. And yet one of the sisters showed signs of superiority in her social contacts almost from the start. It could be anticipated that she would have been found to be the most intelligent of the five, or perhaps the largest and strongest physically. Neither supposition turned out to be true. She was not at the top in the mental tests or in weight. What, then, was the secret of her dominance, so early and surprisingly manifested? In other words, what impels one individual in a group to take the lead? The baby quints did not furnish the answer, nor has it been found even now, nearly thirty years later.

Self-assurance seems to be an essential, but among animals, too, some subordinates are larger, heavier, and stronger than the dominant animal in a group, and insofar as their intelligence has been tested, some have proved to surpass the one in authority. No one knows, either, why those who are actually oppressed never rebel or retaliate — or why, in most cases, they do no more than threaten the ones of still lower rank. With such continual aggravation one might expect the tempers to break out finally in orgies of ruthless slaughtering. That does not happen. The nips and pecks with which dominance is asserted are sometimes painful but almost never are lethal. Typically the cruelty is mental and it is passed along in kind.

In the reports of those who were observing the Dionne sisters there is no indication that the leader gained her position by unpleasant tactics. That is the case, however, with animals living in too crowded a space. Literal space in terms of square feet does not seem as important as the stress of being in contact with too many others; there does seem to be some quite unbearable strain in that situation, which the animals solve if they can. Perhaps the need for a degree of solitude is the reverse side of the instinct that draws sociable animals to one another — like the nourishment instinct, which, in most species, also prevents over-eating. But crowding is frequently a condition about which they can do nothing. Some of their frustration can be imagined by human families who buy second homes in remote areas, only to find that others have had the same idea, so that soon the new neighborhood has become as congested as the old.

All the higher animals stimulate one another when they are in close proximity. The deaths that result from overcrowding may simply mean that the stimulation has become so intense that the animals' stress-mechanisms can't handle it. (There is also a situation called "emotional death," in which an animal is believed to die from the sheer difficulties of living.)

The foregoing mild pages report what actually are some revolutionary discoveries. These findings unquestionably are authentic — they have been confirmed, now, by too many trained observers, both in the wild and in laboratories, to be doubted. And to what does this recent, revised knowledge add up? The conclusion that fighting is not an inescapable urge in the animal temperament. It is not one of the basic instincts.

The new definition of instinct, discussed in Part I, requires that an instinct be motivated internally. It is an inborn drive that will arise without being triggered by any external circumstances. It is unavoidable, and if it is not satisfied, an animal suffers obvious "unease or distress." There are other conditions which have to be met before an animal's behavior can be called truly instinctive, but the innate and insistent quality of the urge is enough to rule out aggressiveness.

As mentioned earlier, there probably are no more than five primary instincts: nutrition, reproduction, social relations, sleep, and care of the body surface. Animals of various kinds have been kept in environments where they had opportunities to eat, sleep, mate, keep themselves clean, and share some sociability — but not too much — with their fellows, and when they have been able, thus, to fulfill these instinctive needs without fighting, they showed no aggressive drive and no distress of the central nervous system because an innate urge was being denied expression.

When animals do attack, they do it so swiftly and effectively that it seems only logical to call their actions instinctive. It is true that any species' *method* of fighting has been inherited. It is a technique, one of several means by which food may be defended or a mate may be secured. It is one of the elements of the "behavior pattern" through which an instinct achieves its purpose. However, the animal does not feel deprived if one of these elements is not called into play. They are useful but not innately essential. As John Paul Scott phrases it, fighting is not a "hunger." It is not an end in itself.

There are differences in the provocation that will cause an animal to attack. One opponent may arouse his anger more quickly than another. The place is a factor: whether an animal is on his own ground, neutral ground, or a rival's. Weather apparently has an influence on the belligerence of many creatures. An animal's own condition may cause him to be more aggressive or less so; and then, temperamentally some individuals seem to be more inclined to react than others — some are phlegmatic, some will fight at the drop of a hat, or in their case the lowering of an opponent's ears. Also, a tendency to fight may become habitual, probably due to early experiences or prolonged irritations later. But these variations in animals' aggressiveness do not change the fact that none of them fight because of any inherited, innate need.

When these scientific conclusions become better known, will they modify one of mankind's favorite myths? The human imagination is a marvelous faculty, perhaps most marvelous in its technological inventiveness because there it does not distort facts. It also is skilled, however, in inventing fantasies — fantasies such as the idea that men are "fundamentally" bestial and aggressive because we have inherited those tendencies from our animal ancestors.

When the earliest manlike primate came down out of the trees and for his more active and ambitious life needed nourishment that was more concentrated than fruit and leaves, perhaps he had some sense of guilt about killing animals, for that was something he had not done before. And then, by a well-known psychological dodge, it may have been that he had to hate the victims he was destroying. Before long he devised as part of his pagan religion the ritual of "loading his sins" onto a goat, or cow, or ox, or chicken, and either killing the animal or driving it forth into the forest.

We have the advantage of a few millenniums of sophistication now; we needn't use animals any longer as scapegoats. We can use them as guides to the laws of decency, those laws of nature in which originate human laws. The more we learn about animals, the better we understand how many hints they can give us for the peaceful functioning of our human relationships.

V

PLAY

The Creative Spirit

The Creative
Spirit

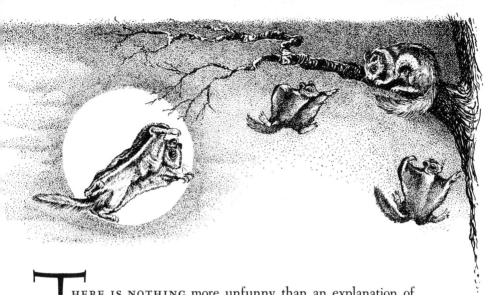

T HERE IS NOTHING more unfunny than an explanation of
why we have laughed at a joke. Though the subject is one
of grave significance to philosophers, to the rest of us any
analyzing of humor is such a desecration of mirth that, hearing it,
we feel we never can laugh again. Similar in their effect have been
the familiar interpretations of play. We listen and at the end feel
wholly deprived of the joy, the fun, the bounce. Is there any way,
then, that we can come to understand play — with the purpose of
having more of it?

It is easy to "expose" play, to define utilitarian uses for it. The
play of young animals and children, it has been said many times,
is practice for grown-up living. Puppies learn how to fight in earnest, as they may do when mature, by wrestling with one another.
Boys, in their games, are developing skill in competition and team-
work; girls playing with dolls are acquiring motherly qualities.
Even the play of human adults is recommended because it is beneficial: it relaxes tensions, it provides a change of pace, it is sub-
limation of a sort, for we often act out in play what we wish we
could do with success on a more serious level. When we have
heard all this, we are in the least-playful mood ever. Play doesn't

seem worthwhile any more, not for us and hardly for puppies. It is all a sham — disguised education or therapy.

Into this arid atmosphere of analysis ("the paralysis of analysis") come the bright modern ethologists with evidence that the utilitarian benefits are no more than side effects. The real meaning of play is something entirely different. It is a spirited message these scientists give us, as they themselves seem to feel, for their words all but sing. They are talking about the play of animals and what they say applies also to human beings. Even to read the explanations can make one feel playful, but before we consider the theories, let's watch some animals playing. We may come part-way to making the new discoveries ourselves.

Witches are riding their broomsticks across the face of the moon — the hunter's moon, which is a whiter disc than the harvest moon, as if it were touched, like the pumpkins, by the October frosts. Count the witches as they are outlined upon its face and then vanish: fifty, a hundred, two hundred witches! Now they are coming back. The sky is full of them. Real witches? Look closely at the next figure sailing across the light. It is a flying squirrel. His body's long axis from pointed nose to the end of his tail is the broomstick, and as he banks in a turn, his upper front foot is the witch's head, his furry drapery her streaming robe. For anyone who has seen flying squirrels gliding around in a moonlit sky, there is no question about how the myth of the Hallowe'en witches arose. Even the season matches, for flying squirrels play in the autumn after their strenuous summer is done. Audubon and Bachman reported watching two hundred of them coasting back and forth through the tops of oak trees in a forest in Pennsylvania. Happily, because they are abroad only at night and therefore are difficult to hunt, flying squirrels still are abundant. The one I saw silhouetted against a moon, looking as much like a witch as anything actual could, was in Jackson Hole.

A flying squirrel is built more like a bat than a bird: like a bat he has membranes of softly furred skin which extend out at the

sides from his wrists to his ankles. A bat can flap these, fast enough
so he can fly more than 25 feet a second, and he can move in any
direction, including up. The squirrel's flaps do not flap; he can
only glide more or less slowly down, although he can turn, in even
a 90-degree angle, by changing the tilt of his body and tail. After
taking off from the top of a tree, he can glide as much as 125 feet,
but land he must, pretty soon, and by inherited preference on the
trunk of another tree. His flying, although it is effortless, therefore
requires great skill in adjusting his rate of descent, his direction,
and landing speed, which must not be too fast if he doesn't want
all his wind to be knocked out of him.

A young squirrel is clumsy at first. He makes all his flights from
low altitudes and often drops onto the ground, until after a few
months he learns the knack. The launching: on a high bough,
with his feet close together, his sharp little nose stretched far out
and his eyes on the distant goal, he rocks back and forth, faster and
faster, gathering strength and perhaps courage, then *springs* into
the air. At once his legs spread to the sides, opening his chute, and
he drops fairly level. If a big bough is in his way, he can manoeuvre around it, but he cannot turn fast enough to glide through
dense leaves and he therefore must land on the trunk of a tree
under the lowest branches. At the end of the glide he makes a quick
upward flip with his rudderlike tail and catches onto the trunk with
his head towards the top, ready to scramble aloft if an unsuspected
enemy should be there on the ground. His skill is almost an art
and, as he is soon to discover, it is a wonderful means of play.

A thing absolutely new to the young squirrel happened yesterday:
the leaves all flew off the trees. The leaves were gone quickly,
during a few hours of boisterous wind, and now the trees are entirely different: he can see through them! He can see the trunks
all the way to the top. All their vertical lengths are available, and
a young squirrel will be tempted to glide through the naked trees
endlessly.

Although the new openness is no novelty to the older squirrels, they too seem pleased with it. It is a season for play anyway, with food gathered for winter, the nests repaired, and the year's offspring old enough now to look after themselves. At exactly this time, with responsibilities lifted, the dense covering on the trees is gone, the moon is full, and as if by a pre-arrangement, the neighboring squirrels gather here to glide back and forth together, crossing and recrossing, in and out of the bare boughs like leaves themselves blowing — an aerial carnival.

Very different and yet with a similar satisfaction perhaps was the play of a dozen or more of the great black whales that were jumping and splashing during a summer midnight up near the Arctic Circle. With one of the officers I was watching them from the bridge of a Coast Guard cutter, crossing the Bering Sea. Most photographs, especially pictures of the large whales when stranded on beaches, make them look utterly stolid — gigantic ridges of flesh that could not, surely, be described ever as graceful. But the whales' bodies are exceedingly limber when they are in the water. They have spines that are called elastic — all the vertebrae loosely attached, and with discs, too, that are pliable. Even the whales' ribs are not fastened rigidly to the spine or breastbone. All this living mechanism is so arranged that the whale can bend and twist and turn as if he were made of rubber. No doubt his flexibility is an aid in swimming through waves and undersea currents, and it also gives him a chance to use his body for sheer delight.

Some of the whales in the Bering Sea were turning somersaults at the surface. A head would submerge, the huge dark line of the back would hump out of the water and curve nearly double; there would be a thrust of the mighty flukes of the tail for momentum, the flukes were out of the surface briefly, then they slipped under again and an instant later the top of the whale's head reappeared and he blew the steam out of his lungs to take in a new breath and sometimes to do a new somersault the next minute.

Others jumped out of the water completely. Unbelievably the immense black, glistening body rose head-up from the waves, more and more of the giant form out until all of it, even the flukes, were in the thin element of the air. Gradually the whale turns down and the snout cuts back into the water, the body and tail following ever so slowly, so slowly as not to seem natural, as if gravity had been canceled for the whale in the air as, very nearly, it is in the sea. Some leaps were made with almost no splashing, only the sinuous rising and seemingly delayed falling. At other times the flukes wildly flailed as they hit the water in their descent, and the animal left a geyser to prove he had made this jump. And sometimes the splashing seemed the whole point of the fun. The enormous animal leapt from the water and let himself fall on it flat, and the mind of a watcher boggled at an effect so preposterous.

Watching the whales at play, in the beautiful glossy dusk of the midnight sun, I thought of the swimming of my own species — how hard we try to achieve speed, in an accepted style of course, of how our different kinds of dives each has a conventional form, and how foolish we'd feel if we simply tumbled and splashed, although children are apt to do that if their parents are not in a great hurry to have them develop techniques.

Of all the jolly possibilities which exist in *motion*, flying squirrels and whales have two of the best because the buoyancy of the air and water allows them to feel so free. (This is a hint of one element in the new conception of play.) The solid earth has advantages too, as gamboling lambs discover in spring when a soft green meadow invites them to romp. Deer apparently love to make their great arching leaps, a soaring, a coming down for a quick, elastic thud on the loam of the forest floor, and a spring up again. I do understand that they jump to see over the brush, to find out whether any enemy is approaching, but deer seem to bound for enjoyment too. Even buffalos, bulky beasts weighing as much as a ton, like to jump. They have been seen leaping off a low bank of a pond into shallow water, repeatedly climbing back up to dive off again.

Otters catch fish so expertly that feeding themselves is a task quickly over, and they can spend most of their time in play, which for them means, best of all, the delight of *sliding*. Beginning with the first winter snowfall, they travel over the land by coasting across it — taking two or three quick little steps for a push and then a long slide exactly as children do on an icy sidewalk. An otter will cover miles in that way. Whenever he finds a ridge of snow, or even a good-sized drift, he stops and slides down it again and again, usually with companions. They all seem so merry, no one can watch them without feeling envious. In summer they make their slides on the banks of brooks and ponds, preferably on clay soil, which soon becomes slick from the otters' wet fur. Audubon and Bachman said that otters construct those summer slides, which may be several feet wide, by clearing them of rocks, moss, roots, and all other obstructions. Recognizing that this making of "apparatus" shows a surprising amount of intelligence, the authors hoped to silence doubters by pointing out that other naturalists have made the same observation.

Seton calls this kind of play the delight of speed without effort. Skiers know about that; in fact, so do motorists, and all children with sleds. Other animals with less initiative than otters often take any free rides that are available. B. B. Roberts, writing about the birds of Iceland, described eider ducks shooting the rapids. That they did this for fun was proved by the way they kept at it, riding down through the swift, swirling water, climbing out where the stream became tranquil, to walk back up along the bank and launch themselves into the playful current again.

It is not surprising that ducks, so used to the vagaries of flowing water, should have found that joining the rapid movement was fun, but there is a much more remarkable incident, told by E. A. Stoner, in which an Anna's hummingbird made the same discovery. This tiny creature, seeming the least aquatic of birds, saw a little stream running down a lawn from a garden faucet and sensed a new opportunity. He could coast on that water! Alighting, he let the current carry his small, emerald and ruby self down to the end, and then many times he flew back to enjoy the unprecedented sensation. To have seen such a possibility and taken advantage of it means that the bird's mind was out of all ruts, was exploring his world and responding to the chance for a new experience. (We are coming closer now to the ethologists' definition of play.)

The enjoyment of motion seems the very simplest of pleasures by human standards. It is simple by animals' standards too, for some of them have developed much more complex types of play. They have "play" which seems in essence similar to the highest kinds of expression in man. Not quite of this maximum sort, but still elaborate in some cases, are animals' games that involve give and take between individuals. These are of great variety.

Wrestling is frequent. Many species enjoy these mock fights; especially young animals do but so too do adults. In his description of Kenya wildlife in *Roadless Area*, Paul Brooks reports vividly on this kind of play between two male lions: "By now we saw his objective: another mature male with an even fuller, dark-tipped mane, waiting sleepily in the grass. Approaching him, the first lion broke into a trot and joined his friend with a great display of affection. They rubbed necks and tumbled about with feet in air, finally . . . settling down side by side, heads swaying in unison, eyes closed to the sun."

Animal psychologists do not down-grade the restraint of creatures who thus fight for fun. That is exactly what some of them call it: restraint. But there are newer interpretations for the lack of ferocity. None of the five basic instincts are involved in such play, and since combats like these are not prompted by competition for anything, not for food, a mate, or a homesite, there is no stimulus to set off a wish to kill.

Learned men have occupied themselves with studies of children's games. They say that some of the most primitive peoples play the same games that are standbys in any twentieth-century suburb, and they make the fascinating comment that group games in which circles are formed have as their underlying theme sowing and harvest or love and marriage, while the line type usually imitate warlike situations. Such are the ritualized children's games. For those that are not so formal, the origins are more remote than even the simplest human society. They go back to the primate species, some back beyond primates, some even beyond the mammals. Two of the favorite activities of children are played by fishes. In fact some of the things that the children's parents do seem like adult versions of fishes' games, although less like a frolic.

Follow-the-leader is one game with which fish amuse themselves. Swimming in and out of the pond vegetation, pricking the surface — "air-snapping" — dawdling and spurting ahead in single file. Anybody who watches the fish can't help remembering strings of small boys all imitating the one who leads in a jump off a culvert, a crawl through the streamside brush, a leap from one bank of the brook to the other, a snaking out into the grass of the meadow. To follow the leader is a pasttime of many creatures, including birds, all the way up the intelligence scale from the fish.

Another fish game, known only in one species, seems a form of teasing, of playing a joke on someone. The jaculator, or archer fish, is able to shoot a jet of water several feet from the surface. It is a skill ordinarily used to shoot down insect food from vegetation overhanging the water, but in one aquarium the fish often let fly their arrows at an attendant they recognized.

No small number of visitors to zoos have been sprayed by chimpanzees, who fill their mouths at their drinking fountains and minutes later will squirt the water on some unsuspecting human observer. It must be rather humiliating to be the butt of a chimpanzee's joke, although anyone who has been on the other side of the wire in a zoo can understand the temptation. One year in San Francisco I helped to make plaster casts of animals' footprints for a biologist who was writing a book on their tracks. Carey Baldwin, director of the Fleishhacker Zoo, allowed us to work in the animal enclosures for peccaries, bears, raccoons, and others, and we went into those for the elephants and the zebras. When one is among the animals, so alert and so mobile, it is rather astonishing to see the human beings lined up outside. How pale the faces, all seeming to show the same naked expression; how motionless the bodies; how lifeless the whole human company appeared! It was natural that they should, since the people were spectators and we are all quiet when we are interested, but one could not be surprised at a chimpanzee's wish to stir up some action.

Many other animals tease. I think of a tree squirrel, the one called a chickaree in the mountains of California. He was tormenting a resting Sierra grouse by darting up close and chirring saucily in her face. He continued until, slowly, gradually, her bulk started to swell and then suddenly all her plumage seemed to explode. The squirrel retreated in haste. On another occasion, in Jackson Hole, a tree squirrel himself was the object of teasing. A line of pine trees extended behind my cabin, spaced just too far apart for a squirrel to jump. From near the top of one tree a blue jay squawked a challenge to the squirrel, at that time on the ground. He raced up the trunk to show that bird who was what in that pine. The jay waited until the squirrel was within a foot of his perch and then took off with deliberate ease, to alight in the next tree beyond. The squirrel, dashing headlong down the trunk of the first tree, was up into the second, and again the jay let him come within a maddening foot of being the captor. The two proceeded through the whole row of six or eight pines, the squirrel certainly knowing that he was being a dupe but willing to play the jay's game for the fun of it. That it really was fun could hardly be doubted, especially since the day was one of diamond-bright winter weather. A coating of soft new snow covered all branches and twigs, and as the squirrel danced along them, he scattered showers of glittering little stars.

Some animals seem to take pleasure in dizzily dashing about, as if they enjoyed pure nonsense as much as small boys do when they reel around bumping into each other. Stoats, the English species of weasels, spin around thus, only with the curious variation that sometimes they jump, flinging themselves at each other, to collide in midair. Occasionally, a single stoat will run about crazily, but with the purpose of arousing the curiosity of a victim. As soon as the prey — a squirrel or rabbit perhaps — is off guard, the stoat makes a lightning attack. When several of the stoats act together this way, however, it is believed that they have no other objective but fun.

In the area where I live, near the Delaware River, anyone who is awake at dawn, when the sun is just starting to stripe the dew on the grass, may see little companies of cottontails frolicking. Some of them leap up and down in one place while others race round and round, often under the jumpers. Fawns bound over each other sometimes, and my Husky dog loves to jump over the back of another dog, the bigger the dog the better. The jumps he makes seem a kind of teasing, but the sportive rabbits jump whether any others are running beneath them or not. Biologists speak of an excess of energy. Perhaps we could also say that they jump for joy. Children still do it.

Tag is one of the favorite animal games. It may be played by two or several in a group. Sometimes there is an actual touch as the one who is *it* gives that role to another, but animals may assume that the touch has been made if in fact it could have been. The hoofed species, especially, like to play tag. A naturalist who had a tame moose found that the moose was eager to play with his children; the moose had to be denied that fun, however, because his touch sent them sprawling. The moose then invented a sort of solitary game of tag with a croquet ball.

If any children would like to join a game being played by animals, they would feel right at home with badgers, whose play is most like their own. Badgers turn somersaults on the grass. They play leapfrog in exactly the same way that boys do (there is a wonderful photograph of badgers leapfrogging in Ernest Neal's book, *The Badger*); and badgers in England play king-of-the-castle, a game they like so well that some groups of them play it every day. At sundown, when they come out of their dens for the night's foraging, first they go by familiar trails to some stump or the trunk of a fallen tree. One climbs to the top and the others all try to climb up themselves and pull down the king. They continue this game for an hour or more, with the royal succession passing from one to another. The American badgers have a shuffle dance that is very much like the twist!

To the badgers it might seem quite normal if children should play with them, for they have the quality, rare among animals, of forming friendships with other species. They allow coyotes and foxes to move into their spacious burrows, which may be as long as 300 feet, and sometimes a badger and a coyote tenant, or a badger and fox will become almost inseparable. The other species might profit when the badger, a better digger, routs a ground squirrel from his tunnel, but it is hard to see how the badger benefits except in sociability. In Africa there is a mutual advantage in the relationship between a badger and a bird called the honey-guide. The bird may summon the badger by calling to him, or the badger may whistle to the bird, and when they get together both know what to do next. The bird leads the way to a bee tree, where the badger digs out the honey and the bird is rewarded by a feast on the wax, which he especially enjoys.

During the last century a seven-year-old boy, Harry Service, was lost from his family's home in Manitoba and lived for two weeks with a badger in its underground den. When he was found he said that the badger had brought him food several times, and he cried when he was taken away from his badger friend. Perhaps the badger, too, grieved when he lost his new playmate.

Rivalry of one kind or another often typifies animals' social games, a fact that is not surprising since animals must compete for many things that are essential to them. The practice of taking turns (commented upon in Part I) also appears in some of their play. It would seem logical to expect it in only the more intelligent creatures, but the most extraordinary example of it that I have seen occurred in two of the humblest — two of those small rodents, the lemmings, that I kept in captivity in the North. Their little game was unusual in another way: it was not traditional. They had worked it out for themselves, and it therefore was play in a very pure form.

One enclosure where the lemmings were confined was a vivarium, glass-walled on two sides, with an area of about eight square feet. One end of the cage was of plywood, through which a hole had been bored. When a lemming went out through the hole, he found himself in a metered activity wheel, large, about twenty inches in diameter, which turned on ball bearings and could be spun very easily and fast. There was room for several lemmings to run in it at the same time, but since their speed varied, the slower ones had to give it up to the better runners. Two of the lemmings ran at exactly the same pace. At first they would stay in the wheel together, running in tandem; then they adopted a program of alternating.

Let us say Number 1 is in the wheel. He maintains himself in a position a few inches ahead of the hole, so that he runs on a slight upward slant. His tiny legs spin so fast, they are blurs to a human eye, and the whir of the wheel can be heard in adjoining rooms. But now it is Number 2's turn. He comes out of the hole, drops to the floor of the wheel, dashes forward until he is just ahead of Number 1, who then gives up his place and goes back inside the vivarium.

Here, among the small pieces of driftwood, there is one long and gnarled. The first lemming runs from one end of it to the other, where he whirls about, retraces his way on the driftwood stick, comes to the hole — the door to the wheel — goes out again and exactly repeats the behavior of the lemming who had replaced him. And now Number 2 goes inside; and does he stop there for a bite of food or a drink of water, or a playful encounter with one of the other lemmings? No, he runs to the end of the same piece of driftwood, returns by that route to the hole, and goes out into the wheel to take his turn spinning it. These two have changed places as many as twenty-two times without stopping and with no variation in any element of their routine. Most remarkable, also, was the precise rhythm that they maintained in the speed of the wheel. There was a slight, very regular pulse in the wheel's momentum, as if a lemming, racing ahead, caught his breath at short intervals. The pulse was the same for both lemmings, and when they changed places the same pulse was maintained and the same overall speed of the wheel. This precision was such that unless I was watching, I could not tell from the sound that the lemmings were alternating.

There were never any conflicts, never any protests from one that wanted to stay in the wheel, never any cheating. The game would end because one of the players, tired perhaps, stayed inside the vivarium. The other would run the wheel alone for a minute or two and then he often would simply stop and lie in the bottom of the wheel, rocked by it briefly, and go fast asleep.

Incidentally, when the two first developed their game, the vivarium stood in front of a window. During the colder part of the winter it was moved to an inside wall and there the lemmings no longer played the game, although they ran the wheel separately. In the spring, when the cage was moved back to the window, on that very day they resumed the game. Close association with any species of animals is full of surprises like this.

In amusing themselves as the flying squirrels and the whales were doing, individual animals are not subject to challenge by others. Each animal does what he likes, meanwhile having the sociable sense of being surrounded by his companions, who also are streaming about through the trees or jumping or splashing. There is no give and take in this kind of play. However, in games something more is required of a player, and that extra demand must help him to make discoveries about himself vis-à-vis others. To the extent that a winner achieves status, however, games are not play in its purest form.

Less competitive and therefore more truly playful is the activity by a whole group as a unit. Examples are the patterned swimming of fishes in schools and the wheeling of flocks of birds. This behavior is one of the mysteries of the natural world, for it is not known how the creatures co-ordinate their beautiful, often elaborate motions.

Sometimes as one sits in a boat on a quiet lake and looks down into the sun-lighted depths, one discovers a truly aesthetic performance there. Dozens or hundreds of fish, translucently green, are moving about in the water as if they were one single organism. They are moving as gracefully as the flow of water itself, and for a moment may be mistaken for reeds in a current. Watch them turn, compressing the form of the group on the inner side, widening on the outer side. See how they all surge ahead with one purpose, or slackening speed, become quiet. This is not a follow-the-leader game; no one fish is guiding the others; and the fishes' motions are not identical, not mechanical, but are synchronized into a lovely design. How do they do it, by what means of communication? There have been guesses but no explanation is widely accepted. The current word for that kind of behavior is "allelomimetic," from two Greek words meaning mutual mimicry, although it is admitted that the fish do not really imitate one another. Their actions are simultaneous.

Wheeling flocks of birds are allelomimetic. I used to watch arctic terns on the shore of the Bering Sea, where a large flock left their nests every summer day as the light was diminishing towards the sundown at midnight. The birds flew around in a rather close circle, back and forth over the beach. On one side of their swing the white bellies were gilded by the sun's rays, on the other the birds merged, blue-gray, into the blue-gray sky so that the flock seemed to disappear. The changing colors must have been even more evident to the terns than to us below, and was the smooth alternating of sparkle and dullness a pleasure also to them? Or was the grace of the motion the whole reason for the experience? The birds, like the schools of fish, apparently had no leader. This was a group performance, one familiar to many watchers of birds, everywhere, and how it functions, as well as why it does, is not known.

There are several human activities which are suggestive. I once was a member of a group that performed Laban dances, that type of allelomimetic dancing which was developed in Germany after the First World War as a means of helping shell-shocked veterans to relate themselves emotionally to others. Our group, organized in San Francisco, danced only for pleasure: twelve men and girls, with a director who did little more than beat a gong and suggest a general form that a dance might take. It could be "campers discovering a forest fire and fleeing from it," or, "a Chinese funeral procession climbing a hill": we never knew in advance what would be proposed. And we made no plan, and yet there was always an astonishing degree of organization in the dances as they developed. Some onlookers called them beautiful, but I don't believe we were striving very consciously for an aesthetic effect. The unit of twelve seemed to have its own purpose, unspoken yet vividly felt: an impulse to carry out a group movement simply took hold of the dancers. I can only describe the experience subjectively and say that it gave one a sense of liberation. Members of jazz groups, improvising together, must feel the same thing. Groups playing chamber music don't improvise but their interpretation is a mutual expression; and on a purely intellectual plane, it may be that the joint work of teams of experimenting scientists provides a widening out of self that adds something to the satisfaction of an individual working alone. Common sense suggests that the schooling fish and the wheeling birds carry out those complex kinds of group play because the creatures enjoy them in much the same way that human beings do their own allelomimetic games.

Some birds and animals dance in groups that do not have an intention so unified. In human terms it could be the difference between a Laban interpretation of a Chinese funeral procession and a square dance in which each individual fits into the general pattern but may introduce his own variations. One thinks of the clowning oldster, tossing his feet around and swirling his partners exuberantly. One of those looser dances is that of chimpanzees, who like to circle some object in single file and in step, all coming down hard on one foot and wagging their heads in a primitive kind of rhythm. There was a chimpanzee clown in one such dance described by Wolfgang Köhler: "As the whole group were joyously trotting round a box, little Konsul stepped to one side outside the circle, drew himself up to his full height, swung his arms to and fro in time to the trotting, and each time that fat Tschego passed him, caught her a sounding smack behind."

What do they have in common, the dancing apes, flying-squirrel revelers, wrestling lions, and teasing fish; the badgers, lemmings, wheeling terns — as well as boys flying kites, little girls playing hopscotch, and men sailing boats? All of these playing animals do share one quality — this: they are free. They, and we, are free from the driving demands of instincts. We have escaped, temporarily, from those activities which make sure that we will survive. Most human beings probably think of pressures as coming from the outside — pressures from social requirements, from employers, or families. But the demands that most rigidly limit our actions are the internal ones, the insistent proddings of instinct.

Undoubtedly instincts determine most of what animals do. Intelligent men always have recognized that fact, and when machines became such a prominent part of civilization, we saw many similarities between machine operations and animals' actions. Neurological structures, we began to say, pull the levers, and animals have no choice but to respond. We still know that that observation is partly true, although more and more we resent the analogy between lifeless mechanisms and creatures that follow the cycle of living: being born, reproducing themselves, and dying. Machines do not have that kind of eternal significance. As far as being at liberty to choose voluntarily between one activity or another, most of the simpler animals probably do not have the chance. They eat, sleep, copulate, clean themselves, and move nearer, or farther away from, their fellows depending on which of the five primary instincts is the one most compelling at the particular moment. Such automated behavior may be all that is possible to frogs, insects (as far as we know), earthworms, snails, and all the multitudes of even more primitive creatures. When we look in the other direction, at the higher animals, we find that they are able to satisfy the instinctual needs and have time left over. They have both the time and the more elaborate nervous systems which prompt them to use it for sheer enjoyment.

A hawk coasting around in the sky illustrates the difference between the predetermined and the playful, or free, activity. Watch the hawk cruising above a meadow, not very far up. He changes direction frequently. Now and then he dips down a little and rises again: he has seen a small shadow that seems to move, or some grasses that quiver. That could be living prey. And the hawk is hungry. What he is doing is an example of appetitive behavior — a random searching required in this case by a literal appetite, by an empty stomach. We don't know how conscious a bird may be of the fact that he is in need of food, but whether he is aware of why he is doing it, or not, he is hunting. When he finally sees an unmistakable mouse, he drops faster than any stone.

In the Sierra Nevadas of California I spent many months at a large granite outcropping, Beetle Rock, several acres in width. When the sun shone on those slopes, its heat was absorbed by the evergreen forests surrounding the Rock but was reflected upward from the light, cream-colored stone. Hawks loved to sail on that updraft. They would ride on it very high, around and around the edge — one could map the boundaries of the Rock by the hawks' circling, although they were in the sky. The hawks sometimes would ride on the column of heat thus for hours: playing. Obviously they were not hungry then, or if they were, that instinct for nourishment was not really demanding.

In Los Angeles, where airplanes streak through the sky constantly, carrying people on urgent "appetitive" missions, a television reporter interviewed one of a team who were preparing for mass balloon flights from Catalina Island across to the mainland. Since so much flying is based on the wish for speed, the reporter obviously was puzzled. What, he asked, is the point of the balloonists' new hobby? What makes it worthwhile, what is its *purpose?* "It hasn't any purpose," said the balloonist. "That's why we do it — because it's so aimless. In this country we're all so driven, everybody's trying so hard to reach a goal, that we just like to get out of that pattern and float around in the sky."

The next day they went up in their pretty striped balloons, which looked like small circus tents. One balloonist, Mrs. Barbara Keith, a grandmother of ten, felt the spirit of true playfulness well enough to say, "It will be wonderful to be part of the wind." But the wind was gusty that day. It caught Mrs. Keith's balloon and hurled it down into the sea, and she lost her life. True play often does involve risks; perhaps danger heightens the pleasure for human beings by sharpening sensibilities. The hawks circling above Beetle Rock did not have that hazard; they could be part of the wind and yet save themselves from its rougher currents. The balloonists and hawks, however, were playing in similar ways.

Psychologists talk of "sex play." To a zoologist that is a contradiction in terms. Real play is escape from all the instinctual drives, and partners in adult sex play do not have that kind of freedom. Sex play can be fun, obviously — maybe even a chase like tag, or a wrestling match — but there are boundaries to it. It moves on a narrow path which instinct defines to an end already known. Though it may be delightful, even humorous, adult sex play never is aimless.

Adolph Murie described the wrestling of grizzly bear lovers: "I saw a large, dark male, with a huge, shaggy head, following a much smaller, straw-colored female. He kept herding her from below, as though his objective was to keep her up the slope. When she traveled, he traveled on a contour below her. Once, when a sharp ridge hid her from him, he galloped forward and upward to intercept her, but she seemed to have anticipated this and had doubled back . . . She made no real effort to escape, and he was soon herding her from below again. At noon they lay down about twenty yards apart, and a little later, when he went into a dip to feed, she hurried away as though she were playing a coy game with him . . . The chase continued all day."

And of another pair: "I saw them breeding on May 20. They were together most of the time and were often playing together and hugging. . . . Later they wrestled again and the male grabbed the female with his jaws back of an ear and tried to mount her, but she rolled over. They continued to wrestle and play for some time."

It was the female who set the tone of this play, at least its duration, and as long as his suspense lasted, the male probably felt that the game was far from stereotyped. But this was not open-ended play. In contrast, watch one of Dr. Murie's bears with her cubs:

"The mother rolled over on her back with all four feet waving and kicking in the air. She reached up at the willow with her forepaws, clawing at it and pulling down the lower branches. She was in a playful mood, but the cubs stood apart and she played alone . . . Life in company with the lone youngster was more intimate. It sought its mother for play and she responded generously. Sometimes the play continued for fifteen or twenty minutes, the mother lying on her back and the cub biting at her feet, head, and neck; sometimes they faced each other and sparred with open jaws. The mother seemed to enjoy the play as much as the little one."

That frolic, which was true play, could have taken any turn possible to grizzly bears. There weren't any rules, any more than there are when bear cubs play by themselves. Then they bump one another off logs, tease, tumble, romp, fool around, do anything that their fancy suggests, and there is no other object.

Although play does not move towards any pre-set, definite goal, there is a kind of search in it, a wandering hunt without knowing what one is looking for. The thing finally found will be most satisfying if it is somewhat new: a new sensation, a new, enjoyable kind of motion, a new game with fellow creatures or an old game with a new twist. The more unexpected, the better it is, and so to find it, one must move around, open-mindedly, feeling one's way.

Play thus might be called a blind-finding, and men must have recognized that groping quality since so many children's games require blindfolding: blindman's buff, pinning the tail on the donkey, etc. Actually the search, in play, is part of the fun, if not most of the fun. Once the pleasurable way to have fun is found, animals, like ourselves, begin almost at once to introduce variations. They are still searching. For this reason some biologists, notably William H. Thorpe, who has made a most perceptive study of animal play, say that play too is "appetitive behavior," even though the appetite in this case is not directly related to the satisfaction of any instinctual need.

Play is considered by Thorpe to be closely related to exploration, at least in the more complex animals. The simpler ones do not explore, or, as mentioned before, play at all. If we can judge, there is no impulse to play in any animals below vertebrates. The vertebral column, the bony tube which encloses and protects the spinal cord, is the structure that makes possible a more elaborate nervous system and therefore a more complex type of behavior. However, even some vertebrates do not play; it appears that snakes never do. Fish do not play as much as birds; birds not as much (probably) as foxes; foxes not as much as porpoises or chimpanzees. The higher up in the scale of nervous and cerebral development, the more, in most cases, the animal plays. And the greater his ability to play, the more it resembles exploration.

Anyone who has spent much time in the woods, observing wild animals, reaches a point where it seems possible to recognize the exploring type of behavior. An animal that is exploring, just out to see what he can see, smell what he can smell, acts differently from the animal that is hunting for prey, or a male in the rut that is prowling around trying to find a promising female scent, or an animal searching with a peculiar numbness in its movements for a place to lie down and go to sleep. There is another kind of roaming around in which all the senses obviously are alert. In an animal thus exploring there is no obvious tension: the animal is just getting to know its environment better. Such an animal therefore is most often young, not yet acquainted with all its neighborhood.

The impulse becomes noticeable in an older animal when it is in a new place. It was especially well developed in both of my Husky dogs, both closely related to wolf ancestors and one in whom the wolf blood was recent. They were both well-mannered dogs, with a sense of "decorum," but when they were taken into strange houses, the wish to know all about that new building was so intense, it could be embarrassing. Without damaging anything the dogs looked under all the beds, went through all the closets, investigated behind every piece of furniture: places where there was no sight or scent that could possibly be related to any of the dogs' instinctual drives. When they had seen absolutely everything, they would lie down quietly near my chair; their curiosity had been satisfied. But that curiosity, so unproductive of anything valuable to a dog except knowledge, could not be denied.

The same tendency, to explore for no reward except information, has been shown in laboratory experiments with animals. P. Crowcroft discovered that some strains of mice will even interrupt fighting if given a chance to reconnoiter. But as Thorpe says, it is easiest to study a creature's curiosity about his environment if he is at least semifree. For example, fanciers who raise homing pigeons know how important it is to release their young birds at greater and gradually greater distances: the pigeons' investigation of the countryside increases their homing skill.

An animal may explore by observing while he is quiet — visual exploring, as the biologists describe it. This too is enjoyed by some of the higher species.

Monkeys will "work" for a chance just to watch, as R. A. Butler and H. M. Alexander found in a fascinating experiment. The monkeys were confined in a room from which they could look out only if they would exert themselves to hold open a door. Six rhesus monkeys, tested for ten hours a day, spent approximately 40 per cent of the time keeping that door open. Although they were especially interested when they could see a toy train running around a track, they held the door open longest when another monkey outside was in sight. Human analogies come to mind. It is slightly enjoyable to watch a big train go by; far, far more enjoyable to watch a good skier come down a hill. I think of the Eskimos, whom I joined in one of their villages for a year. When a hunter brought in a seal, we all would stand in a circle around his wife while she skinned it, and our eyes followed with pleasure every adept turn of her knife.

I believe it can be assumed that many animals below the primate level also enjoy observing. When deer can lie in a place where they feel secure, where they can't be attacked from behind, they don't merely relax and doze; their faces are wonderfully alert. They are always on guard, but their eyes, expressive and knowing, show that they see the harmless as well as suspicious happenings; their ears continually turn, and their nostrils respond subtly to any scents on the passing breeze. Do these sensations bring them no satisfaction? That is hard to believe. The wolves in Alaska are fond of getting up on some knoll, where they will stay for long periods with half-lowered eyelids shading their keenly perceiving, gold-colored eyes; and their ears and nostrils move constantly. In describing this kind of observing as *visual* exploring, the biologists may have been influenced by the fact that most human beings look before they listen, and listen before they sniff. Nine-tenths of us are said to be eye-minded, only one-tenth ear-minded, and all of us ignore almost all odors except those of cooking, although we are warned by the smell of smoke from a fire. (For those who wonder why garden flowers seem to have lost their fragrance, there is an explanation. Nurserymen are breeding the fragrance out because many gardeners have the erroneous idea that it is fragrance which causes allergies. In reality, the discomfort is due to minute pollen grains, drawn into the nose.) Some animals, quite inactive at the time, may explore their surroundings far more by their olfactory sense than by their eyes. Bears probably do, and that kind of observing may be as interesting to them as watching was to the monkeys who worked in order to see the little train run around.

Another kind of exploring play: a few animals find it entertaining to handle and manipulate objects. Many "handle" things, sometimes with mouths and beaks, for practical reasons, as in feeding themselves and making their burrows and nests. We do not mean here that kind of handling but, rather, handling in the sense of playful investigation. Some, in their search for what they can do with an object, turn it into a toy. Many birds like to throw around things like twigs, pieces of moss, and pine cones; then, if they are the hunting species, they pounce on them. The white-winged chough, an Australian bird, incorporates play with sticks and bunches of leaves into an elaborate follow-the-leader game. Richard S. Peterson says that fur seal pups dive down in the sea and bring up strands of kelp, with which they play at length, tossing them, tugging them. And the dolphins at the Marine Studios in Florida have devised various games with the feathers shed by the pelicans that share their tanks. One dolphin would drop a feather near the inflow, where a strong current comes out of the pipe, and would then swim away, wait, and catch the feather as it was streaming by. The dolphins use the feathers in playing catch with each other. They like to play catch with human observers too, but for this fish are better objects than feathers. A man watching may find that he is the target for a fish that comes hurtling out of the tank. If he takes the assault in the right spirit, he throws the fish back to the dolphin, who will return it. The man, not the dolphin, is likely to be the first to tire of the game.

Play with an object especially delights the primates, like the pet monkey described by Richard Carrington who always would spin an orange before she would eat it, and such play in a primate is often exploratory, inventive. This chimpanzee has been given a bamboo stick. What could you do with that? Well, you can hit the floor with it — that makes a good noise, especially fine if somebody else is startled. With a stick you can poke your companion.

When he takes hold of the other end, you can wrestle the stick between you. Sticks can be twirled. And used as canes. You can vault with them — jolly! Two sticks? The chimpanzee has been given another, and he finds that the end of the smaller one can be fitted into the hollow end of the larger, making a pole twice as long. With this he can knock that banana down off the rack, where it has been out of reach. The two sticks, now of pole length, have become a tool.

In the higher animals play can lead to such valuable discoveries, but biologists argue among themselves about whether all play is utilitarian. Some of them won't admit that an animal ever engages in any activity that does not now, or will in the future, lead to the satisfaction of one of his primary instincts. They say that an animal moving about in his environment, "aimlessly" as it appears, is learning where he can later find food, sex, a homesite, or protective contact with his own species. Undoubtedly such encounters do result from an animal's roaming, but is that the sole purpose of exploratory play? Yes, say the so-called Dynamic Psychologists, and they include in "exploring" an animal's quiet observing and his manipulation of objects.

L. A. Thacker is one who disagrees with a view so restricted. Although he too considers that play is learning, he says that it "may have no discoverable specific objective goal whatsoever." He believes that even a subhuman creature may have an impulse to know — just to know, to form an organizing, enlarging conception of things-as-they-are, quite aside from any utilitarian benefits from such knowledge.

Dr. Thorpe emphasizes that play has several functions. On the lowest level play helps to develop "a young animal's motor-habits." But, he says, "play is much more." Play "is performed for its own sake," and in describing the play of birds, he writes that they "make it difficult to avoid the conclusion that there is some element of fun in the performance." That conclusion seems only logical to a layman; yet some biologists write whole treatises on the play of animals without mentioning the word *fun*. Thorpe enumerates some of the many ways that play can add to the animals' knowledge of their environment, but like Thacker he gives them credit for "a general curiosity" — curiosity which presumably enables them to include much interesting but "useless" information along with the practical facts. Thorpe uses R. S. Woodworth's phrase, "the will to perceive." And he finally quotes R. Söderberg, who saw a "pre-aesthetic quality" in the play of some animals.

There is no reason why play cannot have all these functions. If we may be allowed to think of the animal's own, subjective reasons for playing, including exploring, it is hard to believe that he doesn't play as a means of enjoying himself. No contradiction exists — or at least should exist — between pleasure and learning. Children have the same, spontaneous impulse to explore, observe, and manipulate that animals do. They express it in playing; and those interests are also used systematically in their education by teachers. There is a summer camp near Poughkeepsie whose directors recognize that exploring in natural, wooded country, seemingly without guidance, can be of great value, and they make this experience possible to the young campers (with safeguards which are not obvious). Besides the treasures that the exploring child often collects, curious rocks, broken birds' eggs and such, he usually brings back something else: questions. He has been reaching out with his mind, reaching forward — searching, the truest element of play.

When the chimp knocked the banana down, he moved a short way towards becoming a man. For much of our human play, unfortunately, is closely related to our "survival." When we play games for stakes, we are trying to get the banana. Or we play games with the hope of improving our social status, which is the same thing. None of these is the pure play that skating is, or collecting records of folksongs, or carving, or hiking, or watching birds.

Play can lead towards bananas — or it can lead in another direction.

In the case of some animals, at some times, the enjoyment may be a deeper and richer experience than mere fun is. It must have been more for the monkeys and apes that made those paintings so widely publicized in the last few years, paintings facetiously ridiculed because grossly misunderstood.

It was a startling thought that apes had made paintings. Was man not to be left with even a shred of uniqueness? Chimpanzees' pictures, shown in big-city galleries, sold for prices that might have supported a human artist, threadbare in his loft, for a year. Ape "art" indeed! Most of the paintings looked as though a brush had been put in the chimpanzee's hand while he was having a tantrum.

These were some of the more mocking comments:

The paintings were rigged; those that show any quality were snatched away from the ape before he could spoil them. The ape was just waving his arms around. His enjoyment of painting was muscular, the same as if he were throwing things or bashing companions. The painting was only a form of exhibitionism, a way of getting attention from zoo visitors, television technicians, or trainers. The ape only produced the pictures because he was given rewards of food he especially likes.

We'll see by the following facts how many of these impressions were justified.

The earliest investigation of subhuman art was made by a scientist, Mme. Nadjejeta Kohts of Russia, before 1916. It was an incidental part of a study of chimpanzee intelligence. The animal, Joni, made drawings and made enough to prove that his pencilwork (he did not make paintings) definitely improved with practice. It began as large flowing lines, but after a time, during which he "constantly fiddled with a pencil," his pictures consisted of carefully drawn, stronger lines all crisscrossed by very short lines at right angles. Such crisscrossing is a stage in drawing that small children also reach, but not until they have passed through some preliminary levels of simpler scribbling. The detail, the crisscrossing, requires finger work and does not, of course, involve the satisfaction of using large muscles.

Mme. Kohts's project was primarily a comparison of the development of an infant ape and a human child. The human subject was her son, Roody, and she was the first to note that a small ape never reaches the stage which came naturally to Roody when he was three or four years old: that of making pictures, symbols, which represent persons and objects. The same observation, that children but not apes spontaneously achieve this later stage, was made by Winthrop N. Kellogg, a biologist, and his wife at the University of Indiana. The Kelloggs also made a comparative study of a young ape, the female chimpanzee Gua, and a child, their son Donald.

The Kelloggs' project was carried out in the 1930's. Twenty years later much more extensive studies were being made: of apes' intelligence as revealed in their aesthetic efforts, of the progress that children make in their drawing, and — by Desmond Morris, a biologist, curator of mammals at the London Zoo — a detailed comparison of the two. Perhaps no other work in biology has more clearly and fascinatingly shown what is the quality of our own minds that is "human." It is a long-needed complement to the many studies of tool-making and use of language.

Investigations of the way that children's drawing abilities grow have shown that these abilities develop by very definite and predictable steps. Several such studies have been done. The one described by Desmond Morris in his book *The Biology of Art* was by Mrs. Rhoda Kellogg of the Golden Gate Nursery Schools in San Francisco. She has compared 200,000 drawings by very young children in fourteen countries, and from these she has charted the types of drawings, or scribbles, that children make. These drawings were all done spontaneously, without any instruction whatever, and there is a remarkable uniformity in the stages by which they become more complex. Some children may advance faster than others, but all seem to make the same journey.

Mr. Morris's absorbing discussion indicates that children, usually when three or four years old, reach a point which leads directly into a representation of the human face; and that is the stage beyond which no ape ever has gone. Up to that point, *a chimpanzee makes the same progress, by the same steps, as a child does.* Congo, the chimpanzee studied the longest and most intensively, by Mr. Morris, came to the end of his drawing ability when he was making a very good circle and filling it with small marks. This is the stage in a child's development where he begins trying to represent a human face. Would Congo have gone on to start drawing what he saw — the figure of an ape, for example — if his art work had continued? At the time he stopped he had been drawing for more than two years and had produced 384 pictures. They all came out of his inner resources, none being any sort of copying or promotion by the investigator, but beyond that circle with spots inside he could not go. At the time when he had developed that far, he wanted the larger activities available to him in playground equipment. Was his restlessness at this time also due to a sense of frustration because his chimpanzee mind could not make the next step, into drawing representational symbols? With the apes studied by other scientists, all of them, that is the stage at which the pre-human mind cannot go any further.

The scientists who are conducting these studies distinguish between the lines themselves, the calligraphy, and the composition of a picture, that is, the position of the scribbles, whether they produce a balanced form, well-placed on the area of the paper. At the start a chimpanzee makes a firmer line than a child does, probably because his muscular development is more advanced. A child, however, is actually more interested in a line than an ape is. For a child it seems as if the line were an experiment: where will it go? He is "taking a line for a walk," as Paul Klee expressed it — or perhaps the child and the line move together. A blind-finding: the method of all creative endeavor.

This is the impulse that will lead in a few years to the child's picture of a man with head, body, arms, and legs.

In composition, as opposed to lines alone, an ape definitely takes the lead, and he shows an astounding subtlety of feeling for placing his forms (configurations) in the center of the page, of balancing one side against the other, of filling in all corners if any are filled, and of surrounding a center form with others. It is details such as these that were not often analyzed when the chimpanzees' paintings were first shown in galleries, although these are exactly the kind of elements that are pointed out as admirable in the paintings of some modern artists. And in this connection it is interesting to compare the apes' feeling for form with the fundamental tendencies that Jung found in drawings, presumably motivated in the subconscious, that were made by his adult patients. He lists dual configurations, the opposition of light and dark, of upper and lower, right and left, the square, cross, circle, and finally the centering process. Of these he called the centering process the "never-to-be-surpassed climax." A centering process is one of the strongest tendencies in ape artists.

Different apes have different characteristic preferences in their forms — so distinctive that the scientists, shown an unidentified picture, could tell at a glance which of the apes under his care had produced it. Congo's favorite was a fan shape, on which he made many variations. All of them show his awareness of keeping the fan symmetrical and of centering it on the paper. Some of his most pleasing pictures are of fan shapes with curving bases, with the center portion omitted and filled in with dots or splashes. Once he started a fan too far to one side, and in order to maintain the balance of which he was conscious, he spread one side of the fan far to the left to better fill in the space that would otherwise have been blank.

Other apes, too, have shown this awareness of composition. When they were given a sheet of paper that already had a configuration, such as a square, drawn upon it, they either have filled in the square or surrounded it with their own marks; or, if the square was off-center, they have placed a balancing form of their own on the opposite side.

Up to 1961 twenty-three chimpanzees, three orangutans, two gorillas, and four Capuchin monkeys have made drawings which have been studied by scientists, either casually or intensively. The paintings, the productions in color, have only been recent. The first were finger-paintings, but those have been largely abandoned, in part because the tactile sensation of paint on their hands distracted the animals: they were inclined to suck it or wipe it off. But finger-paintings were the ones that first attracted the unexpected public attention. In the winter of 1957–58 an exhibition of "ape art" was held at the Institute of Contemporary Arts in London. It was a showing of finger-paintings by the chimpanzee Betsy, of the Baltimore Zoo, and by the London Zoo's Congo. A serious study of Congo's artistic development was already under way and the zoo wished to keep his paintings as part of a series. Very high prices therefore were placed on the twenty-four shown in the exhibition, but "to our consternation," says Desmond Morris, nearly all of the paintings sold, as did many of Betsy's. The new fad was on: ape art, profitable to several zoos, had taken the fancy of many collectors.

It was easy to say that the people who bought the paintings were the affluent and fashionable who wanted something new for themselves and their guests to talk about. Some no doubt did buy the paintings because ape art seemed amusing, but such would not be the reason why they were acquired by some very discriminating collectors, by Picasso and the great critic Sir Herbert Read. Understandably some biologists would want them, as Sir Julian Huxley did. But many pictures have been purchased by people for whom the investment required a sacrifice, and the sober fact is that the paintings, and the drawings as well, often are undeniably pleasing. Some, quite simply, are beautiful. They seem to express a striking sense of release, which is communicable. And in all there may be a different kind of satisfaction: it is a moving experience to reach back with one's mind to the mind of a subhuman creature who has worked terribly hard to produce his picture, and in the process, it seems, inadvertently has reached forward to us.

The ape "worked terribly hard"? That he did will surprise many who have assumed that all the monkey and ape artists have painted like the ones who have been exploited on television. No doubt the chimps that appear on TV do have fun. The bright lights, the big machine, the attentive technicians, and all those visitors' faces turned towards *him* dipping his hands into the gooey paints — for a born show-off, as many chimpanzees are, this is *great!* He overacts then, like all exhibitionists.

For other chimpanzees it is great too, in a quieter and more intense way, when his friend, the biologist, takes him out of his cage to the test room and puts him in a chair with a table in front of him and on that table sheet after sheet of smooth white paper on which he can make marks with a pencil or crayon in his hand. The biologist is forgotten, everything is forgotten except that white surface and the picture that he can put on it: *his own kind of picture.* The animals concentrate to a degree that had not been considered possible for them. All the biologists comment upon this characteristic. Bella, a chimpanzee in the Netherlands, had "a strikingly high level of motivation." She worked "at full intensity" and with "an unheard-of degree of perseverance for Bella." Other chimpanzees have shown unmistakably that drawing, as a spontaneous activity, has tremendous importance for them — "as significant to them as the graphic response is to us." The animals are angry if they are stopped; and if a picture is taken away from them while they are working on it, usually they go into the wildest tantrums.

They seem to have some deep recognition of what the picture, in their terms, should be. If a drawing was removed from Congo's board while he was working on it and later was returned to him, Congo took up the design at the point where he had been interrupted. It is clear also that the apes have a distinct sense of the stage when a drawing or painting is finished. On the rare occasions when attempts were made to encourage Congo to continue working on a picture that he considered "finished," rather than on a new one, he lost his temper, whimpered, screamed, or, if persuaded to go on, proceeded to wreck the picture with "meaningless or obliterative lines."

How large a part have their trainers played in starting their art activities? No part at all, other than placing a pencil in the animal's hand and putting it down on a piece of paper. As soon as the ape discovered that pencils make marks, his impulse to draw was born. Some of them closed all their fingers around the pencil, as they would hold a stick, but others, especially if they continued long enough, learned for themselves the position we all use in handling a pencil, with the forefinger curled around it. After that they were likely to draw with a motion only of fingers.

Apes who had seen another animal drawing, or even a human writing, did not need to be shown anything. Like Alpha, a female chimpanzee who used to beg the attendants for their pencils and notebooks, they knew at once what a pencil would do. And yet to an ape a pencil and paint-brush are, of course, artificial implements, and some of these animals have made pictures, from their own spontaneous impulse, in other ways. Gua, the Kelloggs' ape, used to draw with the tip of her finger or fingernail in mist that her breath deposited on the windowpane. Sir Julian Huxley, when he was director of the London Zoo, three times saw Meng, a young gorilla, trace with his forefinger the outline of his shadow on the wall. It seems fascinating to think of this new thing, this sensation in a hand, even in a forefinger, coming into evolving minds. It is not in the forepaw of even the smartest dog.

The most interesting animal that started to draw without any prompting was a Capuchin monkey. The monkeys ordinarily are considered well below the great apes in intelligence. P-Y, the Capuchin artist, could solve mechanical problems that are beyond the capacity of most chimpanzees; she is conceded to have been rare, however, and has been called a subhuman genius. It has been observed many times that such outstanding animals do exist, and not only among the primates.

P-Y was born in Peru and was purchased from an Indian by an oil-company geologist "because of her pleasant personality." When she was about eight years old she found her way into the hands of Heinrich Klüver, an eminent psychologist at the Institute for Juvenile Research in Chicago. She was called P-Y for Princeton-Yale, though R-W for Radcliffe-Wellesley, or S-V, or B-B.M. might have been more appropriate, for she was unusually small and delicate and apparently very feminine. By now she is a famous monkey not only because of the astonishing intelligence she displayed, and her spontaneous impulse to create drawings, but because her brain was analyzed after her death in 1938, and it was found to have a very high ratio of weight to her body weight, and to have had "an especially high degree of specialization in the operculum of the insula, where human 'speech centers' seemed already discernible." This discovery might not have been surprising, because P-Y was extraordinarily vocal. She even "talked" to the numerous kinds of implements that were supplied for her tests.

In the rather large laboratory where the tests were made, she was restricted by an iron chain fastened to an iron post. A piece of banana would be put on the floor or hung over her head, always out of her reach, and various kinds of objects were left in her orbit with which she could pull the food to her if she could figure out how to do it.

Some of the implements were the standard sort: a T-stick, wire, rope, etc. Many less conventional objects were given her also, such as a sack, leather belt, floor brush, newspaper, and pieces of cardboard. P-Y used all these things successfully to whip food within reach. One of the most unusual "objects" was an albino rat, tied to a heavy box with a string long enough to allow the rat to run past the banana. The rat apparently was not interested in it himself, but P-Y threw him again and again towards the food until in this way she finally pulled in the food. She was also extremely smart in solving her problem when it required the use of more than one tool or both of her hands. In all, she was tried in 207 tests. Tested again after three years had passed, P-Y remembered all the solutions to the problems that she had worked out before.

She died when only eleven years old, half the normal age span of a Capuchin monkey; and was she so sensitive that she wore herself out? The intensity with which she applied herself to the problems put to her was remarkable. When one was exceptionally difficult, she would strive for an hour or more to solve it and usually would stop only because she was exhausted. Sometimes, however, she was so intrigued by the implements given her that, ignoring the food, she would handle the objects, examine them, carefully dismantle them, or, turning them into toys, would play with them at great length and very inventively. Of all the evidence of intelligence she displayed, however, nothing is more significant than the fact that, of her own wish and initiative, she drew pictures.

In the beginning she drew on the concrete floor of the laboratory, using a wire, nail, or stick. The pictures were not random scribblings here, there, or anywhere. P-Y would make a set of lines, which obviously had a relationship to one another, and when she had completed them, she would move to a different part of the room and make a new set of marks. She worked at these as though she knew what she wanted, and as if she knew when a given picture had reached that point and was finished.

The kinds of drawings she made were, from the beginning, not the most elemental that are ever attempted by animals. Usually they were combinations of more or less parallel lines, horizontal or perpendicular, either curved or straight. Often, then, she would cross these with other lines; and she would make S's. Later when she was given chalk, she drew on the floor with that. With colored chalk she filled a center space solidly red and surrounded it with separate forms of green, blue, and yellow—a very advanced type of form for a pre-human primate. Later still she made drawings with crayon and pencil on paper. In all cases she drew "with her whole body," swaying from head to foot to follow the line of her hand—an example of true action painting.

She was apt to draw when she felt frustrated because one of the mechanical tests was too hard for her, but she drew at other times also, on days when no tests were given her. How much drawing meant to her was proved by the emotion that her sketches aroused in her when she saw them again after an interval. If she was brought into the laboratory before the pictures on the floor had been scrubbed away, she would drop down before each one and touch it, lick it, and apparently try to smell it. Nothing else in the laboratory affected her in the same way, but nothing else was hers in the sense that the drawings were. *She had made those pictures.*

No other monkeys except Capuchins have shown any impulse to draw. Three besides P-Y have done very well: Claro, a male, and Cobra, a female, studied recently by Mme. Kohts in Russia (fifty years after her first work with the chimpanzee Joni); and Pablo, belonging to Professor Bernhard Rensch in Germany. A drawing by Cobra is an abstract design so full of grace and light that a human artist could well be proud of it.

The hundred years during which the evolution of man has been known and studied have been a time when tools, mechanisms, have been a paramount human interest. Since the scientists have been men of their time, it is not surprising that the advance of animal life towards human life has been defined, almost always, as a growing proficiency in the use of tools. In the laboratories an animal's skill in mastering problems with locks, mazes, and gadgets has been the accepted measurement of intelligence. An example, admittedly rather far out, has been the attempt to teach pigeons to type.

Even during these years it has been acknowledged — without being taken much into account — that man's great advances have come through a different quality: his perception, his insight. Early men learned to gather the seeds of wild grasses and plant them: a process in which tools such as plows were a help, but the idea of crop-cultivation was not born of using a tool. Men assembled wild animals into herds that they could control. Tools had little to do with that development. No longer needing to wander in search of food, people could settle into communities. Tools helped them to build their houses there, but the real achievement was social, the restrictions accepted in forming governments. If the concept of evolution had come to birth at any time except the industrial age, animals probably would have been studied for other abilities than the mechanical, and other aspects of animal intelligence would have been emphasized in charting the evolution of minds.

Now, well after the middle of the twentieth century, many thinkers are becoming disenchanted with tools and gadgets. Many are not; computers and spacecraft still seem fascinating beyond the importance of what they can do, and yet an impression is growing that in the end mechanisms are boring, no more than useful means for accomplishing goals which are more significant. This being true, it is natural that, just at this time, there is a small start towards studying animals for those qualities which eventually evolved into rational thought and aesthetic creativity.

Tests with Capuchin monkeys will illustrate the difference. Though the little genius, P-Y, handled her implements well, some other Capuchins have made a very poor showing with them. When, however, W. E. Galt tried Capuchins, rhesus monkeys, and a gibbon with a problem which required that they match cards marked with black and white dots, the Capuchins surpassed all the others. Whereas the rhesus monkeys and gibbon made their selections impulsively, the Capuchins "frequently turned their heads, looking at one card and then the other," and the investigator believed that this comparison tended to improve the accuracy of their choices. Experiments such as these give us some intimation of the origins of true thoughtfulness. And there have been others. Some of the most illuminating have shown the animals' reactions to abstract forms.

Many species are keenly aware of forms — patterns, that is — which resemble the ones in nature that are important to their survival. Baby birds will call to a small round sphere placed at the edge of a larger sphere: to the nestlings the circles apparently represent a parent's head on a body. And young chicks are extremely agitated by a crude paper model that looks like a bird of prey. What is much more surprising is the fact, recently learned, that some birds and animals have an awareness and even aesthetic feeling for abstract designs which have no counterpart in the wild.

The ability to distinguish between stylized patterns such as circles, triangles, and squares has been proved for wasps, turtles, fishes, and a variety of the higher animals. And, incidentally, it has been found that most of them have the same reaction that we do to optical illusions, those pairs of two equal figures, for instance, in which one seems to be larger because of the way it is placed in relation to the other, or because of surrounding lines. The animals also are fooled by these.

In such tests the subjects have learned to discriminate between patterns because they were rewarded with food for making their choices. But Eleanor J. Gibson and her associates have found that rats form a lasting impression of designs on the walls of their cages when no effort has ever been made to direct the rats' attention to them. After the rats had thus been exposed to black cut-outs of circles and triangles, they were much more quick to identify those designs in tests, rather than others.

Surprises continue. Professor Bernhard Rensch has discovered that some animals have their preferences between abstract designs, and that they choose the ones that are better organized, the ones, that is, which have balance or symmetry, or are smooth or parallel. That a bird, for example, would have any interest in such designs seems remarkable; that he would choose the more orderly one, in test after test, is astonishing.

Rensch prepared various pairs of cards, each pair consisting of one card with a well-organized pattern on it, the other with the same black and white elements but arranged in a jumble. The balanced forms included three bars in a sequence matched with a card that showed three bent, irregular bars; a card on which there were several small squares inside one another, shown at the same time with a card scribbled aimlessly; a circle on which equal triangles radiated from the center of a circle had as its opposite a circle with the triangles scattered hit or miss; and a circle with a smooth outline was presented with a rough circle whose outline was wavy. There were four other similar pairs.

Pablo, the Capuchin, selected the organized pattern in all of eight choices. An African guenon monkey (a species believed more primitive) made the aesthetic choice in five out of eight. But a crow picked up the orderly one six times out of eight, and so did a jackdaw. Except in one instance all the "misses" were not a preference for the untidy designs; they were simply a failure to show any preference at all. The tests, incidentally, were performed more than 300 times before Professor Rensch considered that they were reliable.

Fishes preferred the irregular patterns. The reason might be that the currents of water in which they live break up many outlines of shapes in their world.

In trying to understand why a crow is attracted by straight lines rather than bent ones, and a perfectly round rather than an irregular circle, it is almost impossible not to assume an aesthetic tendency in the bird. Before drawing further conclusions, however, let us see what other hints there may be that animals have artistic sensibilities.

A fair number of birds and animals have forms of "artistic" expression which obviously are intended to dazzle the opposite sex. Can it be assumed that there is no aesthetic content in these? Insofar as they are related to the reproductive instinct they are not playful in the sense that true play is release from instinctual pressures; but it seems sometimes that some songs and dances are on a borderline. They are meant to attract, and yet they appear also to be enjoyed by the performer for himself alone.

Ornithologists have a kind of grab-bag labeled "Display" into which they put a variety of birds' activities. A bird displays — literally — when he struts or turns or in other ways calls attention to his spectacular adornments. A peacock is displaying when it raises and fans out its marvelous tail. A male grouse displays by inflating the usually hidden bright yellow air sacs on its neck which then become circled with conspicuous feather borders; and at the same time the tail is lifted and spread. There are special movements which the bird makes at that time, also attention-getting. I have had a Sierra grouse display to me, whom he evidently considered a friend, and the effect is indeed impressive — so startling that I imagine it might well throw a hen grouse off guard.

The bowerbirds of Australia and near-by islands are birds in which a few species have beautiful feather structures but most of the males are quite drab. As is well known, they build trysting bowers to which they hope to lure the females; and it has been noted that the least handsome males construct the most elaborate bowers. Ornithologists have therefore taken to calling the bowers a substitute form of display: lacking gorgeous crests, which the males may once have had, they collect as much gorgeousness as they can in the form of flowers, shells, pebbles, silvery leaves, and such, to flash before the eyes of desired mates.

The comment seems reasonable; and yet there is more to be said. For the bowers are not only conspicuous: many are trimmed with what unquestionably seems aesthetic taste. Can we therefore rule out the thought that the decoration of these meeting places gives the male bird no personal pleasure?

Eggs are not laid in the bowers, which are strictly settings for love-making. They are of several kinds. "Avenue bowers" are like tunnels: into a mat of plant fibers patiently laid down on the ground, the male inserts many grasses and twigs, in such a way that they quite or nearly bend over and form an enclosure. It is a remarkable fact that such bowers almost always are placed in a north-south direction, the purpose being, it is thought, that the bower will be filled with sunlight during all the daytime hours.

And then there are "tepee bowers," built up around the trunk of a sapling to a height of three feet or more; and also some roofed structures which look like miniature cottages. A great deal of work goes into making all types of the bowers. Sometimes their construction takes four or five months.

Some are covered with growing orchids; in other cases they are decorated with flowers stuck into the walls. And always there is a "display area" around the entrance which is strewn with any objects that have appealed to the owner. It is in the arrangement of these that the pre-aesthetic quality of the whole is most evident. For however bright and therefore conspicuous the objects may be, there is a definite attempt to select colors and to space out the objects in certain ways. In some cases small piles of flowers are deposited here and there on the display arena. One ornithologist experimented with the preferences of a brown-gardener bowerbird. S. Dillon Ripley, in *Trail of the Money Bird*, tells how he placed some flowers of different colors on the bird's display area. The bird threw out all but one, a red orchid. What to do with that? The bird, orchid in his mouth, hopped this way and that until "with many darts and flourishes" he placed it on top of an assortment of pink flowers. "The best matching job that could be done," commented Ripley. Some species have a penchant for certain colors; when it can, one blue-eyed bird chooses only blue objects.

A few of the birds paint their bowers. They make a paste by chewing up strong-colored substances such as berries or charcoal, and one, the satin bowerbird, makes actual paint-brushes by stripping off fibers from the inner bark of trees and then dips these fibers in "paints," especially the juice of berries. The use of the fiber brushes is one of the most notable uses of a tool by an animal. It has often been said that birds and animals may occasionally use natural objects as tools but that tools themselves never are made. The bowerbird's brush contradicts that comment. (Another instance, recently reported by the English biologist Jane Goodall, is the making of drinking cups by chimpanzees who fold leaves into cone shapes.)

Some bowerbirds lay freshly cut leaves over their display spaces, turning the leaves upside-down so their silvery sides are uppermost. That this habit is not accidental was proved by an ornithologist who turned all the leaves over: the bird soon reversed them so that the silvery sides were upward again. Such leaves, and also the cut flowers that decorate bowers, are replaced as soon as they wither, usually as often as once every day.

Finally, after all the preparation, the time comes when the females start wandering through the forest. They seem to inspect the bowers, and when one has been selected, the female enters the little enclosure and the male's work is rewarded. The female does not remain there to lay her eggs. In a nest that she may build as high as forty feet up in a tree, she raises her family without help from the male. But when the young birds are fledged, often she takes them back to their father's bower, and there the whole family goes through a kind of ritual display to one another.

All during the time of the egg-laying and early care of the young, the male has continued to maintain and beautify his home. For weeks the new flowers are gathered each day, or the pattern of new leaves is laid down on the ground. Yet the courtship is over — and what motivates all this work unless it is the male's enjoyment? There is nothing sure about the female's return with the family. Sometimes she does not come back.

The songs of birds are in some ways analogous. Many ornithologists have noted that songs are performed, with what seems attempts at skill, long after the sexual phase of the birds' life is over. On this subject Thorpe has listed the opinions of several scientists: of E. P. Bicknell, who considers that the late summer and autumn songs of many American birds are superior to those of the breeding season; of R. Noble, who has discovered that the skylark sings its longest songs in September and October; of A. A. Saunders, who has called attention to the elaboration and sometimes complete change in the song of American birds after the nesting season; and of V. Haecker who has found the same thing to be true in the autumn and winter singing of Central European songbirds. H. Boker, examining the testes of birds that sing in autumn and winter, found no high level of sex hormone production to suggest a reproductive motivation for the late singing.

Wallace Craig, one of the most respected students of bird song, quotes the general opinion that the twilight song of the eastern wood pewee is neither a territorial nor a mating song. He describes its "great length and continuity, its complex and highly musical structure, its superiority to the daytime singing . . ." And to explain these qualities he says that psychological factors undoubtedly have to be recognized.

That all birds do not always sing to further their mating activities seems to be proved finally and conclusively by the songs of the various species that imitate other birds. It would not serve any romantic end for a mockingbird to sing the wistful torch song of a mourning dove.

A surprising number of mammals sing. Sometimes enough chipmunks and squirrels, including flying squirrels, learn to do it so that they sing together in what could be called a chorus. I once had a singing mouse that was inspired to sing by hearing radio music. The little voice would continue for some time after the electronic music stopped, a song very fluent and more bell-like than a canary's. During the last century there was a spate of articles in nature journals by people who were reporting the singing of mice. One by W. O. Hickey in the *American Naturalist* described a mouse which, having filled an overshoe in a closet with popcorn, would sit among his corn and "sing his beautiful solo" for ten minutes at a time. "His song was not a chirp but a continuous song of musical tone, a kind of to-wit-to-wee-woo-woo-wee-woo, quite varied in pitch." (People who can find human syllables for animal sounds fill me with awe.) Mr. Hickey thought his singer was "the prairie mouse, *Hesperomys michiganensis*," but apparently mice of any species may sing.

Anyone who has heard a chorus of wolves, gathered on some moonlight night to sing from the top of a tundra knoll (not a love call, since this is group singing), will be haunted for life by the thrilling wild harmonies. When my part-wolf Husky, Bobo, sang, he seemed plainly to try for a certain effect, particularly for one high, clear, ringing note almost on perfect pitch. His most familiar song rose by a quick succession of notes to that climax and then slid away in a series of undulating falls, and if he could not reach the high note the first time, he made the attempt again and again before he finished the song. Earlier, in 1947, I had made an experiment with a Norwegian elkhound that belonged to the naturalist-brothers, Olaus and Adolph Murie. Being alone with the dog on their ranch one day, I played on the piano a dozen or more selections of varying mood to see if the dog would respond to them. The dog, Chimo, wailed with seemingly deep distress during Tschaikovsky's "None but the Lonely Heart"; he frisked around during a Spanish dance, and during some short selections by Mozart and Bach he lay down near the piano but with his head up alertly and his ears turned towards the sound. One sometimes hears people say that dogs howl when they listen to human music because the sounds hurt their ears. Perhaps their howling seems to them like reciprocal singing — or maybe they simply dislike the selections.

The perception of differences in tone would surely have to precede any musical expression on the part of an animal. Much fascinating work is now being done on this question. Most amazing to me was the information that some minnows can learn to discriminate between halftones. And the tiny fighting fish (*Betta splendens*) has been trained to distinguish rhythmical beats of three and five seconds.

Wolfgang Köhler, who studied chimpanzees for four years at Tenerife, describes in his book *The Mentality of Apes,* a biological classic, the very origin of an impulse to dance. One ape stamps her feet alternately, pretending that she is angry; another stamps back at her but then starts *springing* from one foot to the other; and next begins turning, pirouetting as she alternates her steps. A further stage is to spin around with both arms extended horizontally, and finally to progress over the ground as she spins. The rhythmic motions become contagious: the first ape is now also spinning around the play area.

Or two apes will be wrestling and tumbling about near a post. Again that inchoate impulse: they will circle the post. They will circle it with a marching rhythm. Others join them. The dance (what Köhler calls a motion-pattern) becomes more involved and the march encircles *two* posts, with the emphasis in the steps becoming stronger and stronger.

In all this interesting description, however, the most significant detail seems to be an additional comment: that when the female ape Tschego is marching in a circle with the others, she begins of her own accord to elaborate the rhythm. In other cases, says Köhler, rhythm becomes of secondary importance and she concentrates on the form of the movements that she is making.

The dances of many birds are often mutual performances; the female as well as the male joins in. It is true that they usually are part of the mating ritual — in contrast to the dances of the chimpanzees, which seem rather to be a kind of creative play. Is it impossible, then, that the birds also enjoy them in some pre-aesthetic sense? Human love songs and sonnets have sometimes been composed "with a reproductive motivation," but it certainly cannot be said that the composers and poets were therefore deprived of the pleasure of expressing their emotions beautifully.

Caution is necessary, for we don't want to fall back into the Victorian habit of attributing exclusively human mental processes to creatures other than human. It does appear, however, that some animal minds are progressing along paths that are familiar to us because we have trod them ourselves in the long past; and if one of the stages they reach on that journey is a beginning of creativity, we should be willing to recognize that our species may not be the only one ever to come to that point.

This much is unquestioned: that the animal activities we now, tentatively, call aesthetic give them satisfaction, and that they engage in them exactly as if they were play. Insofar as they extend beyond routine and ritual behavior, they *are* play. The animal artists are groping for something that is not known until it is found, a process which is the very essence of play — and of human creativity: the writer reaching, but not straining, for the idea that he will know is right when it reveals itself; the painter whose hand often seems to guide his mind; the composer who hears his song at a moment when he is not even thinking of music; and the great experimenters who work in pure science — all these have at times described what they do as play. They do not mean that the work takes no effort, but that the search seems to furnish its own energy, and the final result is *discovered*, not captured, or won, or built if it is of the best quality.

The animals painting, singing, and dancing show some signs at times of being moved by a similar, spontaneous impulse. It is true that the art they produce is simple and limited, but so too are the drawings, songs, and dances of very young children, and yet we recognize that a creative urge prompts them. What is added by the adult human artist is self-discipline, the acceptance of drudgery in order to polish, correct, and perfect.

The animal artists obviously enjoy what they are doing, but more significant, so it seems, is the evidence of their innate sense of order. The apes working for balance in the compositions they draw, the crow preferring organized patterns, the birds and mammals that make repeated attempts to achieve a clear tone are not what we might expect when we watch the casualness of the animals' ordinary behavior — and yet there they are, these hints of an impulse to express some faint sense of organization and harmony. The effort is not long sustained but the impulse is there. The philosopher Suzanne K. Langer speaks of "this unconscious appreciation of form" as being "the primitive root of all abstractions, the keynote of rationality, which lies deep in our pure animal experience."

There can't be much mystery about where an unconscious appreciation of form originates. The animals are surrounded by symmetry in their own bodies and those of their fellows; by balance in almost all plant life; by the rhythm of speeding wings, feet, and fins, and the larger rhythms of days and seasons. They are exposed every moment to proofs of an ordered universe. The touching thing is that so many animals of the higher orders are moved to try to express their innate, though unreasoned, experiencing of nature's laws.

Night falls and winter comes for us as it does in the wilderness. Nature's pulses, however, don't reach us with very much impact — we have insulated ourselves too well. And yet we, too, know some regularity in our lives, much of it of our own making. We know the good regularity of schedules in schools and offices, of public transportation, of many services, and the provision of supplies that mean civilized comfort and elegance. Even today personal living occasionally has the form of a work of art. But we also create, deliberately it sometimes appears, a degree of irregularity that nature never would tolerate. We take risks that result in sudden and shocking tragedies; we endure situations that cause the unstable to turn to violence; international tensions that could be talked away are allowed to deteriorate into wars. In general, because of indifference, fatigue, or perplexity, we permit the shrillness of regularly recurring emergencies. We have accepted senselessness as a kind of mad norm. Animals could not stand such disorder; nor in fact can we. Insanity is a human development. So far as we know, animals in the wild do not have mental illness; except for brain injuries and infections, all are sane.

Dr. Thorpe writes of "activities which, though originating in 'play,' have produced real advances in knowledge and comprehension of the scheme of things, and which may, for all we know, offer vistas of advance in the millennia to come, compared to which our present understanding will seem exceedingly puny and childish." For many of us, however, the vistas of brighter millennia are confused and dim. Looking out on our urban scenes, we often believe that life is absurd, which is to say without a chance of achieving coherence.

Can one reason for our discouragement be that we have divorced ourselves from the patterns and rhythms and the renewals of the natural world? It may be that it is not enough to know nature's laws — as we do fairly well now — in terms of physics and chemistry. Perhaps the individual's inner security has to stem from knowledge he gains with his own, concrete senses. To be reassured by the order in nature we may have to stand, literally, with our feet on actual soil (that element where death and life are so exquisitely balanced). Possibly it is necessary to measure the growth of some trees on successive years by their lengthening shadows; to feel in oneself, deeply, the changes of mood that are paced by the seasons; and to watch, for more than five minutes at a time, the fabric of stars drawn smoothly across the sky.

To know — in the same way that we know the touch of chromium handles, the sight of glass walls, the smell of polluted air, and the taste of anchovies — to know in as intimate ways as these the proofs of nature's enduring program might give us back our lost sense of meaning.

The stars are not absurd.

DEFINITIONS

REFERENCES

Definitions

Action Pattern, or Behavior Pattern. The traditional series of steps by which an instinct achieves its objective. An action pattern is as typical of a particular species as the structure of the bird or animal itself. Sometimes species are even identified by their action patterns.

Agonistic Behavior. A more familiar term is Antagonistic.

Allelomimetic Activity. Behavior performed by a group of birds or animals acting in almost identical fashion without obvious communication between them. Wheeling flocks of birds are an example. There is no proven explanation of the means by which they co-ordinate their movements.

Appetitive Behavior. The restless, often vague, searching of an animal with an instinctive urge and as yet no external stimulus to trigger direct action.

Block. The term used for the internal element which restrains an instinct until it may suitably be released by some stimulus (internal, such as hunger; or external, such as parasites in the fur). Without such blocks all the instincts might try to express themselves at the same time, with resulting chaos.

Commensalism. A relationship of mutual benefit between differing species.

Consummatory Act. The final stage by which each of the instincts fulfills its drive. It is the least variable act in the behavior pattern.

Directive Behavior. Behavior so developed by evolution that it favors the survival and reproduction of the individual animal. The definition does not include any intimation of conscious purpose.

Displacement. When the fulfillment of an instinctual urge is frustrated – either by external circumstances or by a competing instinct – an animal may make substitute motions, often irrelevant and futile, which are called Displacement Activity. Sometimes (less frequently now) this substitution has been described as Sparking Over. In human beings many restless "nervous habits" are displacement activity. Or sleep may be: the drowsiness that overwhelms some people when facing unpleasant tasks.

Drive. A useful term when used to mean a general state of tension impelling an animal to some kind of action. For a number of years Drive was used instead of Instinct, but it has had to be abandoned in that sense because it did not clearly set off the basic urge from the action pattern. For a while there were comfort drives, social drives, escape drives, fleeing drives, sex drives, mating drives, nest-building drives, and many others – drives in such numbers that all sensible meaning was lost.

Epimeletic Behavior. "Care-giving": either to a young animal or to a distressed individual of any age; by parents or by others.

Ethology. The study of animals' normal behavior, whenever possible in their natural environment with natural social relationships. Strict new techniques have been devised with the purpose of eliminating an ethologist's subjective impressions; and field observations are later confirmed, if they can be, by laboratory experiments. Through such careful methods the knowledge and understanding of animal behavior has advanced enormously during the last fifteen years.

Hierarchy. (1) *Behavior*. A social order in which rank is established by combat, threat, or other domineering approach. "Peck order." (2) *Anatomy*. A series of related animal – or insect – functions with rising levels of complexity. In mammals, the various elements of the nervous system, grading from the simplest sensory neuron through the spinal cord to the most elaborate centers of the brain, are called a hierarchy, although it may be that these stages are not literal structures but modes of operating.

Imprinting. The mechanism by which many birds and animals identify with an individual they see shortly after birth. Since this is usually the mother, the young creature thus gains the sense of belonging to its own species; but in artificial circumstances animals can be "imprinted" by human caretakers or even by inanimate objects. The period in which imprinting is accomplished is short — a few days in chicks, a few weeks in some mammals. The effects are believed to be irreversible in most cases.

Innate Releasing Mechanism (IRM). The internal "device" (little understood) by which the Block is removed and an instinct is allowed to go into action.

Instinct. An inborn, that is, innate, impulse to seek a particular satisfaction. Some specialists in animal behavior now limit the Instinctive urges to five. To be classified as instinctive, an urge must arise without external stimulation, and it must create stress, or "misery," in the animal until it is expressed in action.

Learned Behavior, or Acquired Behavior. Such activity is absorbed from the example of parents or is learned through experience; it is not inborn. Some birds, as an instance, only sing what they have heard around them, even though the songs may be those of totally different species. Such singing is learned behavior. Other birds are born with the songs of their own species already formed in their Action Patterns, and they will sing these typical songs even if they are reared in isolated, sound-proof rooms.

Morphology. The form and structure of an animal or plant, or of its parts. Also the study of these.

Niche. A bird's or animal's total environmental situation, including habitat, and social and nutritional opportunities.

Prostasia. A social order maintained by domineering aggressiveness. The cause is usually an artificial environment (captivity) and/or overcrowding. Most free-ranging animals prefer independence or voluntary attachment to a wise leader.

Purposive Behavior. Behavior in which perception, memory, and finally anticipation may cause an animal's activity to take one course rather than another. To what extent this is possible, and in what species, is one of the most stimulating questions now being investigated by biologists.

Reproductively Isolated. Said of species that do not interbreed. If they nevertheless are nearly identical morphologically, these are called Sibling Species.

Social Releaser. An action or a physical quality that causes a response in another member of the same species. Examples would be the bugling challenge of a bull elk, or the begging posture of a young bird wanting food from its parent.

Species. A division of animals that do not interbreed, the reluctance believed due to differences in body odor, structure, voice, courtship rituals, or other less obvious factors. Formerly, but no longer, species were always assorted according to structure and/or color. Subspecies, and the similar classification of Races, are groups that vary in observable ways but do interbreed and produce fertile hybrids.

Spontaneous Behavior. Innate; independent of exterior stimulation.

Stimulus. Some new development, internal or external, which activates the behavior pattern of an instinct. When it is external and incites the animal's consummatory act, it is called a Sign Stimulus.

Supernormal Stimulus. One which surpasses the normal potency usually needed to arouse an instinct. A birdhouse, which some species prefer to trees or bushes, is a supernormal stimulus.

Vacuum Activity. Behavior which seems to be part of an instinctive action pattern but actually is irrelevant at the time. It is vacuum activity when an owl, fed to satiation, yet pounces on a mouse.

References

THE REFERENCES below are in two separate lists: (1) sources chiefly scientific, and (2) those of more general interest. The division is not absolute. Some of the scientific sources would be interesting to almost anyone, and the general references contain material that any scientist might find useful.

To a large extent the more recent a source is, the more reliable are its facts. There are good reasons, however, for including some of the older reports. Many are still entirely dependable; for example, C. R. Carpenter's study of gibbons never has been, and probably never will be, superseded. In some cases, too, it is worthwhile to know about earlier work that has provided the data for later discoveries, such as the statistics about embryonic pathology gathered by G. W. Corner, who could not explain the reason for the birth accidents he had found — that analysis had to wait for R. J. Blandau with his exquisitely fine techniques. And some biologists like Ernest Thompson Seton have been listed because they wrote at a time when a scientist's style permitted his personal interest in his animal subjects to show, and it is still a delight to read the observations of one who did not find it necessary to restrain human warmth in order to be authentic. Nevertheless, the mass of biological knowledge is constantly being revised, and the older sources should be checked against later references. For summaries of what is now most widely accepted, no books are more to be trusted than Nikolaas Tinbergen's The Study of Instinct and W. H. Thorpe's Instinct and Learning in Animals.

The guide books included in the general list are those that I personally have found helpful when observing birds and animals in their natural surroundings. Some other field guides are equally good, and any biological library will furnish information about them.

SCIENTIFIC SOURCES

Alderstein, A., and Elizabeth Fehrer
1955. "The Effect of Food Deprivation on Exploratory Behavior in a Complex Maze," *Jour. Comp. Physiol. Psychol.*, Vol. 48, pp. 250–253.
Allee, W. C.
1936. "Analytical Studies of Group Behavior in Birds," *Wilson Bull.*, Vol. 48, pp. 143–151.
1938. *The Social Life of Animals.* New York: Norton.
1950–1952. "Dominance and Hierarchy in Societies of Vertebrates," in *Colloques Internationaux du Centre National de la Recherché Scientifique XXXIV, Structure et Physiologie des Sociétés Animals* (Pierre P. Grasse, Ed.). Pp. 151–181.
Allee, W. C., A. A. Emerson, O. Park, T. Park, and K. P. Schmidt
1949. *Principles of Animal Ecology.* Philadelphia: Saunders.
Andersson, C. J.
1873. *The Lion and the Elephant.* London: Hurst & Blackett.
Armstrong, E. A.
1947. *Bird Display and Behavior.* New York: Oxford University Press.
1950. "The Nature and Function of Displacement Activities," *Symp. Soc. Exp. Biol.*, Vol. 4, pp. 361–387.
1951. "The Nature and Function of Animal Mimesis," *Bull. Anim. Behav.*, No. 9, pp. 46–58.
Asdell, S. A.
1934. "The Reproduction of Farm Animals," *Cornell Extension Bull.* No. 305. Ithaca, N.Y. Pp. 3–27.
1946. *Patterns of Mammalian Reproduction.* Ithaca, N.Y.: Comstock.
Austin, C. R.
1961. *The Mammalian Egg.* Springfield, Ill.: Thomas.
Baerends, G. P.
1950. "Specializations in Organs and Movements with a Releasing Function," *Symp. Soc. Exp. Biol.*, Vol. 4, pp. 337–360.
1955. "Egg Recognition in the Herring Gull," *Proc. 14th Int. Congr. Psychol.*, Montreal. Pp. 93–94.
Banham, Katharine M.
1950. "The Development of Affectionate Behavior in Infancy," *Jour. Genet. Psychol.*, Vol. 76, pp. 283–289.
Barnett, S. A.
1958. "Exploratory Behaviour," *Brit. Jour. Psychol.*, Vol. 49, pp. 289–310.

Beach, F. A.
1945. "Current Concepts of Play in Animals," *Amer. Naturalist*, Vol. 79, pp. 523–541.
1948. *Hormones and Behavior*. New York: Paul Hoeber.
Beach, F. A., and Julian Jaynes
1954. "Effects of Early Experience upon the Behavior of Animals," *Psychol. Bull.*, Vol. 51, pp. 239–263.
Bela, Bodnar
1934. "Le Spalax de Hongrie (*Spalax hungaricus*)," *Terre et Vie*, Vol. 4, pp. 423–433.
Benedict, F. G.
1936. *The Physiology of the Elephant*. Washington: Carnegie Institution of Washington.
Berlyne, D. E.
1950. "Novelty and Curiosity as Determinants of Exploratory Behaviour," *Brit. Jour. Psychol.*, Vol. 41, pp. 68–80.
1955. "The Arousal and Satiation of Perceptual Curiosity in the Rat," *Jour. Comp. Physiol. Psychol.*, Vol. 48, pp. 238–246.
Berlyne, D. E., and J. Slater
1957. "Perceptual Curiosity, Exploratory Behavior and Maze Learning," *Jour. Comp. Physiol. Psychol.*, Vol. 50, pp. 228–232.
Blandau, R. J.
1954. "The Effects on Development When Eggs and Sperm Are Aged before Fertilization," in *Ann. New York Acad. of Sciences*, Vol. 57, pp. 526 ff.
Blandau, R. J., and W. C. Young
1939. "The Effects of Delayed Fertilization on the Development of the Guinea Pig Ovum," *Amer. Jour. Anat.*, Vol. 64, pp. 303–329.
Blatz, W. C., E. Millichamp, and M. Charles
1937. "The Early Social Development of the Dionne Quintuplets," in *Collected Studies on the Dionne Quintuplets*. Toronto: University of Toronto Press.
Bonin, Gerhardt von
1938. "The Cerebral Cortex of the Cebus Monkey," *Jour. Comp. Neur.*, Vol. 69, No. 2.
Bowlby, J.
1952. "Critical Phases in the Development of Social Responses in Man and Other Animals," in *Prospects in Psychiatric Research* (J. M. Tanner, Ed.). Oxford: Clarendon Press.
1958. "The Nature of the Child's Tie to His Mother," *Int. Jour. Psychoanalysis*, Vol. 39, pp. 1–24.
Brown, F. A., Jr., M. F. Bennett, H. M. Webb, and C. L. Ralph
1956. "Persistent Daily, Monthly and 27-Day Cycles of Activity in the Oyster and the Quahog," *Jour. Exp. Zool.*, Vol. 131, pp. 235–262.

Butler, R. A.
   1957. "The Effect of Deprivation of Visual Incentives on Visual Exploration Motivation in Monkeys," *Jour. Comp. Physiol. Psychol.*, Vol. 50, pp. 177–179.
Butler, R. A., and H. M. Alexander
   1955. "Daily Patterns of Visual Exploratory Behavior in the Monkey," *Jour. Comp. Physiol. Psychol.*, Vol. 45, pp. 247–249.
Calhoun, John B.
   1963. *The Ecology and Sociology of the Norway Rat.* U.S. Dept. of Health, Education and Welfare.
Cannon, W. B.
   1929. *Bodily Changes in Pain, Hunger, Fear and Rage.* Boston: Branford.
Carpenter, C. R.
   1934. "A Field Study of the Behavior and Social Relations of Howling Monkeys (*Allouata palliata*)," *Comp. Psychol. Mono.*, Vol. 10, No. 2, Serial No. 48.
   1940. "A Field Study in Siam of the Behavior and Social Relations of the Gibbon (*Hylobates lar*)," *Comp. Psychol. Mono.*, Vol. 16, No. 5, Serial No. 84.
   1942. "Sexual Behavior of Free-Ranging Rhesus Monkeys (*Macaca mulatta*)," *Jour. Comp. Psychol.*, Vol. 23, pp. 113–162.
   1942. "Societies of Monkeys and Apes," *Biol. Symposia*, Vol. 8, pp. 177–204.
Chapman, R. M., and Nissim Levy
   1957. "Hunger Drive and Reinforcing Effect of Novel Stimuli," *Jour. Comp. Physiol. Psychol.*, Vol. 50, pp. 233–238.
Christian, J. J.
   1956. "Adrenal and Reproductive Responses to Population Size in Mice," *Ecology*, Vol. 37, pp. 258–273.
Church, R. M.
   1959. "Emotional Reactions of Rats to the Pain of Others," *Jour. Comp. Physiol. Psychol.*, Vol. 52, pp. 132–134.
Collias, N. E.
   1944. "Aggressive Behavior among Vertebrate Animals," *Physiological Zool.*, Vol. 17, pp. 83–123.
   1952. "The Development of Social Behavior in Birds," *Auk*, Vol. 69, pp. 127–159.
Collias, N. E., and E. C. Collias
   1956. "Some Mechanisms of Family Integration in Ducks," *Auk*, Vol. 73, pp. 378–400.
Collias, N. E., and Martin Joos
   1953. "The Spectrographic Analysis of Sound Signals of the Domestic Fowl," *Behaviour*, Vol. 5, pp. 175–188.

Comstock, J. H.
1924. *An Introduction to Entomology.* Ithaca, N.Y.: Comstock.
Corner, G. W.
1923. "The Problem of Embryonic Pathology in Mammals," *Amer. Jour. Anatomy,* Vol. 31, pp. 523–545.
1942. *The Hormones in Human Reproduction.* Princeton: Princeton University Press.
Craig, Wallace
1943. "The Song of the Wood Pewee, *Lycochanes virens* Linnaeus: A Study of Bird Music," *New York State Mus. Bull.* No. 334, pp. 1–186.
Crook, J. H.
1953. "An Observational Study of the Gulls of Southampton Water," *Brit. Birds,* Vol. 46, pp. 386–397.
Daanje, A.
1950. "On the Locomotory Movements in Birds and the Intention Movements Derived from Them," *Behaviour,* Vol. 3, Part I, pp. 48–98.
Dember, W. N.
1956. "Response by the Rat to Environmental Change," *Jour. Comp. Physiol. Psychol.,* Vol. 49, pp. 93–95.
Dethier, V. G.
1957. "Communication by Insects: Physiology of Dancing," *Science,* Vol. 125, pp. 331–336.
Dice, L. R.
1940. "Breeding Structure of Populations in Relation to Speciation," *Amer. Naturalist,* Vol. 74, pp. 232–248.
Du Brul, E. L.
1958. "Brain and Behavior," *Anat. Rec.,* Vol. 132, No. 3, pp. 428–429.
Dunn, L. C.
1939–1940. "Heredity and Development of Early Abnormalities in Vertebrates," *Harvey Lectures,* Series 35, pp. 135–165. Cold Spring Harbor, L.I.: Carnegie Institution.
Elton, C. S.
1942. *Voles, Mice and Lemmings: Problems in Population Dynamics.* Oxford: Clarendon Press.
Emerson, A. E.
1928. "Communication Among Termites," *Proc. IV Int. Congr. Entom.,* II.
Emlen, J. T.
1952. "Flocking Behavior in Birds," *Auk,* Vol. 69, pp. 160–170.
Engle, E. T., Ed.
1946. *Conference on Fertility, New York Academy of Medicine.* Princeton: Princeton University Press.
Errington, P. L.
1951. "Concerning Fluctuations in Populations of the Prolific and

Widely Distributed Muskrat," *Amer. Naturalist,* Vol. 85, pp. 223–238.

Essapian, F. S.
1953. "The Birth and Growth of a Porpoise," *Natural Hist. Mag.,* Vol. 62, pp. 392–399.

Etkin, William
1954. "Social Behavior and the Evolution of Man's Faculties," *Amer. Naturalist,* Vol. 88, pp. 129–142.

Ewer, R. F.
1957. "Ethological Concepts," *Science,* Vol. 126, pp. 599–603.

Farris, E. J.
1956. *Human Ovulation and Fertility.* Philadelphia: Lippincott.

Fielde, Adele M.
1904. "Power of Recognition among Ants," *Biol. Bull.,* Vol. 7, pp. 227–250.

Fisher, Edna
1939. "Habits of the Sea Otter," *Jour. Mamm.,* Vol. 20., pp. 21–36.
1940. "Early Life of a Sea Otter Pup," *Jour. Mamm.,* Vol. 21, pp. 132 ff.

Frisch, K. von
1950. *Bees, Their Vision, Chemical Senses and Language.* Ithaca, N.Y.: Cornell University Press.

Galt, W. E.
1939. "The Capacity of the Rhesus and Cebus Monkey and the Gibbon to Acquire Differential Response to Complex Visual Stimuli," *Genet. Psychol. Mono.,* Vol. 21, No. 3, pp. 387–455.
1940. "The Principle of Cooperation in Behavior," *Quart. Rev. Biol.,* Vol. 15, pp. 401–410.

Gannon, R. A.
1930. "Observations on the Satin Bower-Bird with Regard to the Material Used by It in Painting Its Bower," *Emu,* Vol. 80, pp. 39–41.

Gerard, R. W.
1942. "A Biological Basis for Ethics," *The Philosophy of Science,* Vol. 9, pp. 102 ff.

Gibson, Eleanor J., R. D. Walk, H. L. Pick, Jr., and T. J. Tighe
1958. "The Effect of Prolonged Exposure to Visual Patterns on Learning to Discriminate Similar and Different Patterns," *Jour. Comp. Physiol. Psychol.,* Vol. 51, pp. 584–587.

Goldfarb, William
1943. "The Effects of Early Institutional Care on Adolescent Personality," *Jour. Exp. Educ.,* Vol. 12, pp. 106–129.

Gray, P. H.
1958. "Theory and Evidence of Imprinting in Human Infants," *Jour. Psychol.,* Vol. 46, pp. 155–166.

Green, R. G., and C. A. Evans
1940. "Studies on a Population Cycle of Snowshoe Hares on the Lake

Alexander Area," *Jour. Wildlife Manag.*, Vol. 4, pp. 220–238, 267–278, 347–358.

Griffin, D. R.
1940. "Notes on the Life Histories of New England Cave Bats," *Jour. Mamm.*, Vol. 21, No. 2, pp. 181–187.

Hall, E. Raymond
1946. *Mammals of Nevada.* Berkeley: University of California Press.

Harker, Janet E.
1958. "Diurnal Rhythms in the Animal Kingdom," *Biol. Rev.*, Vol. 33, No. 1, pp. 1–53.

Harlow, H. F.
1953. "Higher Functions of the Nervous System," *Ann. Rev. Physiol.*, Vol. 15, pp. 493–514.
1959. "Affectional Responses in the Infant Monkey," *Science*, Vol. 130, pp. 421–432.

Harlow, H. F., N. C. Blazek, and G. E. McClearn
1956. "Manipulatory Motivation in the Infant Rhesus Monkey," *Jour. Comp. Physiol. Psychol.*, Vol. 49, pp. 444–448.

Harlow, H. F., M. K. Harlow, and D. R. Meyer
1950. "Learning Motivated by a Manipulation Drive," *Jour. Exp. Psychol.*, Vol. 40, pp. 228–234.

Harlow, H. F., and Margaret K. Harlow
1961. "A Study of Animal Affection," *Natural Hist.*, Vol. 70, No. 10, pp. 48–55.

Harris, V. T.
1952. "An Experimental Study of Habitat Selection by Prairie and Forest Races of the Deermouse, *Peromyscus maniculatus,*" in *Contributions from the Laboratory of Vertebrate Biology*, No. 56. Ann Arbor: University of Michigan Press. Pp. 1–53.

Heck, L., Sr.
1930. "Das Affenpalmenhaus des Berliner Zoologischen Gartens," *Zool. Gart.*, Vol. 2, pp. 173–184.

Hediger, Heini
1955. *Studies of the Psychology and Behavior of Captive Animals in Zoos and Circuses.* New York: Criterion Books.

Hickey, W. O.
1889. "Musical Mouse," *Amer. Naturalist*, Vol. 23, pp. 481–484.

Hinde, R. A.
1953. "Appetitive Behaviour and Consummatory Act," *Behaviour*, Vol. 5, pp. 189–224.
1959. "Behaviour and Speciation in Birds and Lower Vertebrates," *Biol. Rev.*, Vol. 34, pp. 85–129.
1961. "The Establishment of the Parent-Offspring Relation in Birds, with Some Mammalian Analogies," in *Current Problems in Animal Behaviour* (W. H. Thorpe and O. L. Zangwill, Eds.). Pp. 175–194.

Hobhouse, L. T.
1951. *Morals in Evolution*. London: Chapman.
Hooper, C. L.
1897. *A Report on the Sea-Otter Banks of Alaska*. U.S. Treasury Dept. Doc. No. 1977.
Hornaday, W. T.
1879. "On the Species of the Bornean Orangs, with Notes on Their Habits," *Proc. Amer. Asso. Advanc. Sci.*, Salem, 20th meeting. Pp. 438–455.
1886. *Two Years in the Jungle*. New York: Scribner.
1915. "Gorillas Past and Present," *New York Zool. Soc. Bull.*, Vol. 18, pp. 1181–1185.
Howard, H. E.
1920. *Territory in Bird Life*. London: Murray.
Huxley, Sir Julian
1934. "A Natural Experiment on the Territorial Instinct," *Brit. Birds*, Vol. 27, pp. 270–277.
James, William
1890. *Principles of Psychology*, 2 vols. New York: Dover (Authorized Edition, 1950).
Jaynes, Julian
1956. "Imprinting: The Interaction of Learned and Innate Behavior: I. Development and Generalization," *Jour. Comp. Physiol. Psychol.*, Vol. 49, pp. 201–206.
1957. "Imprinting: The Interaction of Learned and Innate Behavior: II. The Critical Period," *Jour. Comp. Physiol. Psychol.*, Vol. 50, pp. 6–10.
1958. "Imprinting: The Interaction of Learned and Innate Behavior: III. Practice Effects on Performance, Retention, and Fear," *Jour. Comp. Physiol. Psychol.*, Vol. 51, pp. 234–237.
Keenleyside, M. H. A.
1955. "Some Aspects of the Schooling Behaviour of Fish," *Behaviour*, Vol. 8, pp. 183–249.
Kellogg, Rhoda
1955. *What Children Scribble and Why*. San Francisco: Privately printed.
Kellogg, W. N., and L. A. Kellogg
1933. *The Ape and the Child*. New York: McGraw-Hill.
Klüver, Heinrich
1933. *Behavior Mechanisms in Monkeys*. Chicago: University of Chicago Press.
1937. "Re-examination of Implement-Using Behavior in a Cebus Monkey after an Interval of Three Years," *Acta Psychologica*, Vol. 2, pp. 347–397.
Koehler, O.
1950. "The Ability of Birds to 'Count,' " *Bull. Anim. Behav.*, No. 9, pp. 41–45.

Köhler, Wolfgang
1931. *The Mentality of Apes*, 2nd ed. New York: Harcourt, Brace. (Paperback ed.: New York: Vintage Press, 1959.)

Koford, C. B.
1963. "Group Relations in an Island Colony of Rhesus Monkeys," in *Primate Social Behavior* (Charles H. Southwick, Ed.). Princeton: Van Nostrand. Pp. 136–153.

Kohts
The work of this author will be found — in accordance with Russian practice — under a variety of names:

Kohts, Nadie   Kohts, N. N. Ladygina
Kohts, Nadjejeta   Laduigina-Kots (Nadezhda Nikolafona)

All refer to the same woman, an eminent specialist in primate psychology at Moscow.
1921. "Berichte des Zoologischen Laboratoriums beim Darwin-Museum für die Zeit 1914–1920," *Staatsverlag.* 1923. *Untersuchungen über die Erkenntnisfähigkeiten des Schimpanzen.* Moscow: Museum Darwinianum. (German translation of summary, pp. 454–492.)
1928. "Recherches sur l'intelligence du Chimpanzé par la méthode choix d'après modèle," *Jour. de Psychol.,* Vol. 25, pp. 255–276.
1935. "Infant Ape and Human Child," *Sci. Mem. Mus. Darwinianum,* Vol. 3. (In Russian with English summary.)
1958. *The Development of the Mind in the Evolutionary Process of Organisms.* Moscow.

Kuroda, Ryo
1931. "On the Counting Ability of a Monkey," *Jour. Comp. Psychol.,* Vol. 12, pp. 171–180.

Lack, David
1954. *The Natural Regulation of Animal Numbers.* Oxford: Clarendon Press.

Laing, J. A.
1957. "Female Fertility," in *Progress in the Physiology of Farm Animals,* Vol. 3, Ch. 17. London: Butterworth.

Lippitt, R.
1940. "An Experimental Study of the Effect of Democratic and Authoritarian Atmospheres," *Univ. Iowa Stud.,* Vol. 16, No. 3.

Lorenz, Konrad
1937. "The Companion in the Bird's World," *Auk,* Vol. 54, pp. 245–273.
1950. "The Comparative Method of Studying Innate Behaviour Patterns," *Sympos. of Soc. Exp. Biol. on Physiological Mechanisms in Animal Behaviour,* Cambridge, Eng., Vol. 4, pp. 221–268.

McBride, A. F., and D. O. Hebb
1948. "Behavior of the Captive Bottle-Nose Dolphin, *Tursiops truncatus*," *Jour. Comp. Psychol.,* Vol. 41, pp. 111–123.

McCabe, T. T., and Barbara D. Blanchard
  1950. *Three Species of Peromyscus.* Santa Barbara, Calif.: Rood Associates.
McCulloch, T. L., and G. M. Haselrud
  1939. "Affective Response of an Infant Chimpanzee Reared in Isolation from Its Kind," *Jour. Comp. Psychol.,* Vol. 28, pp. 437–445.
Maier, N. R. F., and T. C. Schneirla
  1935. *Principles of Animal Psychology.* New York: McGraw-Hill.
Mall, F. P., and Franz Keibel, Eds.
  1910–1912. *Manual of Human Embryology,* 2 vols. Philadelphia: Lippincott.
Marshall, A. J.
  1954. *Bower-Birds.* London: Oxford University Press.
Mayr, Ernst
  1963. *Animal Species and Evolution.* Cambridge: Harvard University Press.
Medawar, P. B.
  1960. *The Future of Man.* New York: Basic Books.
Miles, R. C.
  1958. "Learning in Kittens with Manipulatory, Exploratory and Food Incentives," *Jour. Comp. Physiol. Psychol.,* Vol. 51, pp. 39–42.
Morgan, C. Lloyd
  1894. *Introduction to Comparative Psychology.* London: Contemporary Science.
Montgomery, K. C.
  1954. "The Role of the Exploratory Drive in Learning," *Jour. Comp. Physiol. Psychol.,* Vol. 47, pp. 60–64.
  1955. "The Relation between Fear Induced by Novel Stimulation and Exploratory Behavior," *Jour. Comp. Physiol. Psychol.,* Vol. 48, pp. 254–260.
Montgomery, K. C., and Marshall Segall
  1955. "Discrimination Learning Based upon the Exploratory Drive," *Jour. Comp. Physiol. Psychol.,* Vol. 48, pp. 225–228.
Morris, Desmond
  1956a. "The Feather Postures of Birds and the Problem of the Origin of Social Signals," *Behaviour,* Vol. 11, pp. 75–113.
  1956b. "The Function and Causation of Courtship Ceremonies," in *L'Instinct dans le Comportment des Animaux et de l'Homme.* Paris: Fondation Singer-Polignac. Pp. 261–286.
  1962. *The Biology of Art.* New York: Knopf.
Murie, Adolph
  1937. "Some Food Habits of the Black Bear," *Jour. Mamm.,* Vol. 18, No. 2, pp. 238–240.
  1940. *Ecology of the Coyote in the Yellowstone: Fauna of the National Parks of the United States,* No. 4. U.S. Department of the Interior.

1944. *The Wolves of Mount McKinley: Fauna of the National Parks of the United States,* No. 5. U.S. Department of the Interior.

Murie, O. J.
1935. *Alaska-Yukon Caribou: North American Fauna,* Vol. 54. U.S. Department of Agriculture.
1940. "Notes on the Sea Otter," *Jour. Mamm.,* Vol. 21, p. 119.
1951. *The Elk of North America.* Harrisburg, Pa.: Stackpole and Wildlife Management Institute.

Neal, E. G.
1948. *The Badger.* London: Collins.

Needham, Joseph
1942. *Biochemistry and Morphogenesis.* Cambridge, Eng.: Cambridge University Press.

New York Times
June 26, 1963. "Radioactive Paths Show Ants Trading Food with Fellows." Report of Symposium organized by the International Atomic Energy Commission and the United States Food and Agriculture Organization.

Nice, Margaret M.
1943. "Studies in the Life History of the Song Sparrow," *Trans. Linn. Soc. N.Y.,* Vol. 6, pp. 1–328.

Peterson, Richard S.
1964. *Behavior of the Northern Fur Seal.* Doctor of Science thesis filed in Department of Pathobiology, Johns Hopkins University.

Pittendrigh, C. S.
1958. "Perspectives in the Study of Biological Clocks," in *Perspectives in Marine Biology* (A. Buzatti-Travers, Ed.). Berkeley: University of California Press. Pp. 239–268.

Ramsay, A. O., and E. H. Hess
1954. "A Laboratory Approach to the Study of Imprinting," *Wilson Bull.,* Vol. 66, pp. 157–234.

Ranson, S. W.
1934. "The Hypothalamus: Its Significance for Visceral Innervation and Emotional Expression," in *Trans. of the College of Physicians of Philadelphia,* Vol. 2, pp. 222–242.

Rensch, Bernhard
1957. "Asthetiche Faktoren bei Farb- und Formbevorzugungen von Affen," *Zeitschrift für Tierpsychologie,* Vol. 14, pp. 71–99.
1958. "Die Wirksamkeit Asthetischer Faktoren bei Wirbeltieren," *Zeitschrift für Tierpsychologie,* Vol. 15, pp. 447–461.
1960. *Evolution Above the Species Level.* New York: Columbia University Press.

Révész, G.
1944. "The Language of Animals," *Jour. Genet. Psychol.,* Vol. 30, pp. 117–147.

Ricketts, E. F., and Jack Calvin
1948. *Between Pacific Tides.* Stanford, Calif.: Stanford University Press.
Ripley, S. D.
1942. *Trail of the Money Bird.* New York: Harper.
Roberts, Brian
1934. "Notes on the Birds of Central and South-East Iceland," *Ibis* (13th Ser.), Vol. 4, pp. 239–264.
Robinson, A.
1921. "Prenatal Death," *Edinburgh Med. Jour.,* Vol. 26, pp. 137–209.
Salman, D. H.
1943. "Note on the Number Conception in Animal Psychology," *Brit. Jour. Psychol.,* Vol. 33, pp. 209–219.
Schaller, G. B.
1963. *The Mountain Gorilla.* Chicago: University of Chicago Press.
Schevill, W. E., and Barbara Lawrence
1949. "Underwater Listening to the White Porpoise," *Science,* Vol. 109, pp. 143–144.
Schiller, Paul
1951. "Figural Preferences in the Drawings of a Chimpanzee," *Jour. Comp. Physiol. Psychol.,* Vol. 44, pp. 101–111.
Schneirla, T. C.
1946. "Problems in the Biopsychology of Social Organization," *Jour. Abnormal and Soc. Psychol.,* Vol. 41, No. 4, pp. 385–402.
1949. "Army Ant Behavior under Dry Season Conditions," *Bull. Amer. Mus. Nat. Hist.,* Vol. 94, No. 1, pp. 1–81.
Schultz, A. H.
1926. "Studies on the Variability of the Platyrrhine Monkeys," *Jour. Mamm.,* Vol. 7, No. 4, pp. 286–302.
1931. "Man as a Primate," *Scient. Mo.,* Vol. 33, pp. 385 ff.
1933. "Observations on the Growth, Classification and Evolutionary Specialization of Gibbons and Simangs," *Human Biol.,* Vol. 5, No. 2, pp. 212–255; No. 3, pp. 385–444.
1937. "Proportions, Variability and Symmetries of the Long Bones of the Limbs and Clavicles in Man and Apes," *Human Biol.,* Vol. 9, pp. 281–328.
1939. "Notes on Diseases and Fractures of Wild Apes," *Bull. Hist. Med.,* Vol. 7, No. 6, pp. 571–582.
Scott, J. P., and Emil Fredericson
1951. "The Causes of Fighting in Mice and Rats," *Physiol. Zool.,* Vol. 24, pp. 273–309.
Scott, J. P., Emil Fredericson, and J. L. Fuller
1951. "Experimental Exploration of the Critical Period Hypothesis," *Personality,* Vol. 1, pp. 162–183.

Scott, J. P., and M. V. Marston
1950. "Critical Periods Affecting the Development of Normal and Maladjustive Social Behavior in Puppies," *Jour. Genet. Psychol.*, Vol. 77, pp. 25–60.
Shadle, A. R.
1944. "The Play of American Porcupines," *Jour. Comp. Psychol.*, Vol. 37, No. 3, pp. 145–150.
Shadle, A. R., Marilyn Smelzer, and Margaret Metz
1946. "The Sex Relations of Porcupines," *Jour. Mamm.*, Vol. 27, No. 2, pp. 116–121.
Shapovalov, L.
1940. "The Homing Instinct in Trout and Salmon," *Proc. 6th Pacific Sci. Congr.*, Vol. 3, pp. 317–322.
Shaw, C. E.
1948–1951. "The Male Combat 'Dance' of Some Crotalid Snakes," *Herpetologica*, Vol. 4, pp. 137–145; Vol. 7, pp. 149–168.
Skinner, M. P.
1922. "The Pronghorn," *Jour. Mamm.*, Vol. 3, pp. 82–105.
Skutch, A. F.
1935. "Helpers at the Nest," *Auk*, Vol. 52, pp. 257–273.
Söderberg, R.
1929. "Genesis of Decorative and Building Instincts of Bower-Birds with Some Notes on the Problem of the Origin of Art," in *Verh. 6, Int. Orn. Kongr.*, Copenhagen, 1926. Pp. 297–335.
Sokolowsky, Alexander
1923. "The Sexual Life of the Anthropoid Apes," *Urol. Cutan. Rev.*, Vol. 27, pp. 612–615.
Sollberger, D. F.
1940. "Notes on the Life History of the Small Eastern Flying Squirrel," *Jour. Mamm.*, Vol. 21, No. 3, pp. 282 ff.
Spemann, Hans
1938. *Embryonic Development and Induction.* New Haven: Yale University Press.
Stellar, Eliot
1954. "The Physiology of Motivation," *Psychol. Rev.*, Vol. 61, pp. 5–22.
Stoner, E. A.
1947. "Anna Humming-Birds at Play," *Condor*, Vol. 49, p. 36.
Sumner, F. R.
1932. "Genetic, Distributional, and Evolutional Studies of the Subspecies of Deer Mice (*Peromyscus*)," *Biblio. Genetica*, Vol. 9, pp. 1–106.
Swanberg, P. O.
1951. "Food Storage, Territory and Song in the Thick-billed Nutcracker," *Proc. 10th Int. Congr. Orn.*, Upsala. Pp. 545–554.

Thacker, L. A.
1950. "An Investigation of Non-Instrumental Learning," *Jour. Comp. Physiol. Psychol.*, Vol. 43, pp. 86–98.
Thompson, W. R.
1953. "The Inheritance of Behavior: Behavioral Differences in Fifteen Mouse Strains," *Canad. Jour. Psychol.*, Vol. 7, pp. 145–155.
Thorpe, W. H.
1943. "A Type of Insight Learning in Birds," *Brit. Birds*, Vol. 37, pp. 29–31.
1943–1944. "Types of Learning in Insects and Other Arthropods," *Brit. Jour. Psychol.* (Gen. Sect.), Vol. 33, pp. 220–234; Vol. 34, pp. 20–31, 66–76.
1945a. "Further Notes on a Type of Insight Learning in Birds," *Brit. Birds*, Vol. 38, pp. 46–49.
1945b. "The Evolutionary Significance of Habitat Selection," *Jour. Anim. Ecol.*, Vol. 14, pp. 67–70.
1948. "The Modern Concept of Instinctive Behaviour," *Bull. Anim. Behav.*, Vol. 1, No. 7, p. 12.
1958a. "The Learning of Song Patterns by Birds, with Especial Reference to the Song of the Chaffinch (*Fringilla coelebs*)," *Ibis*, Vol. 100, pp. 535–570.
1958b. "Ethology as a New Branch of Biology," in *Perspectives in Marine Biology* (A. Buzatti-Travers, Ed.), Berkeley: University of California Press. Pp. 411–428.
1961a. "Comparative Psychology," *Ann. Rev. Psychol.*, Vol. 12, pp. 27–50.
1961b. Introduction to "Studies of Problems Common to the Psychology of Animals and Men," in *Current Problems in Animal Behaviour* (W. H. Thorpe and O. L. Zangwill, Eds.). Cambridge, Eng.: Cambridge University Press. Pp. 167–175.
1961c. "Sensitive Periods in the Learning of Animals and Men: A Study of Imprinting with Special Reference to the Induction of Cyclic Behaviour," in *Current Problems in Animal Behaviour* (W. H. Thorpe and O. L. Zangwill, Eds.). Cambridge, Eng.: Cambridge University Press. Pp. 194–225.
1963. *Learning and Instinct in Animals*, 2nd Ed. Cambridge: Harvard University Press.
Thorpe, W. H., and B. I. Lade
1961. "The Songs of Some Families of the Order Passeriformes," *Ibis*, Vol. 103, pp. 231–259.
Tinbergen, Nikolaas
1936. "The Function of Sexual Fighting in Birds; and the Problem of the Origin of 'Territory,'" *Bird-Banding*, Vol. 7, pp. 1–8.
1939. "On the Analysis of Social Organization among Vertebrates, with

Special Reference to Birds," *Amer. Midl. Naturalist,* Vol. 21, pp. 210–234.

1942. "An Objectivistic Study of the Innate Behaviour of Animals," *Biblioth. Biotheor.,* Vol. 1, pp. 39–98.

1953. *The Herring Gull's World.* London: Collins.

1955. *The Study of Instinct.* Oxford: Clarendon Press.

1963. *Social Behaviour in Animals.* New York: Wiley.

Tinklepaugh, O. L., and C. G. Hartman

1932. "Behavior and Maternal Care of the New-Born Monkey (*M. rhesus*)," *Jour. Genet. Psychol.,* Vol. 40, pp. 257 ff.

Tolman, E. C.

1941. "Motivation, Learning and Adjustment," *Proc. Amer. Phil. Soc.,* Vol. 84, pp. 543–563.

Torre-Bueno, J. R. de la

1905. "Notes on Collecting, Preserving and Rearing Aquatic Hemiptera," *Canad. Ent.,* Vol. 37, pp. 12–24.

Tucker, M. A. R.

1938. *Past and Future of Ethics.* London: Oxford University Press.

Verplanck, W. S.

1955. "An Hypothesis on Imprinting," *Brit. Jour. Anim. Behav.,* Vol. 3, p. 123.

Walker, E. P.

1941. *Animal Behavior.* Smithsonian Institution Annual Report for 1940. Pp. 217–313.

Walker, E. L.

1951. "Drive Specificity and Learning: A Demonstration of a Response Tendency Acquired under a Strong Irrelevant Drive," *Jour. Comp. Physiol. Psychol.,* Vol. 44, pp. 596–603.

Woodrow, Herbert

1929. "Discrimination by the Monkey of Temporal Sequence of Varying Number of Stimuli," *Jour. Comp. Psychol.,* Vol. 9, No. 2, pp. 123–157.

Wright, Sewall

1940. "Breeding Structure of Populations in Relation to Speciation," *Amer. Naturalist,* Vol. 74, pp. 232–248.

Wynne-Edwards, V. C.

1962. *Animal Dispersion in Relation to Social Behaviour.* New York: Hasner.

Yerkes, R. M.

1939. "Social Dominance and Sexual Status in the Chimpanzee," *Quart. Rev. Biol.,* Vol. 14, No. 2, pp. 115–136.

1943. *Chimpanzees: A Laboratory Colony.* New Haven: Yale University Press.

Yerkes, R. M., and M. Tomilin

1935. "Mother-Infant Relations in Chimpanzees," *Jour. Comp. Psychol.,* Vol. 20, pp. 321–359.

Yerkes, R. M., and Ada W. Yerkes
   1929. *The Great Apes.* New Haven: Yale University Press.
Young, W. C.
   1941. "Observations and Experiments on Mating Behavior in Female Mammals," *Quart. Rev. Biol.,* Vol. 16, pp. 135–156, 311–335.
Zuckerman, Sir Solly
   1932. *The Social Life of Monkeys and Apes.* London: Routledge and Kegan Paul.

SOURCES OF GENERAL INTEREST

Adamson, Joy
   1960. *Born Free.* New York: Pantheon.
   1961. *Living Free.* New York: Harcourt, Brace & World.
Alexander, W. B.
   1963. *Birds of the Ocean,* 2nd Ed. New York: Putnam.
Allee, W. C.
   1951. *Cooperation Among Animals, with Human Implications.* New York: Schuman.
Allen, Arthur A.
   1939. *The Golden Plover and Other Birds.* Ithaca, N.Y.: Comstock.
Anthony, H. E.
   1928. *Field Book of North American Mammals.* New York: Putnam.
Armstrong, E. A.
   1955. *The Wren.* London: Collins.
Audubon, John James, and John Bachman
   1851. *The Quadrupeds of North America.* New York: V. G. Audubon.
Borland, Hal
   1959. *The Enduring Pattern.* New York: Simon and Schuster.
Bossard, James H. S.
   1956. *Parent and Child.* Philadelphia: University of Pennsylvania Press.
Bourlière, François
   1962. *The Natural History of Mammals,* 2nd Ed. New York: Knopf.
Brooks, Paul
   1964. *Roadless Area.* New York: Knopf.
Bowlby, John
   1951. *Maternal Care and Mental Health.* Geneva: World Health Organization.
Burton, Maurice
   1956. *Infancy in Animals.* London: Hutchinson.
Cahalane, V. H.
   1947. *Mammals of North America.* New York: Macmillan.
Carrighar, Sally
   1944. *One Day on Beetle Rock.* New York: Knopf.

Carrighar, Sally *cont'd*
1947. *One Day at Teton Marsh*. New York: Knopf.
1953. *Icebound Summer*. New York: Knopf.
1959. *Wild Voice of the North*. New York: Doubleday.
Carrington, Richard
1959. *Elephants*. New York: Basic Books.
Carson, Rachel L.
1951. *The Sea Around Us*. New York: Oxford University Press.
Caton, John Dean
1877. *The Antelope and Deer of America*. New York: Hurd & Houghton.
Clark, Austin H.
1953. *The Ecology, Evolution, and Distribution of the Vertebrates*. Smithsonian Institution Annual Report for 1952, pp. 283–305.
Conant, Roger
1958. *A Field Guide to Reptiles and Amphibians*. Boston: Houghton Mifflin.
Corner, G. W.
1944. *Ourselves Unborn*. New Haven: Yale University Press.
1961. "Science and Sex Ethics," in *Adventures of the Mind*, 2nd Ser. (Richard Thruelson and John Kobler, Eds.). New York: Knopf. Pp. 205–221.
Crisler, Lois
1958. *Arctic Wild*. New York: Harper.
Darwin, Charles
1872. *The Expression of Emotions in Man and Animals*. London: Murray.
Essapian, Frank S.
1953. "The Birth and Growth of a Porpoise," *Natural Hist. Mag.*, pp. 392–399.
Ford, Clellan S., and Frank A. Beach
1953. *Patterns of Sexual Behavior*. New York: Harper.
Goldschmidt, Walter, Ed.
1960. *Exploring the Ways of Mankind*. Now York: Holt, Rinehart & Winston.
Hamilton, W. J., Jr.
1939. *American Mammals*. New York: McGraw-Hill.
Harlow, Harry F., and Margaret K. Harlow
1961. "A Study of Animal Affection," *Natural Hist.*, Vol. 70, No. 10, pp. 48–55.
Hausman, L. A.
1946. *Field Book of Eastern Birds*. New York: Putnam.
Hoffmann, Ralph
1927. *Birds of the Pacific States*. Boston: Houghton Mifflin.

Hooton, Earnest
1942. *Man's Poor Relations.* Garden City, New York: Doubleday, Doran.

Hornaday, W. T.
1922. *The Minds and Manners of Wild Animals.* New York: Scribner.

Huxley, Aldous
1963. *Literature and Science.* New York: Harper & Row.

Huxley, Sir Julian
1944. *Man in the Modern World.* New York: New American Library.

Klots, Alexander B.
1951. *A Field Guide to the Butterflies.* Boston: Houghton Mifflin.

Lack, David
1943. *The Life of the Robin.* London: H. F. & G. Witherby.

Langer, Suzanne K.
1942. *Philosophy in a New Key.* Cambridge: Harvard University Press.

Lorenz, Konrad
1952. *King Solomon's Ring.* New York: Crowell.
1955. *Man Meets Dog.* Boston: Houghton Mifflin.

Lutz, Frank E.
1935. *Field Book of Insects.* New York: Putnam.

Maritain, Jacques
1958. *The Rights of Man.* London: Bles.

Milne, Lorus J., and Margery Milne
1962. *The Senses of Animals and Men.* New York: Atheneum.

Morgan, Ann Haven
1930. *Field Book of Ponds and Streams.* New York: Putnam.
1955. *Kinships of Animals and Man: A Textbook of Animal Biology.* New York: McGraw-Hill.

Murie, Adolph
1961. *A Naturalist in Alaska.* New York: Devin-Adair.

Murie, Olaus J.
1954. *A Field Guide to Animal Tracks.* Boston: Houghton Mifflin.

Needham, J. G., and J. T. Lloyd
1937. *The Life of Inland Waters.* Ithaca, N.Y.: Comstock.

Nice, Margaret M.
1939. *The Watcher at the Nest.* New York: Macmillan.

Ordish, George
1960. *The Living House.* New York: Lippincott.

Peterson, Roger Tory
1947. *A Field Guide to the Birds: Giving Field Marks of All Species Found East of the Rockies.* Boston: Houghton Mifflin.
1961. *A Field Guide to Western Birds,* 2nd Ed. Boston: Houghton Mifflin.

Peterson, Roger Tory, Guy Mountfort, and P. A. D. Hollom
1954. *A Field Guide to the Birds of Britain and Europe.* Boston: Houghton Mifflin.
Progoff, Ira
1959. *Depth Psychology and Modern Man.* New York: Julian.
Pycraft, William P.
1912. *The Infancy of Animals.* London: Hutchinson.
1913. *The Courtship of Animals.* London: Hutchinson.
Reik, Theodor
1957. *Myth and Guilt.* New York: Braziller.
Rennie, James
1844. *The Elephant.* New York: Harper. (Originally published by the British Society for the Diffusion of Useful Knowledge.)
Reynolds, Vernon
1964. "The Man of the Woods," *Natural Hist.,* Vol. 73, No. 1, pp. 44 ff.
Rodahl, Kaare
1963. *The Last of the Few.* New York: Harper & Row.
Schmidt, K. P., and D. D. Davis
1928. *Field Book of Snakes.* New York: Putnam.
Scott, John Paul
1958. *Animal Behavior.* Chicago: University of Chicago Press.
Schaller, George B.
1964. *The Year of the Gorilla.* Chicago: University of Chicago Press.
Seton, Ernest Thompson
1909. *Life-Histories of Northern Animals.* New York: Scribner.
Sherrington, Sir Charles
1953. *Man on His Nature.* Cambridge, Eng.: Cambridge University Press.
Smith, Homer W.
1955. *Man and His Gods.* Boston: Little, Brown.
Sumner, Lowell, and Joseph S. Dixon
1953. *Birds and Mammals of the Sierra Nevada.* Berkeley: University of California Press.
Taverner, P. A.
1949. *Birds of Canada.* Toronto: Musson.
Teale, Edwin Way
1962. *The Strange Lives of Familiar Insects.* New York: Dodd, Mead.
Thorpe, William H.
1961. *Bird-Song.* Cambridge, Eng.: Cambridge University Press.
1962. *Biology and the Nature of Man.* London: Oxford University Press.
Tomlinson, H. M.
1924. *Tide Marks.* New York: Harper.

Welty, Joel Carl
   1962. *The Life of Birds.* Philadelphia: Saunders.
Williams, Lt.-Col. J. H.
   1950. *Elephant Bill.* Garden City, N.Y.: Doubleday
Witherby, H. F., Ed.
   1947–1948. *A Handbook of British Birds,* 5 vols. London: H. F. & G.
   Witherby.
Van Tyne, Josselyn, and Andrew J. Berger
   1959. *Fundamentals of Ornithology.* New York: Wiley.

Index

Tschego, chimpanzee, 200, 230
Tucker, M. A. R., *The Past and Future of Ethics*, 44
Tuno, Husky dog, 143, 194, 206
Turkeys, domestic, 81
Turtles, 157, 222

U.S. Coast Guard, 188

Vacuum Activity, defined, 240
Vertebrates, *see* Aquatic animals, Reptiles, Birds, Mammals
Victorian approach to biology, 26
Voices of animals, 124; gibbons, 123–24; vocalization of Capuchin monkey, P–Y, 218. *See also* Song, Bird song

Walstrom, Allan G., 41
Wapiti, *see* Elk
Warblers, 162
Warfare, as attacks on one's own species, occurs only in harvester ants and men, 167
Wasps, 222
  Chalybion, 58
  Hornets, 57, 59
  Mud-daubers, 56
  Paper-wasps, 56
  Social wasps, 58
  Sceliphron, 58
  Trypoxylon, 58
Water hens (gallinules), 82
Water-bugs, *Belostoma*, 53
Waterhouse, George Robert, 130
Watson, J. B., 27, 37
Weasels, 76, 112; stoats (English weasels), 194
Westermarck, E. A., 45
Whales, 6, 11, 188–89; killer, 67
White, Gilbert, 25, 160–61
Winter, preparation for, 7–10
Wisconsin, University of, 78
Wolverines, 166

Wolves, 7, 11, 76–77, 110, 113, 138, 139–40, 143, 165–66, 174, 207; behavior suggesting honor and self-respect, 44–45; care of young, 84–85; described in *Arctic Wild*, 148–49; sing, 228–29; territories of, 164
Wood pewees, 228
Woodchucks, 174
Woodworth, R. S., 210
Wrens, 40
Wyoming, 107, 144, 153

Yale Laboratories of Primate Biology, 118
Yerkes, Robert M., 90, 117–18
Young: mother-infant relationship, 79–80; paternal care of, 54–55, 58, 59; education of birds, 63–64; of mammals, 64–77. *See also* Animal Parents, Part II (47); Celibacy, Emotional weaning of young, Foster care, Imprinting
Yukon River, 54

Zagarus, A., 21
Zebras, 193
Zenodotus, 160
Zoos, reluctance of animals to mate in, 25
  Baltimore Zoo, promotion of ape art, 215
  London Zoo, research into primate aesthetic tendencies, 212–18 passim
  Philadelphia Zoo, research into deaths from stress, 174
  San Diego Zoo, research into rattlesnake combats, 151
  San Francisco Fleishhacker Zoo, 193
Zuckerman, Sir Solly, 119, 178